THE SUCCESS SECRETS OF THE WORLD'S
SUPERACHIEVERS REVEALED

THE TRIUMPH OF AUDACITY

**HOW ORDINARY PEOPLE BECOME
INSANELY SUCCESSFUL SELF-MADE**

COACH GREB

CONTENT

The Shield of Audacity...5

Introduction 6

Chapter 1: The Audacity of Insanity..11

Chapter 2: The Audacity of Change...38

Chapter 3: The Audacity of Purpose 58

Chapter 4: The Audacity of Imagination..................................87

Chapter 5: The Audacity of Expectation 113

Chapter 6: The Audacity of Sacrifice.....................................132

Chapter 7: The Audacity of Execution 164

Chapter 8: The Audacity of Resilience 205

Chapter 9: The Audacity of Giving 230

Conclusion 256

Acknowledgements..258

About Coach Greb 259

Books By Coach Greb..261

Powerful Books That Inspired Me...262

To

Auzie Leonie

A MOTHER WHO LIVED TO LOVE.

THE SHIELD OF AUDACITY

"Here's to the crazy ones. The misfits. The rebels. The troublemakers. The round pegs in the square holes. The ones who see things differently. They're not fond of rules. And they have no respect for the status quo. You can quote them, disagree with them, glorify, or vilify them. About the only thing you can't do is ignore them. Because they change things. They push the human race forward. And while some may see them as the crazy ones, we see genius. Because the people who are crazy enough to think they can change the world are the ones who do."

— **Rob Siltanen**

INTRODUCTION

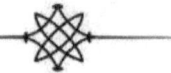

> **WHAT IF YOU HAD A LITTLE BIT MORE AUDACITY?**

On the sunny day of December 15, 2013, the universe halted its course for a moment and turned its glare on Qunu, a Xhosa village in Eastern Cape Province, South Africa, to pay homage to a life lived. The military sounded the trumpet, and twenty-one gunshots saluted the man who had deliberately stepped down from power after a short five-year term when many dictators elsewhere continued to savagely torture and bury whole nations to hold on to power for eternity.

The crowd of 4500 guests and dignitaries went silent. Then came the most dreaded time: when the man had to leave all that he had known to return and enter eternity, alone. As the soldiers loaded him onto a gun carriage and escorted him to the gates of infinity, the world watched in awe, mourned, and saluted a man of character, a man who was born with the audacity to say "No." That man knew the power of "No, thank you" when most people would have traded their selfhood for a little bit of comfort.

It was a man who did not ride in a Lamborghini or fly private jets. It was a man who saw little wealth in the world's riches, yet Nelson Mandela lived the richest and most fulfilling life any human being I know has ever lived. Rolihlahla Mandela, also known as Nelson Mandela, could have spent eternity on earth; unfortunately, life on earth is rationed. As the lights dimmed on his life, we questioned: has the man fulfilled, well done, and achieved what he came on earth to accomplish?

Introduction

Flipping through the different news channels, including NBC, CNN, ABC, and BBC, I heard nothing but the same central question, exposing the man to the human court of justice, which scare me a bit, thinking of how I would answer those questions before the Great Judge. That gave me a cheat sheet and a preview of the possible questions on the heavenly entrance exam each one of us will have to answer. Think for a moment, standing before God and being asked these questions. Scary, right?

"What do we remember of the man, and what has he done with his life?"

"What has he accomplished for humanity?"

"How has he impacted the lives of the black South Africans oppressed by the brutal Apartheid regime?"

"What did he contribute to society as a whole?"

Surprisingly, no one cared what fleet of cars Nelson Mandela left behind, nor the harem of girls or women he married. No one even asked how much money, private islands, or the ledger of expensive properties he owned.

While hedge fund managers, singers, football stars, and fast-lane drivers spent their time counting, ranking, and comparing their latest contracts, deals, acquisitions, gadgets, cars, jets, mansions, and net worth, Mandela saw little value in those perishables. Trained as a lawyer, Mandela could have chosen to stay in his little corner to savor the joy of life, unconcerned with his fellows' suffering. But no! Mandela cared little about worldly treasures that send many to an unforgiving and dizzying rat race and a spiral of quests for more and bigger.

Mandela saw little wealth in amassing riches, advocating for the crooked, pitiless, and unscrupulous robbers of public treasures. Instead, determined to pay the price with his own freedom, Nelson Mandela hung his life onto the painful cross of supplice to fight for justice and equity for millions of voiceless black South Africans.

With the utmost bravery and courage, Mandela vowed to stand firm like a soldier in front of the Apartheid regime. *How dare you steal and dispossess me of my father's land and treat me like a "no human,"* Rolihlahla thought. He could not stand by and watch millions of his fellows being snatched out of life by a ruthless, dehumanizing, segregationist, and systematic pauperism machine of the white supremacists who stole and lorded over South Africa's riches.

That made me throw my own question:

What do you remember of the man: his life as South Africa's president or suffering as the world's most famous prisoner?

How do you rise from a 27-year jail cell to the presidential palace if not that God wants to lecture the world about the power of selflessness? Initially sentenced to the death penalty, Mandela rejected not one but three release offers and refused to compromise his conviction in exchange for conditional liberty, saying:

> *I have fought against white domination, and I have fought against black domination. I have cherished the ideal of a democratic and free society in which all persons live together in harmony and with equal opportunities. It is an ideal which I hope to live for and to achieve. But if needs be, it is an ideal for which I am prepared to die.*

(Speech from the Dock quote by Nelson Mandela on 20 April 1964)

What is the price to pay for the prize to win the jackpot? What does it take?

Jesus earned to sit at the father's right because he accepted giving away his life to save humanity. Doesn't the Holy Book teach that he who saves his life loses it, but he who loses it saves it (Matthew 16:25)? What about Reverend Dr. Martin Luther King? Why would someone sacrifice the luxurious life he could have afforded to dare the brutal force and brave the violence and inhuman treatment of the white southern segregationists? Why would someone fearlessly confront, barehand, the riffle of the heartless supremacists to end up falling to its bullets?

I wonder why a young girl would prefer to leave the playground to stand against a robust Taliban regime, claiming the right to education for many young girls in her country, as did Malala Yousafzai. She escaped several assassinations attempts during her audacious enterprise to see her fellow girls earn the fundamental right to education.

What does it take to become an Aliko Dangote, a Steve Job, or an Elon Musk when the odds are all against you? How do you show up in the closed circle of the superrich when you were raised in deep poverty, as Oprah Winfrey did?

The other question that remains is: what is left of the human being when you have stripped him of his titles, the Nobel Prize, the exquisite mansions, the sumptuous park of ultimate driving machines, the private jets, the multimillion-dollar yacht, the fat bank accounts, and the glamour of the spotlight? What do you become when you have been stripped of the royal crown, the golden chair, the commander garment, or the princess's robe? I'll let you figure that out. So why the needless suffering for a piece of makeup? The most significant game-changers of our times concern themselves not so much with a bottle of Perignon or the stomach's satiety but with humanity's burden. They know they cannot do it alone, so they reckon they are the one rock. Small-minded people focus on finite pursuits. Legendary achievers devote their lives to the manifestation of infinity. This is what this book invites you to explore.

> **INSPIRED TO EMPOWER, THIS BOOK WILL CHANGE YOUR LIFE.**

The nine chapters of *The Triumph of Audacity* explore the idea that audacious individuals often challenge conventional wisdom and pursue ideas that may seem insane to others. Through storytelling, this book invites you to experience the audacity of ordinary people who became phenomenal, unstoppable, and highly successful self-made: Elon Musk's audacious vision for SpaceX, Vincent van Gogh's unconventional art, and Steve Jobs' relentlessness in creating the iPhone are a few legends you will soon enjoy reading.

The Triumph of Audacity inspires you to embrace audacity, even when your ideas seem outlandish, and challenge societal norms that stifle creativity. The book empowers you to embrace unconventional thinking, dare to be different, and believe in your audacious ideas even when others doubt you.

Through a spiral of historical, technological, economic, and spiritual accounts, *The Triumph of Audacity* discusses the spiritual, emotional, psychological, and practical framework of wealth-building and calls each of us to push the boundaries beyond human limits.

Written under divine inspiration, guidance, and authority, the book is a cocktail of unconventional inquiries, witty humor, and risky stylistic verbiage, enticing you to get out of your comfort zone to discover and believe in your abilities. The book will inspire you to reach within you what it takes to dig and unleash the divine gift to accomplish marvels upon this earth.

The Triumph of Audacity will uncover the untruths and half-truths and help you bust self-defeating beliefs. Many ill-purposed teachings and deceptive maneuvers have kept so many in abject poverty, a formidable weapon in the hands of autocratic powers and oligarchies to drive and maintain 95 percent of the earth's population under their control.

The Triumph of Audacity will equip you with spiritual wisdom, knowledge, economic insights, and practical strategies to discover and manifest your calling as it did for me. Since I found my purpose, my life has never been the same. I have become more fulfilled as I am now confident and enthused to share God's message of hope, rehabilitation, and growth. How is this possible? I knew little about his words and did not lead a prayerful life. You might question yourself: "How can God use me, so ridden with imperfection, uneducated, and born in poverty?" That is the same question Moses asks himself, but that should be none of your worries.

What this book is not about. Many who expect this book to teach investment strategies, real estate investment, and the like will be disappointed. I have a "Teach Me Money Series" collection, a hands-on money education program to build wealth from scratch. The book in The Power to Triumph series are motivational, inspirational, habit-formatting, and life-changing coaching programs.

This book aims to wake you up: if you keep dreaming the bootleg dream, you and your descendants will continue serving on the plantation. However, if you alter your mindset, paradigm, surroundings, habits, relationships, and activities, you could be one of the rare ones who yank themselves out of the ingeniously orchestrated, planted pauperism scheme.

You, too, can become self-made if you surrender to your calling. Paul was not an angel when God appeared to him. Yet he became the uncontested vocal advocate of Christ. God is not concerned about how perfect or imperfect you are. He delights in turning the feeble into a hero, a demon into an angel, and the poor into rich. God does not make any difference in whom He chooses for His mission.

THE AUDACITY OF INSANITY

EXPRESS THE POWER OF UNCOMMON SENSE

Achievers are not born talented, but they possess the " I can do attitude."

– Gladys Bejani

> ## ENCHAINED IN THE MIDDLE...CLASS BY A BOOTLEG DREAM

A man passing by a herd of elephants in a village stopped, amazed by what he saw. He noticed that these elephants were attached to a rope and dared not move, so he asked the trainer,

"Why aren't these elephants moving?"

"They are attached," replied the trainer.

"How so?" asked the passerby, "I see nothing but a little rope,"

"That is the problem," laughed the trainer, then added: "When they were young, these elephants were attached to the rope. Even when they grew up and are now multifold stronger than the rope, they still think the rope to be too strong to be broken."

The man sighed and walked away, shaking his head in a loud soliloquy like a madman. I will discuss this scene in a future book titled *Comedies of Our Lives: The Ill-measures of Humankind and The Inconsistencies of Human Life*. What these animals experienced is no different from what humans go through. By the power of dictatorial propaganda, mercantilist bandwagons, cultural norms, religious dogmas, political indoctrination, and corporate standard operating procedures and codes of conduct, the original self is erased and thrown into the abyss. People line up, shackled to a way of life they abhor but must live by or else.

The middle class is lured and enchained by debt, job security, retirement accounts, promotion opportunities, bonuses, perks, and unnumerable predatory incentives. With this much-rationed liberty, what room is left to think about *making yourself*? *Self-madeship* and obedience to societal mandates seem to be mutually exclusive. How can you be yourself while conforming to mainstream dictate? Either you break one or uplift the other, each choice carrying its weight of consequences. Either you die as a free-spirit butterfly, conform to bandwagon behavior, and live an average life, or accept to pay the price to be the exceptional You.

Coming to the crossroads of life takes more than a wish, a dream, or a parchment. It takes a truckload of audacity to seize your freedom to be YOU, not the name tags or title "Mr. XYZ, Sales Manager," or "Ms. ABC, Store Manager."

The essential question is: Why do so many people subject themselves to such an unnecessary ordeal? Why do many choose to live a half-life?

> **THE STRANGEST SECRET:
> PEOPLE FAIL BECAUSE THEY
> DON'T THINK. THEY CONFORM.**

Earl Nightingale is a household name among those who pioneered the famous law of attraction and personal success. Born and raised in the decade of the Great Depression, Earl was an eyewitness to what a shortage was. His most significant contribution is known as the *5 Percent Rule*. Where did this come from? As a radio host, in 1956, Earl laid out a finding he called the 5 Percent in a recorded audio cast titled *The Strangest Secret*. In his conclusions, Earl noted the results of a survey he conducted on a hypothetical group of one hundred young men aged twenty-five. Earl asked the one hundred young men at the start of their adult lives what they thought their lives would be like in forty years when they turned sixty-five. The hundred young men were all overly optimistic about their future. Unfortunately, the findings said otherwise.

Here is what hypothetically happened. Based on the theory, one man out of the one hundred would have become wealthy, the same 1 percent we talk about today, and four would become financially independent—that is, they could live comfortably independent of work. What about the 95 remaining? Five people would have continued working, thirty-six departed from the earth, and fifty-four would be broke and become dependent on handouts from public services or family members.

What do we learn here? Only five percent of people would have made it financially. How did they make it, and what did the 95 percent do wrong? According to Earl, the reason people fail is that they conform. Earl argues that most people do not think much, so the easiest way is to do what others do. "Why reinvent the wheel?" says the adage. The average individual is afraid of breaking the rules imposed upon them.

True power lies not in dull conformism but in self-assertion and the power of BEING YOU and not *everyone* else.

What is the problem in our society of approval, laws, ordinances, standard operating procedures, and codes of conduct? People live the expectation of others, not the exception. Afraid to be on the wrong side of Main Street, people dilute themselves in dull conformism because of obscurantism that keeps the light away from them. That is the greatest threat to our society, more arduous than terrorism, more than the fiercest pandemic, the desire to control others, subject the majority of the planet's citizens to the dictates of capitalistic, religious, cultural, and political oligarchies, a tiny few hungry for power. Why?

HOW DO YOU BECOME AN ALIKO DANGOTE, THE RICHEST BLACK SELF-MADE MAN ON EARTH?

French philosopher Pierre Corneille said, *"For souls, nobly born valor doesn't await the passing of years."* How do you become the world's richest black man, racking a $14 billion fortune? Ranked 136 by Forbes Magazine, Aliko Dangote teaches us one viable life lesson: You do not need to flip someone's burger before starting your own. You do not build a life being someone's debenture worker. You will leave nothing on this if your idea of living is to be a tool in making someone's family legacy.

I often ache when I see brilliant minds line up to apply for a job at Big Company when they could well create Big Company themselves. How many people dare to think of jumping into entrepreneurship right after college?

Upon losing his father at the wee age of eight, Aliko knew he had to take matters into his own hands if he were to make it in this life. The founder and CEO of the Dangote Group, a conglomerate of diversified industries, was adopted by his maternal grandfather, a businessman in Nigeria. Surrounded by entrepreneurial minds, Aliko quickly realized his love of business. In a Forbes Magazine interview, he said, *"When you are raised by an entrepreneurial parent or grandparent, you pick that aspiration, it makes you be much more aggressive — to think anything is possible."* Like any predestined billionaire, Aliko knew early on what it takes to make money: **give people what they want and be paid for it**.

Aliko needed no degree in business to start making money. He figured out his own way of earning money right from the playground, selling sweets to other kids. Aliko was not born in poverty like many rags-to-riches stories, but his legend is worth paying heed to. It is one of my visionary audacity, action, resilience, discipline, sacrifice, and gratitude. Upon graduating high school, Aliko was admitted to Al-Azhar University in Cairo, Egypt, where he obtained a Bachelor of Business degree in 1977. Upon returning to Nigeria, unlike most graduates, Aliko did not line up to seek employment with Big Corp. He did not think starting a business at 21 was too risky or challenging.

Success does not bow to your grey hair. Especially in business, success is not about your age, parchment, hair texture, or skin color. It is about using your natural gift to solve people's problems as efficiently as possible. Aliko said, *"Every morning, when I wake up, I make up my mind to solve as many problems as possible before retiring home."* True entrepreneurship aims to solve people's problems and reach as many people as possible. When satisfied, people will reward them and ask for more. That is the whole genius of being in business. Conversely, uninspired, fly-by-night entrepreneurs say they go into business to make money. Wrong. Every business aims to solve people's challenges, pain, needs, and wants. As a result of their contribution, the entrepreneurs are rewarded with wealth.

SECRET CODE #1
LIVE BY DESIGN, NOT PRESCRIPTION.

Nothing could stop Aliko when he decided to realize his dream of becoming an entrepreneur. He would charge forward in the pursuit of his passion. As his biography reads, as soon as Aliko encountered the business of sugar, he fell in love with it and had a plan for it. He said, *"You must have a vision, and not just a vision, but you must have a plan that will help you fulfill that vision."* He saw a different way to impact people's basic needs: sugar, cement, oil, flour, and more. The easiest and most recession-proof businesses deal with people's primary needs: food, shelter, and transportation. Aliko's ascension to wealth caters to one of the human basic needs: food. He did not invent rocket science or embark on something complicated. Aliko's business idea and model were simple: provide sugar to customers most efficiently, cost-effectively, and consistently. Many would-be entrepreneurs struggle and throw in the towel because they get into businesses they and their target market do not know or understand.

Aliko had a vision beyond the $3000 his uncle lent to import sugar. He peeped into the future and saw the untapped potential to build one of Africa's largest food and cement conglomerates. Like many self-made people, Aliko found his core value in social responsibility: seek your neighbor's welfare first, which is the true meaning of a life worth living. Aliko believes that

"The real thing about wealth, which will make you enjoy it and be happy that you are rich, is how many lives you can touch while alive.

I share Aliko's business philosophy as I teach that no business can exist without people with needs. Don't the Holy Scriptures, the holy handbook of life, urge us to love our neighbors and take care of their needs; it is then that we are rewarded for a job well done as it is written in 1 Corinthians 10:24, "Let no one seek his own good, but the good of his neighbor."

Why do so many people fail to live up to this simple task? Below are twenty-one power habits of the few who defy commonsense and audaciously cling to the dictate of their insanity to birth marvels upon the earth.

FIFTEEN POWER HABITS OF INSANELY SUCCESSFUL NERDS

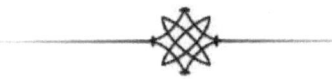

What do you know about self-made, and how are they different from the average Joe? If you observe people around you, you will notice a significant difference. The self-made are a rare species. You will have to search hard to find them because they are not where everybody is.

Conversely, ordinary people run the streets. They are where you can find regular folks. They think and act like everyone, fearing the lonely island of being called different. The average person feels in her comfort zone, doing average work, expecting average results, and leaving nothing behind. The average person sees life in terms of personal gain and personal gratification.

They pursue pettiness, the ephemeral, the easy catch. They prefer to fish in shallow waters and never dare to go into deep waters where they can catch bigger fish. They are in total contradiction with the self-made who are non-content with ordinary life. Ordinary people pursue average careers, work around average people, live in the middle class, and pursue short-sighted dreams. They are afraid to be found on the road untraveled, be called nerd, insane, stupid, or crazy. They are not concerned with creating value for the world. Their motto is "Don't fix it if it ain't broken," "Why reinvent the wheel?" or "A bird in the hand is worth two on the tree."

The self-made are in total contrast to the average folks. They are here to turn the world upside down and care little about what the world thinks of them. In fact, what others say matters little to them. Yet, they are the ones who change our world, and that is what they will spend their life on earth doing.

You've got to be insane to be a self-made nerd. Superachievers are ordinary people passionate about the crazy ideas that obsess them. Why would someone name his baby X2 as Elon Musk did? How crazy was Zuckerberg with FaceMash, a project he launched in 2004 in his dorm at Harvard University? Who in his right mind would pay $200,000 to

acquire a domain name that generally costs between $3 and $19 when the company had not made a cent in profit? With a $41 billion valuation in November 2010, paying American Farm Bureau $8.5 million to acquire the domain name fb.com might not have been a big deal for Facebook. No business school will teach you to deplete yourself from a few resources, especially when all you had to start with was a $ 500,000 initial investment from Michael Thiel. Nerds do not follow common wisdom; they itch to release the beast within.

1. YOU'VE GOT TO BE INSANE

You can't call yourself a superachiever unless you've been dismissed as insane. Zuckerberg was not the only fool to yank out a check from his pocketbook when he barely made any money in 2004. But that's nothing compared to the sale of the domain name business.com. In 1999, Weinbaum eCompanies Ventures purchased the domain name *business.com*, making Marc Ostrofsky a $7.5 millionaire. Jake Weinbaum did not wait too long to flip that domain name eight years later for a dizzying price tag of $347 million, 47 times what he paid. You might wonder what is so much in a domain; why couldn't they find similar domain names? With the Internet becoming an appealing superhighway, domain names have become virtual real estate. Flipping them is no different from flipping a lot or house. Many domain traders have set up shops to snatch all appealing domain names.

The self-made do things the ordinary person will find unthinkable. That explains why there are so few of them. How many average people are out there? A pack for cheap. But nerdy people with a brain, not that many. These people are uncommon in that they think and act differently from the average person. They accomplish what they set out to do regardless of others' opinions of them. A self-made person is an independent thinker who owns and is proudly accountable for his actions and opinions.

2. GET OUT OF THE BANDWAGON: GAME CHANGERS ARE INDEPENDENT, CRITICAL, AND UNORTHODOX THINKERS

We all know the half-truths we are told about how to live our lives, what to buy, how to buy, and why one should not stand on the sideline. We surf malls and the Internet superhighways, looking for sales to buy things we do not need to impress people who hate us. Commonsense wisdom asks you to unquestionably follow what everybody is doing. We want everything other people have right away. We want to act the way others behave. We dare not stop and question their motives and attitudes. We operate on impulse, and thanks to the many systems that promote and induce impulsiveness, we indulge in behaviors that sabotage our ability to be ourselves, think independently, and make a difference, thereby killing creativity and inventiveness. Phenomenal achievers may not be intellectual, but they are knowledgeable and use the utmost power of the brain. ***Intelligence*** *sets apart victors from victims and the poor from the rich.*

3. DARE TO THINK: WALK AWAY FROM THE BRAINWASHED *PUPPET* SOCIETY

With technology becoming pervasive in our lives, we have lost the patience and the ability to ponder decisions. The brain has lost its capacity to evaluate alternatives and make sound decisions. We have become addicted to gadgets such as TVs, smartphones, and tools and now think in our place. I remember years ago when we feared machines would replace humans. Smart technologies and artificial intelligence are progressively and irreversibly replacing human intelligence.

Elon Musk, one of the vocal promoters of Artificial intelligence, does not hide the threat such technology poses to human safety. In an April 2023 interview with former Fox News newscaster Tucker Carlson, here is what Elon said,

> *"AI is more dangerous than, say, mismanaged aircraft design or production maintenance or bad car production, in the sense that it is, it has the potential — however small one may regard that."*

According to a CNN report, Elon even proposed a six-month halt on what he called an "Out-of-control" race toward the proliferation of AI.

French philosopher and mathematician Rene Descartes has been oft quoted for writing in *Discours sur la Methode*, "*Je pense, donc je suis,*" which translates, 'I think, so I am." What did Descartes mean? My understanding is that your ability to ponder is what makes you a human being. In other words, losing the faculty to think deprives you of your right to be human.

Is this not what we observe in places where brutal regimes dehumanize and crush the spirit of those who oppose them? They deprived these people of their ability to voice their opinions, analyze, and say 'No." This is standard practice all over the planet. Some do so with brutality, others with malice.

Consequently, most people have lost their ability to think independently. Very few people can think logically to make a sensible decision because of how we live. You expected your grandma or grandpa to be the source of wisdom. Not so sure. They, too, are victims of thinking deficiency, the ability to think critically and solve problems.

According to Scienceabc.com and Worlpopulationreview.com, Americans' average IQ is 98, with Massachusetts ranking the highest at 104. Intelligence Quotient, while not a predictor of life success, is the ability of a person to solve problems and make sound judgments. The average IQ is 100, ranging from 85 to 115 for ordinary people. It can go above 200 for geniuses or below 70 for mentally impaired individuals.

In their lecture series **Brain Wash**, neurologists Dr. David Perlmutter and son Dr. Austin Perlmutter discuss how our sedentary modern culture has rewired how we think. The sugar-rich diet and the stressful lifestyle deteriorate our physical and mental capacity. For example, the lack of proper sleep, physical exercise, and sedentary indoor living damage your body and brain's decision-making ability. They offer an alternative that includes interaction with nature, a brain-nourishing diet, physical exercise, and human interaction.

Thinking deficiency exposes you to traps that destroy your ability to escape poverty. The Holy book has hammered the importance of thinking right. In his letter to the Romans, Apostle Paul pinned the importance of thinking differently and independently from the world when he wrote in Romans 12:2:

> *And do not be conformed to this world, but be transformed by the renewing of your mind, that you may prove what is that good and acceptable and perfect will of God.*

Be a critical thinker. What is our biggest challenge as humans? Such a question might make you list many answers. Earl Nightingale believes people fail to build wealth because they do not think. Indeed, critical thinking is a challenge for many Americans, especially the younger generations,

In a 2020 survey, MindEge, a company created by Harvard and MIT faculty Jefferson Flanders, released some chilling findings. The research reports that nearly 44 percent of Millennials received an "F" on critical thinking. Over 76 percent of the 1000 respondents surveyed failed to differentiate fake news from accurate information.

In my career as an educator, this has been my most significant concern regarding learning. Our youth seem to be bored with something that demands too much thinking. The World Economic Forum rated this a serious issue. Critical thinking was the second most crucial skill to exhibit at one of its events, second only to complex problem-solving.

Critical thinking is more than just mathematical thinking. While we promote science, technology, mathematics, and engineering in our school systems, we should not neglect all other forms of intelligence. Below are some areas that our school systems need to include in the curriculum if we are to create competitive economies:

- Critical thinking and analytical reasoning.
- Problem-solving and idea generation.
- Emotional intelligence.
- Leadership and team spirit.
- Creative thinking and risk-taking.
- Promotion of independent initiative.

Critical thinking has nothing to do with science or technology. The truth is that critical thinking must be taught across all eight areas of intelligence: mathematical, literary, artistic, linguistic, kinesthetic, musical, social, and naturalistic.

Critical thinking expands the mind's capacity to see the big picture while considering the details; it empowers self-confidence to own your opinion and manifest your uniqueness.

4. CELEBRATE YOUR UNIQUENESS: THERE IS POWER IN BEING DIFFERENT

There is power in being different. Accept being a non-conformist. Nerds like to act in total contradiction to the mainstream. What do you notice when you look at Elon Musk, Mark Zuckerberg, and Jeff Bezos? To me, these three lads are far from being regular humans. They act in ways that the average person would not understand.

What is the next logical thing an average person does after cashing a mere $165 million stake in PayPal from selling your brainchild to giant eBay? A good boy would buy himself a $30-million mansion, then fly to Canada to purchase his mama a lovely estate. Back in the US, with a chest full of cash, he would round up a horde of pals and girls to help him celebrate his new life. Which fool continues renting an apartment when he can buy the apartment complex?

Elon Musk was not interested in things that most people would die for - a house, a stock portfolio, a diamond, or a ruby. No! Elon was more preoccupied with the fire burning inside, more focused on releasing the beast roaring within that wanted to escape, a surge that had been boiling in him in his wee hours of life to a point that worried his parents. But nerds do not always follow parental ordinances, or shall I say, they rarely do. It is not rare to see superachievers crossed with their parents at the start of their folly to follow paths untraveled.

How often have you heard of the self-made who dare their parents to choose an insane path stubbornly? We often talk about Bill Gates, Michael Dell, and many more who threw away their books and pens to strike at life in their wee ages. Gates dropped out of Harvard to pursue his dream of Microsoft, the world's giant in the software industry. Michael Dell dropped out of the University of Texas to create Dell Computer, one of the world's largest computer makers. In our society, *bandwagon behavior* has inhibited many talents.

Conformists are comfortable being dictated how to breathe, think, and walk. They are monitored and expected to act a certain way. Mainstream has mapped out the route to success for them—the middle-class toils for financial security; the rich strategize for economic power. The refrain is known, and your grandmother is an expert at it.

Here it goes, "Grandchild, study hard, get a good degree, get a well-paying job, buy a house, fund your retirement, and retire happy."

But as a respectful grandchild, you dare not ask,

"Grandma, is that why you can barely survive in retirement?"

Ninety-five percent of people, the *majority poor*, are blindfolded to believe the gurus and experts.

Not so for the self-made, whose beliefs and behaviors contradict the rest of society. They are generally lightyears away from the rest of the world. They peep into the future before everyone else.

Employees at the most thriving companies in America, such as Google, Yahoo, Facebook, and Twitter, have ignored the dress code in corporate America. The dark suit, white shirt, and tie seem to be an unnecessary burden to the creative pulse of the millennial employees. They could care less about slacks and dress shoes. They feel very much at ease in their jeans and sneakers. Yet they are the creative geniuses whose inventiveness daily shapes our lives. Billionaire Mark Zuckerberg wears hoodies to work every day. Steve Jobs rarely wore a suit. He introduced revolutionary products such as the iPod and iPad, wearing simple sweaters and jeans.

Be cautioned, however. Being a non-conformist does not mean breaking legal and moral laws. It simply implies doing things differently and becoming an independent thinker. Unfortunately, this has been a leading cause of strife between parents and their adult children.

5. MANIFEST UNCONVENTIONAL AND RELENTLESS STUBBORNNESS

Do you know why over 74 percent of people are reportedly not in love with their careers? Many chose their careers under pressure: their parents or the living conditions urged them to choose the easy or imposed alternative. Do you know why 95 percent of people cannot build wealth? They spend their lives on dead-end jobs they are not passionate about. They only work to make money to pay bills or buy stuff. So, they are dependent on money. No wonder they blow off the money they work so hard for because they want to find happiness in the material stuff surrounding them. Only unorthodox children live to realize themselves.

Parents sometimes tend to un-love their child, who never gets in line; Teachers wish the unruly students get removed from their class. No unconventional student has ever been a teacher's pet. Social order breakers are outcasts and silenced because they hate following rules, norms, and mandates. Yet, they are the ones who spearhead change and innovation in society. These industry leaders are the originators of social progress.

Many parents believe they detain the truth and think themselves more apt to decide what is best for their offspring. Many of them want to live through their children what they have not achieved, so they impose what they believe is best or heard from their colleagues. The typical conversation goes like this:

"Honey, I think you ought to study nursing. It pays good money these days. You know Ms. Hunter, my colleague, who came here for your sixteenth birthday? That's what her daughter studied, and she's already got three job offers," advises the mother.

As for the *knowledgeable* uncle, he nailed the best career choice for his favorite nephew:

"You know, John, cyber security is a hot career choice. Or you may choose computer science. They will pay you $70,000 right out of college."

When the child tries to respond, unimpressed,

"Well, I understand all that, but I only want to study wildlife. That's what I love. That's my passion," the whole family will

rebuttal in unison,

"And how will you pay for the $50,000 student loans with that stupid job?"

Mocking, the uncle would ask, "Animals? That's the best you can do?"

It does not matter what part of the planet you reside in; the millennials and the generations after them are made of breeds of humans in total contrast from their baby boomers or Gen X parents. They are not the keep-quiet-go-to-your-room type of pals. They are free-spirited lads who will rarely put up with their parents' dictates. They are unimpressed by your authority, title, or size. They will unapologetically tell the president of the United States or the king of England where to get off. Below is a dramatized scene that paints generational clashes common in our modern households.

Chief Ojukwu, a highly regarded political leader idolized by many of his constituents from the prosperous Anambra State, Nigeria, was in for a big frustration when he thought he still had parental authority over his US-educated children.

When the overpowering father, sumptuously outfitted in his chamber robe, summoned his foreign-educated children to dictate what they should become, Chief did not expect what he heard from his unorthodox children. After gathering his two sons and daughter and comfortably seated in his royal golden chair of authority, Chief Ojukwu started a litany of reasons why he summoned his children. The youth, who could care less about authoritarian practices and were visibly annoyed by their father's chivalrous conduct, awaited the end of the speech, for they knew what would come of it. And here it was:

"So here is my decision for your careers," the father finally came to the main point:

"Afamefuna, you will be a doctor; Bunkechukwu, you are an engineer. Now turning to Ada softly with a smile and handing out his hands to welcome her, he uttered,

"As for you, My Dear, you will read law."

But as he saw the frowning faces, the father swiftly shifted his mood, hammering,

"That's it! I see nothing else. That's what I have always wanted for my children. That's why I sacrificed my entire life so you, my children, can become people who make me proud."

Interrupting, the free-spirited Atlanta-educated younger son, Bunkechukwu, tried to reason with the father, saying,

"But Dad…," the boy did not have a chance to add another sound when Chief cut him off sharply, growling,

"You must make sure our family name lives on. These are well-respected and well-paying careers. Nothing beats that."

Not welcoming a confrontation from a child, Chief ordered abruptly."

"That's it! You may leave," satisfied he imposed as he always does.

Acting this way is preparing a fertile ground for strife. The students will either give in, be disgruntled, and hate their parents for life, or impose themselves and let the chips fall where they may.

Can you imagine what type of indigestion Mr. and Mrs. Rondeau suffered during a delicious dinner of ribs and mashed potatoes when their sixteen-year-old Chris interrupted their appetite to announce the big news?

"Mom, Dad, I have a surprise!" he broke in.

"Oh yeah, Son?" they marveled, leaning impatiently toward the son.

Then, boldly, the son hammered, "I am quitting school!"

Planet Fitness CEO Chris Rondeau did not beat about the bush when he told his parents what he wanted to do with his life. Resolved to face any consequence, Chris boldly added with a smile,

"I'm calling it quits."

Not giving the parents, a chance to question or argue, the boy interrupted, "Mom, Dad, listen, listen. I've made up my mind. I'm quitting school. Work makes more money than school?"

What do you think the parents did? Did they hug him and sing Alleluia, or did they fight to get him out of his stupid idea of quitting school without a high school diploma?

Forcing our children into our dream careers is a huge mistake that takes success away from them, pushing them to go and die in boring jobs. *An individual's success path is divinely ordained and aligned with his natural gift and interests.* It comes from their natural buildup, which has nothing to do with money or a career. That is the thing which individuals will excel in their lives. Parents' interfering with their agendas and driving their offspring away from their choices can only turn the latter into miserable, dangerous creatures. Disgruntled and angry, they would surf life like wounded beasts until they snatched life out of innocent people one day.

The problem is even more severe when we consider our education systems. Our society is erroneously biased toward science, technology, mathematics, and engineering, frustrating brilliant students gifted with other types of intelligence. Why do you think the Picassos, the Van Goths, and the Mozarts have become rare species in our high-tech world? "*Their contribution is minimal. We don't have enough funding for those extra subjects, you know,*" would justify a well-respected educational decision-maker in our metric-based society.

Harvard University neuropsychologist Howard Gardner released his study of different types of intelligence in his book *Frames of Mind: The Theory of Multiple Intelligences*. Garden built his research on the hypothesis that each child possesses a specific intelligence type and will thrive on it. Gardner found the following eight types of intelligence:

1. *Mathematical-logical intelligence*: puzzle, problem-solving.
2. *Spatial intelligence*: painting, drawing, construction,
3. *Linguistic intelligence*: language, literature, reading, and writing.
4. *Kinesthetic intelligence*: physical expression, dance, and sport.
5. *Musical intelligence*: easiness of playing musical instruments.
6. *Naturalistic intelligence*: love for nature, animals, water, and plants.
7. *Intrapersonal intelligence*: internal, personal power, independent.
8. *Interpersonal intelligence*: social skills, team spirit.

Apart from being stubborn, the self-made fight for their freedom of thought and stretch their view beyond confinement. They see the big picture.

6. ADOPT JEFF BEZOS' BIG-PICTURE MINDSET: BE UNBOUNDED AND REACH INTO LIMITLESS INFINITY

Jeff Bezos, the man who suffers a congenital craving to hold the globe in his palm, has a pathetic propensity to control anything his foolish appetite sends him to. Marching like a giant, he wants to establish supremacy in any industry he preys on—the epitome of unstoppable conquistadors. Jeff sees everything big and is not hurrying to get where he is headed. From books, Amazon wants to be in any industry with over one hundred companies under its roof. From A to Z: retail, book, technology, shipping, grocery, pharmacy, air spaces, news media, movies, entre, entertainment, electronics consumer goods, electronics, clothing, robotics, home security, the list is unending.

Self-made people are not hungry entrepreneurs who see their ventures as their bread-winning storehouse; they have a long-range view. They see the big picture from afar and are willing to shoot in the long-range and wait. How did Jeff Bezos figure out the future of web services? More than anything. Writer Brad Stone, the author of *Amazon Unbound*, researched the company extensively and released some jaw-dropping revelations.

According to Stone's findings, Amazon's earnings do not necessarily come from online sales. The company controls 51 percent of the global online market. Likewise, a study by writer and serial entrepreneur Mal Warwick found Amazon Web Services to be the critical profit center, bringing Amazon over 47 percent of its overall profit.

Launched in 2003, just seven years after Amazon started as an online bookstore, this department was already peeping into the future of computing. AWS controls 32 percent of the world's cloud computing market, ahead of Microsoft and Google, 29 percent and 7 percent, respectively. It took this department years to yield a profit, but Jeff Bezos, with a *forward-thinking and big-picture* mindset, did not think that was a big deal. With the speeding growth of Amazon's second profit maker, Amazon Advertising Services, bringing 10 percent of its revenue and the logistics division, the future has much in store for Amazon.

Big-picture thinking turns the garage dream into a global giant worth 1.7 trillion and employing 1.3 million people worldwide. Yet without a strategy, the entrepreneur can quickly lose control of things like mastodont, as Steve Jobs did. He probably should have borrowed a cheat sheet from Mark Zuckerberg.

7. APPLY ZUCKERBERG'S THEORY OF CONTROL: BE IN THE DRIVER'S SEAT TO YOUR DESTINATION

You cannot own what you do not control, and you cannot control what you do not own. Let no one on your ins and outs.
— **Coach Greb**

"How dare you fire me from the company I created?" Jobs yelled.
In an interview with news media outlet Engage, disruptive marketing expert and now serial investor John Sculley remembered his feud with Steve Job. He said, four decades later, a particular thought never left him:

"He never forgave me for firing him," Sculley uttered thoughtfully.

Who had the guts to fire someone from the company he created from sweat? That's what effective leaders do: make the difficult call.

In 1983, Steve Jobs hired John Sculley, the then-President of Pepsi-Cola, to run Apple Computers. Sculley's mission was to make Apple's Macintosh, lagging IBM and Atari computers, and catch up. As a marketing guru and business executive, Sculley was thinking of a strategy to trouble IBM's waters, taking market share from it. Jobs, on the other hand, was more focused on innovation. Though the two men were close, they disagreed on almost everything concerning Apple's operation. Eventually, Steve accused John of pricing the computer too high, which caused crumbling sales. On the other hand, John accused Jobs of puerile tantrums, which did not help the company's profitability and growth.

The one responsible before the board was not Steve. John was, so he decided to take matters into his own hands and keep Steve out of the decision process: he fired him.

Shocking, isn't it? The CEO's role is to oversee the company's core decisions. John did not blink when his views contradicted Jobs's tantrums. Steve Jobs lost control of the company he had created because he did not put the safeguards in place to maintain control. Maintaining control of your vision is vital. Mark Zuckerberg understood this thanks to the advice of his mentor and business partner Sean Parker, who introduced Zuckerberg to Peter Thiel, the initial investor who put up $500,000 for Facebook. Parker, at one point, served as the president of the company.

Learn to maintain control over your vision. Acting on the advice of Sean Parker, despite his early age of 21, Mark Zuckerberg did not relinquish his decision-making power to another person. He is the majority owner of

Facebook and the chief executive officer of his company, who has the final signature for critical decisions. Nothing gets done without his signature.

8. EXPRESS STEVE JOBS'S FINISH-LINE MINDSET: FOCUS ON FINALITY. GET THINGS DONE.

It doesn't matter where you were born; you are still a genius. What makes Steve Jobs, Mark Zuckerberg, Andrew Carnegie, Sam Walton, and many others unique? They surrender to their passion and live to drive their dream home. Many of the world's super-achievers were born in poverty. John Rockefeller was the son of a con artist. Sam Walton's family was dirt poor. Oprah Winfrey grew up in poverty. Over 75 percent of our world's billionaires and millionaires came from humble backgrounds, from families of welders, millers, farmers, teachers, and salespeople. But they did not become whiners who found great excuses to explain their inability to be successful because they grew up in poverty.

Steve's biological parents abandoned him, but that did not hinder his vision. He became one of the men whose dream changed how we communicate today. Steve Jobs was born to an American mother and a Syrian father, who gave him up for adoption to an American family, who gave him their last name, Jobs. Rejected by his parents, Jobs had a good reason to be a failure. He could have run to the streets of drugs and crime, but he had a passion early on.

Steve saw little interest in pursuing a college degree when he fell in love with computers. He quit his first term at the University of Oregon to find a job. While working at Atari Computer, he joined the Homebrew Club, an organization for computer geeks.

Do not worry about how the rest will play out. When you heed the vision and set yourself into action mode, it will come when you least expect it. At one of the Homebrew Club gatherings, a network organization for computer geeks, Steve Jobs met the other Steve: Steve Wozniak. Wozniak was the computer brain and technology genius behind Apple's initial success. Before joining Jobs, Wozniak had developed a computer prototype with a graphic user interface. This point-and-click desktop icon has popularized the use of the computer and made it pervasive in our lives.

9. BE AN EXPERT AT SOLVING ONE SPECIFIC HUMAN CHALLENGE: MARK ZUCKERBERG BUILT FACEBOOK FROM HIS DORM.

Unlike Steve Jobs, Mark Zuckerberg did not intend to build a business when launching FaceMash initially. What do people do people with white collars in those glass buildings do? What do those people with blue collar in the steel buildings do? They solve people's problems. Businesses and entrepreneurs set out to solve problems. When Mark Zuckerberg launched the original version of Facebook, he was not intent on creating a business. In an interview with Freakonomics Radio article by Catherine Clifford on CNBC.com, Zuckerberg said, *"I never started this to build a company."* He added that he intended to connect people at colleges and schools. The interview showcased the foundational purpose of entrepreneurship:

Zuckerberg had identified an essential need he wanted to satisfy. As an inspired problem-solver and an ace at figuring things out, he had to dig further. He did not stop until he created what would later become Facebook. Zuckerberg added that he could not find any such thing anywhere on the Internet:

> *You could find music, you could find news, you could find information, but you couldn't find and connect with the people that you cared about, which, as people, is the most important thing. So that seemed like a big hole that needed to get filled.*

Mark Zuckerberg's philosophy is common to many pioneers who strike at new ideas that seem weird, remote, and impossible to the average person. British billionaire serial entrepreneur Richard Branson believes that *"Entrepreneurship in its truest form is about identifying a gap in the market and creating a product of use to fill that hole and make people's lives better."*

Likewise, three young men's insane, silly play toy has created a new economy: the YouTube and video streaming industry. How did they do it?

10. LET YOUR INSANITY IMPACT THE WORLD: HOW THREE KIDS' SILLY IDEA REVOLUTIONIZED THE INTERNET.

People like Zuckerberg and Jobs consciously or unconsciously transform our world and build wealth for generations and humankind. As an entrepreneur, you are on a divine mission to participate in the positive transformation of our world. It is an assignment you cannot miss. Innovating is transforming, improving, finding new applications and uses, adding to what already exists, and creating something out of what is already there. The passion of three kids has changed the world of video sharing.

When Jawed Karim, Chad Hurley, and Steve Chen created YouTube in 2005, they did not know it would be a powerful tool to spread learning, fun, and the gospel worldwide. Today, billions of teachings, music, preaching, and fun resources in every industry are available on YouTube—people teaching and empowering others around the globe.

Entrepreneurship is at the origin of wealth creation, and no industry in our recent history has made more wealth than technology innovation. When the three friends and former employees at PayPal met at a party and were inspired by the idea of creating a dating site, they had no idea they were laying the foundation of the world's second most popular social network website and by far the most useful, ahead of Facebook, Twitter, and the likes. The silly idea of posting the unfortunate failing zipper of Janet Jackson at the tsunami gave way to more appetite.

The fast growth of the site could not let any giant go to sleep. From a vi, the site quickly reached in 2006. Google saw this as an opportunity to own the Next Big Thing. In September 2006, while the company was still crawling, Google acquired YouTube for $1.65 billion, giving the founders and Sequoia Capital, the $11.5 million initial investor, a huge payday. Wait! How much did Sequoia walk away with its 30 percent stake? At the time of the acquisition, Wall Street Journal experts estimated that while the founders took home around $100 to $200 million each, they valued Sequoia's profit at $469.6, a 40-fold return from a total of $480 million in less than a year. Their prophecy was correct.

Today, YouTube's straightforward, fun, user-friendly, freedom-based, fee-less, user-generated, remunerable content has made it the go-to place for promoters, teachers, preachers, entrepreneurs, institutions, and merchants of dreams of all stripes. With its 2.7 billion users, a short step behind Facebook's 3.0 billion users as of September 2023.

Entrepreneurs are at the core of national and global development. They spur technological advancements, economic growth, and scientific expansion.

11. ADVERSITY IS A GOLDMINE: UBER & AIRBNB WERE CREATED OF OUT FRUSTRATIONS

Millionaires are pioneers and trendsetters. Data proves that every wealthy entrepreneur has been the pioneer of some trend. They might create a new frame of mind, technology, physical edifice, notion, concept, or idea that impacts our world. Apple invented the iPhone, Microsoft, and Apple the user-friendly GUI (Graphic User Interface.)

Adversity turned into simple ideas that generate billions: Entrepreneurship is not about surfing the space. It is about solving your own problem or the problem of people in your backyard. Repeat and solve the same problem for many more people. That's it. It is not rocket science. How hard was it to think about having people use their cars to give other people a lift?

According to Uber.com, "On a cold winter evening in Paris, Travis Kalanick and Garrett Camp couldn't get a ride. That's when the idea of Uber was born. The two entrepreneurs developed a smartphone app that lets people tap a button and get a ride." Garret Camp and Travis Kalanick figured it out with Ubercab and renamed it Uber in 2009.

How challenging was it to have people rent other people's homes? Brian Chesky, Nathan Blecharczyk, and Joe Gebbia, who tried to find a creative way to pay their rent, created Airbnb in 2008. The concept had always existed in a different form known as bed and breakfast.

Do you want to know why Virgin Atlantic started? When British billionaire Sir Branson found himself stranded at the airport in Puerto Rico en route to the British Virgin Islands, he found a solution: he started his own commercial airline.

The audacity to confront their Goliaths was the only force that made Uber, Airbnb, and Virgin Atlantic build global giants from their adversities. The life stories of these young men teach that they faced challenges and never expected the magnitude of success they experienced. When life threw a lemon at them, they creatively made lemonade out of it.

12. LEVERAGE THE POWER OF PEOPLE: BANK TYCOON J.P. MORGAN SKILLFULLY SWAM THROUGH TO HIS GOLDEN OPPORTUNITIES

When you surrender to your destiny, God will connect you with the man or woman who will be the trigger. Sam Walton would have never started Walmart had he not met Helen, his wife, whose father loaned him $20,000 of the $25,000 seed capital Walton needed to start his store. Bank tycoon J. P. Morgan needed entry into the affluent circle of New York City. Luckily, he had married up. His wife "Memie" Amelia Sturges, the daughter of a wealthy New York merchant, was the woman of destiny who gave J.P. Morgan a chance to meet the top class of New York, whose influence opened doors to him.

Learn to recognize your angel of destiny. My grandmother always taught her grandchildren, saying, "Always be kind and courteous to the stranger you meet, even if the persona does not seem likable. Angels come in various forms."

People make people. Many people think that *Steve* Jobs was a computer genius. That is partly true. He was probably more of a wise business genius than a computer genius. He was not a genius programmer. Steve Jobs was an innovator and a leadership genius who knew how to use the people around him.

It takes one event, one opportunity, to change your life. Microsoft would have probably taken a different direction had it not been for the contract Bill Gates received from IBM to design the PS2 and MS-DOS. Banker J.P. Morgan grew his wealth multifold upon buying Carnegie Steel Company for $480 million in 1901, equivalent to nearly $17 billion in 2022. Countless stories support the view that every great business has had its break.

It is an incredible $1.5 billion contract from US NASA (National Aeronautics and Space Administration) for Elon Musk's SpaceX project, a supply deal, or something that comes along to reshape your business landscape. It can be a mistake that leads to creating your microwave oven, delicious potato chip, fireworks, chocolate cookies, or inkjet printer. It could even be a tragic event like the loss of his wife Lucretia that steered renowned American painter and inventor Samuel F.B. Morse into creating the telegraph to deliver news in a timely fashion.

13. NOTHING CAN WITHSTAND THE FIRE OF PASSION: MICHAEL JORDAN WENT FROM REJECT TO NBA BILLIONAIRE LEGEND

Love what you do or do what you love; in other words, *don't follow money. Follow the honey, and money will follow you.* Honey is what you love. If you focus on excelling at what you love. Eventually, you can turn into a wealth-producing machine. And that's what most successful people. That is the success secret of super-achievers. Success occurs when what you do is an extension of something you enjoy doing. Multiple Olympic swimming champion Michael Phelps spent countless hours in the water, practicing six hours daily. Michael confessed that nothing was wrong with him.

Likewise, basketball legend Michael Jordan started exercising at 5:00 AM and spent five hours training daily. Elon Musk works an average of 95 hours weekly. Over 80 percent of successful people wake up before six, and many work an average of 80 hours a week. Who would spend this much time doing something he does not enjoy?

The self-made didn't become successful whining at boring jobs. To make sure you make it to the top, choose your career wisely. Superachievers enjoy their freedom and will not trade it for anything. They excel because they have fun doing what they love to do. Most millionaires have acquired their wealth doing things they love. For some, it is technology; for others, it is helping others or a personal hobby that turns into a business. Turning your passion into a wealth-building system is the most significant and enjoyable way to build wealth. I do not know any basketball player who does not enjoy playing, nor can I give you the name of a singer who hates singing.

Chinese philosopher Confucius is credited with the quote, *"Choose a job you love, and you will never work another day in your life."* While no clarity is available regarding the ownership of the quote, another version of the idea reads: **'Find something you love to do, and you'll never have to work a day in your life.'** Regardless of who said it, the idea behind the quote is that when you love something, you do not see it as a job or a burden. Hence, you tend to spend a lot of time doing it, which gives you the opportunity develop an expertise at it, why? The way to succeed at anything is to practice, correct your shortcomings, and repeat the steps. Why is it necessary for a tap dancer to keep on practicing? When you are passionate about what you do, you either already have a natural ability and skills or quickly develop and master those skills. You develop expertise and unparalleled genius. You would do it even if you were not paid for it when you love something. You go the extra mile; you transmit your passion to your team and the end user. Something you are passionate about is naturally endowed, so you become an icon, setting you apart for success.

14. DEVELOP PERSUASIVE POWER AND KEEN SALESMANSHIP: SAMUEL PALMISANO ROSE FROM SALESMAN TO IBM CEO

Above all else, become an expert at persuasion. It does not matter what you do in life or whether you are a clerk, manager, salesperson, investor, entrepreneur, educator, scientist, president, or CEO, if you are weak at persuading people, you will have a hard time making headways in your area of expertise. Persuasion and selling have one thing in common: the goal of getting your prospect to buy or buy into your offer. One of the most incredible skills every successful person has is the ability to sell—success is all about selling or trading, giving valuable consideration in return for an equivalent value. The word "sell" broadly means the ability to win others to your purpose. In that sense, aren't we all salespeople? In a 2013 study conducted by the American Marketing Association, 25 percent of corporate CEOs had a background or education in marketing and sales. In contrast, *Fortune* magazine revealed that only 11 percent of CEOs hold a business degree (33 percent of CEOs hold an engineering degree). The sales function is the heart of the business. You may have a fantastic product, but if you lack the sales experts in your organization to sell it, you are just on life support. It won't be long before you close your doors.

Entrepreneurs must develop strong marketing and sales skills or hire professional sales talent. Otherwise, the company will not survive if it cannot generate revenue. The sales function supersedes any other business function. Howard Shultz's Starbucks took off because he was a sales genius. IBM CEO Samuel Palmisano started as a sales agent, and so did Anne Mulcahy, CEO of Xerox. Even timid-looking Bill Gates toured the world to sell Microsoft Windows when it was first launched and unknown to the world.

Political candidates sell their programs and personalities to voters. Workers sell their time, skills, and talents to their employers; entrepreneurs sell their ideas to investors; companies sell their products and services to consumers. Investors sell their money for a profit. Athletes, singers, and artists sell their talents, know-how, and abilities. Even professions such as the practice of medicine, law, and specialized knowledge are all about selling. Celebrities sell their skills and images for profit. In this sense, profit is the added value, the surplus you receive from winning people to your cause.

15. EMBRACE NAPOLEON HILL'S PRINCIPLE OF ENTHUSIASM AND OPTIMISM TO CONQUER ADVERSITY AND THE WORLD.

Science proves that optimism is a gateway to longevity. The Scriptures address the power of positive thinking when they read, "*Keep your heart with diligence. For out of it spring the issue of your life*" Proverbs 4:24.

What happens to people you smile at? They automatically smile back. The contagious nature of enthusiasm will create an atmosphere of positive interaction. Powerful coaches are funny; influential leaders are accessible and relatable. Successful people are positive, energetic, and optimistic. Napoleon Hill profusely discussed the benefits of enthusiasm in his famous *Sixteen Principles of Success* coaching. Enthusiasm is attractive and conducive to more productivity. The self-made thrive on their cheerful demeanor and outlook on life. Enthusiasm is the secret to success; it motivates, creates interest, and inspires employees to perform their best to complete any task without coercion.

Many people fail to realize themselves because they fear being judged or crave belongingness. The lesson here is that you will not make a significant impact if you cannot detach yourself from being and acting like everybody. There is a price to pay for being different, but it is worth the sacrifice.

> **LESSON LEARNED:** *This chapter delves into the idea that true audacity often appears insane to others. Through stories of individuals who defied conventional wisdom and pursued their wildest dreams, the chapter explored the boundary between genius and madness. It is a vibrant invitation and encouragement for you to embrace audacity and think beyond the norm, even if it appears ridiculous to those around you.*

YOUR TURN - DAY 1: THE AUDACITY OF INSANITY

Self-Reflection: *Think about a time when you had an audacious idea that others considered insane. What was it, and what did you learn from that experience?*

- Have you ever pursued an idea or goal that others considered "insane," and if so, what was the outcome?
- How do you typically react when faced with skepticism or criticism regarding audacious ideas or plans?
- What is your comfort level with embracing audacity in your personal or professional life?
- Can you recall any historical or contemporary figures who achieved greatness by defying conventional wisdom?

Application: *Summarize your takeaway from this chapter in the following lines, then answer questions 1-3 in one sentence.*

1. **Challenge Norms:** Identify one aspect of your life or work where you can challenge conventional thinking and take an audacious step. What's holding you back, and how can you overcome those obstacles?
2. **Dream Big:** Write down three audacious goals or dreams you've always had but haven't pursued. Choose one to work on and create a plan to make it a reality.
3. **Inspiration:** Find and read about someone who achieved remarkable success by embracing their audacity. How can their story inspire you to be bolder in your actions?

THE AUDACITY OF CHANGE

EVOLVE & FLY FREE LIKE A BUTTERFLY

"Progress is impossible without change, and those who cannot change their minds cannot change anything."

– George Bernard Shaw

Chapter 1 discussed the power of being self and remaining true to your values and principles. Detaching yourself from the bandwagon will assuredly lead you to break the status quo and open the door to change, innovation, and progress. In this chapter, the examples of Jack Welch, Netflix, Blockbuster, and Nokia will highlight some of the opportunities and challenges of ordinary people who become highly successful game changers.

JACK WELCH'S BOLD DECISION THAT TURNED GENERAL ELECTRIC INTO A GIANT

Decision-making is a vital skill of superachievers. Like many corporate executives, Jack Welch was an inspired decision-maker. He guided the destiny of General Electric, an appliance giant. In his book *Winning*, Jack Welch wrote how he enjoyed the freedom his board gave him to make tough decisions without pressure. As a result, he significantly impacted General Electric's growth until his retirement, raising the company's value from $12 billion in 1981 to $ 410 billion in 2001.

Jack made history with his severance package of $417 million. "What did he do to deserve that much when most employees were earning a tiny bit of that jackpot?" you might wonder.

Jack Welch made several bold, unpopular decisions that eventually benefited the company he grew thirty-fivefold. That's huge. Hired as the youngest CEO of GE, Jack entered the boardroom with a list of challenges to prove he deserved the position. He quickly brought about significant changes, altering the corporate culture and the bureaucratic system. He replaced it with a leaner operation. Jack then changed the Big Corp culture into a more approachable, less intimidating small company atmosphere and promoted it throughout the organization to empower employees. Jack was celebrated for his unparalleled legacy at General Electric on his retirement day.

People like Jack Welch get paid millions to make the most defining decisions for their organizations. A mistake will lead to huge losses and chaos involving the lives of many. A good decision-maker is analytical, informed, and well-advised. Self-made people surround themselves with people who feed them the correct information so they can be self-reliant decision-makers. As the head of a household, even if it is just you, you make many decisions, consciously or unconsciously, every day to change your growth.

But audacity isn't just about thinking differently; it's about acting differently. In the chapter on the audacity of change, we delve into the lives of trailblazers like Jeff Bezos and Mark Zuckerberg, who disrupted entire industries with their bold visions. They didn't wait for change to show up – they created it, challenging norms and reshaping the world.

THE DEMISE OF NOKIA, A GIANT THAT FAILED TO SEE THE FUTURE

How do you fall from a market capitalization of $151 billion in 2007 to a mere $19 billion less than thirteen years later? Founded in 1865, the Finnish company Nokia was once the world leader in the cellular phone industry, with 41 percent of the market share. According to Statista.com, in the first quarter of 2007, Nokia controlled 46.7 percent of the world's cellular phone market, to fall to 3.1 percent in the second quarter of 2013. Today, the company is nothing more than a dwarf compared to giants like Huawei, Samsung, and Apple. Nokia's management did not see that change keeps you in business. You must continually vet the market to know where the trend is going.

With the advent of the millennials, smartphones, and the all-in-one portable do-it-all, Nokia, the patriarch of the phone industry, failed to predict the future. The giant was left in the dust of innovation to eventually go and die at the foot of Microsoft Mobile for the pitiful price of $7.6 billion in April 2014. That is pocket change, knowing the gazillions of patents, skilled engineers, and the opportunity Nokia let go.

How disheartening for those whose wealth depended on Nokia's stocks. In June of 2000, if you owned 100,000 shares of Nokia, you could boast of being a millionaire to the tune of $6,200,000, which is not bad. If you were lucky to sell in November 2007, you would go home with $4,100,000, which is not too shabby. But if you waited too long until April 2014, when Nokia sold its device division to Microsoft Mobile, you could only cash in a mere $730,000, a 5,470,000 loss.

Eventually, Microsoft Mobile went to its grave. Nokia's cell phone department was acquired by Finnish company HMD Global, a young company created in 2016 by Smart Connect and funded by venture capitalist Jean-Francois Baril, a former Nokia executive vice president.

Despite their lawsuit, Nokia shareholders lost money, while surprisingly, the former executives of Nokia regrouped and are now running HMD. Despite all the marketing efforts, Nokia is nowhere on the radar of the world market. Huawei, Samsung, Apple, LG, and Lenovo are now running the game. Nokia's brand reputation and market leadership waned away because its executives failed to see change, adapt, and innovate.

Unlike Nokia, Netflix understood the power of innovation to keep pace with the continuous swing in consumer mood and habits.

KAIZEN, THE JAPANESE'S OBSESSION WITH CHANGE

You cannot grow if you reject change. The concept of change is a hot topic in human organizations. Change is the essence of evolution. All that exists experiences change, yet change is not always welcome. People resist change for one reason or another. They prefer the status quo, the known. Dreading uncertainty, they prefer to stick with the devil they know. It is laughable that humans strive for better lives; they want to achieve success; they want new things yet resist what brings about those things they desire. Isn't this what we call the inconsistency of human nature? By nature, humans evolve, grow, and strive for happiness and success. As your life improves, you feel a sense of self-worth as you achieve milestones. Change, in essence, is the compass of success. That which does not change is lifeless.

> ## SECRET CODE #2
> ## BE TRANSFORMED AND BECOME A GAME CHANGER

How much has your life changed? That is the most critical question at this point in our conversation. Over the past five years or even ten years, how much change have you experienced in your life? Have you earned a new degree or a certificate? Have you completed that program you never finished? Have you learned a new trade? Have you experienced a promotion or a raise? Have your relationship, marriage, or finances improved? Have you added a new member to your family? Have you made new friends? Have you met people who can impact your life? Have you started that book you always dreamed about? Have you started the business that fascinates you? Have you changed those habits you are not so proud of? Have you lost those pounds you are so uncomfortable with? How much have you changed in the last year, the previous five years, or the last ten years?

Where do you see yourself the following year, five years, or ten or twenty years? What are the indicators or predictors of change and growth? Past the New Year resolution, will you resume your life as usual for the next 364 days?

Many people resist change because of the fear of losing self-continuity and dreading the pain of dealing with an unknown reality. If mismanaged, change can lead to chaos. According to a report from Harvard Business Review, 70 percent of mergers and acquisitions fail because people resist change. People in merging ventures cling to their corporate culture. Where two cultures are profoundly dissimilar, the failure rate can reach as high as 90 percent.

To innovate, you must always consider people's self-interests, including personal ambitions, behaviors, preferences, and goals. Resistance becomes fierce when you abruptly alter people's customs and change fails. People must accept for it to take form, for coercion can only cause resentment and brutality.

Change must be incremental, progressive, and continuous to be efficient, ensuring continuity will not abruptly cease. That is why intelligent organizations imply the snowball change principle. They start with scaled improvement in one department, then progressively move to a different one throughout the organization. You cannot alter everything suddenly.

Innovative organizations use the Japanese concept of continuous improvement, known as Kaizen. Kaizen can help create growth in different areas, such as reducing waste by controlling overproduction and improving employee job satisfaction, leading to a higher retention rate.

The chain reaction increases customer satisfaction, reduces job-related accidents, fosters higher team morale, etc. In sum, Kaizen leads the organization to more profitability and an overall climate of satisfaction. After all, change is stubborn, and no matter how you try to prevent it, it cannot be stopped. It will eventually show up uninvited because it has a purpose. It must continue its course and lead to innovation, the essence of progress.

JEFF AND ELON'S TITANS' FEUD IN THE INNOVATION BATTLEGROUND

One would have thought that being a multibillionaire would have made you act civilized. I thought people in the upper lounge would act grown up and courteous, unlike two street-corner thugs. I guess I was wrong. Money does not change people; it magnifies what they really are. Who does not remember Soviet president Nikita Khrushchev's infamous shoes on the table during a UN meeting or President Ronald Reagan's middle finger at California protesters?

The people we call geniuses and hold in high regard are often no different from two middle school kids. Jeff Bezos and Elon Musk don't like each other, and the world knows it, but to the point of throwing jabs at each other, that's low. The same way the Russians and the Americans frowned at each other's plan to conquer space, the same way two Golden Lounge occupants have been mocking each other's space venture for over two decades. Jeff did not appreciate how Elon secured the exclusive right to use NASA's launch pad. Elon threw tantrums when Jeff was granted a NASA patent. My friend Alex, who does not like the two men, said, "As long as they do not provoke the meteorites to come and hit us here on Earth, they can fight all they want." I added as long as their competition improves space innovation for all of us, all the best.

The two men's dislike for each other came from a 2004 dinner. The two rivals met to iron out things, tone down their feud, and clarify the goals of their respective space ventures, Elon's SpaceX and Jeff's Blue Origin. But expectedly, the dinner did not go well when the two men could not agree on how to share the "tiny" space in the upper lounge. "Who will be best of us all?" The two nerds feuded with each other. With all the billions of galaxies in space, why fight over tiny red Mars?

Recently, Forbes Magazine ranked America's most innovative CEO. Guess who came in the top two positions? Jeff Bezos and Elon Musk were tied. How did Elon Musk position himself in late 2020 as the second wealthiest man on earth when he was ranked 35th at the beginning of the year? Inspired leaders know that they must listen to the market and adapt. The market is dynamic and efficient. Innovation-deficient organizations die while innovative ones thrive.

Today, the West does not understand that innovation in Asia is 8taking the world by surprise. Asia is developing at the speed of light, from China to Thailand to Malaysia. At the current rhythm, it is not hazardous to expect Asia to outpace Europe within the next decade, if not sooner. Arrogantly still stuck in their outdated history books, thinking of old, feudal, poor China, many refuse to acknowledge that China no longer plays in their league. Honesty wants us to note that Asia will soon surpass the West if the latter continues to sleep on their laurels, claiming to be the world's best in this and that.

No one, no nation or company holds the monopoly of innovation, and no country is too strong to surpass if its infrastructure and human capital fail to meet the current standards. Likewise, no company is too big to fall if it fails to meet customers' and clients' changing needs and lifestyles. Giant Nokia paid the price for its sluggishness and inability to adapt to the demands of the changing business landscape.

THE RISE OF NETFLIX, AN IDEA THEY SAID "...WILL NEVER WORK"

"The dot-com hysteria is completely overblown?" said John Antioco, the man who oversaw the destiny of Blockbuster, another giant that failed to predict the future in 2000. Do you remember the early 2000s when investors lost money in the dot-com bubble? It was that time Marc

Randolph and Reed Hastings chose to pitch their newfound gold chest idea of online video streaming to Blockbuster executives.

The Power of Pivot. Events following 9/11 that impacted the cost of shipping DVDs affected Netflix's profitability. Hence, the company wanted to pivot and look for a buyer. After turning down Amazon's $14 million offer for the venture, Reed and Mark flew to Dallas to present their proposal to Blockbuster executives.

Despite a well-coordinated presentation highlighting the opportunity for Blockbuster, a brick-and-mortar video rental industry leader, to enter the promising online market, the representatives laughed at the idea. They said, "That will never work."

Never be too comfortable. Keep innovating. Keep pushing. The biggest mistake that crushes people after they have met success is becoming too comfortable. They stop evolving, pushing up and forward. Never underestimate the tiny David. He could send you to your grave or serve as your lifesaver when the appointed time for you to drown comes. Never look down on your assistant or mentee. Never, never be too comfortable.

For a mere $50 million asking price for acquiring a company in which investors had already poured $30 million, Blockbuster, worth $5 billion at the time, let go of an idea worth $230 billion today. After rejecting an opportunity that would have made the company adapt and maintain market leadership, Blockbuster's management was too comfortable to see beyond their sumptuous glass offices. The management team dismissed the small company's offer amid mocking giggles.

Like any fairy tale, Marc and Reed had their last laughs. Blockbuster failed to adapt to the video industry trend. It went to its grave ten years later, and Netflix became the world giant two decades later. History repeats itself and gives us opportunities to wise up, but do we? Every success has a story, and the legend of Netflix is worth reading. Next time you pitch your multi-million-dollar idea, you hear, "You've got to be insane!" "That is the dumbest idea; you know that will never work," pick up your tools and continue your search.

Those refrains are an everyday song for entrepreneurs. They are also the reason people never attempt to think beyond the ordinary. However, visionary entrepreneurs welcome "No" as the first step to "Yes." Billionaire Howard Shultz of Starbucks could lecture you on how to keep going even if your idea got rejected 220 times. Rejection is part of every salesperson's job.

If you ever talk to Marc Randolph, one of the men behind the fantastic legend of Netflix, you will learn a life lesson. He will teach you that developing a good idea takes a dozen terrible ideas. Netflix proved that you could be the one to resurrect, revitalize, and give a new luster to an industry that others think is dying. That's called innovative genius. Ask Marc Randolph to send you a copy of his book *That Will Never Work: The Birth of Netflix and the Amazing Life of an Idea*.

Reading the first-hand account of the founder of Netflix will be worth decades of learning at a top-ranked business school. I will spare you the whole story of Netflix's inception. Instead, let us focus on how innovation can lead entrepreneurs with a motive to abandon everything to start the next big thing. Marc Randolph was such a man. When Marc sold his venture Integrity QA to Pure Atria, a company headed by Hastings, the two men got closer. Marc became the company's Vice President of Marketing, Pure Atria. The two visionaries started scouting for even better business ventures.

Commuting together, the two men joined their assets: one with a head full of ideas, the other a chest full of cash. They went on a spree to find the Next Big Idea. A born entrepreneur, Marc threw out idea after idea.

"Let's create and sell personalized products online," Marc offered.

"What do you have in mind, Marc?" asked Reed.

"Humm, I'm not sure. What about dog food, shampoo, or a surfing board?

"Are you sure that'll work?" asked Reed.

"I'm not sure. Why not?" responded Marc.

I am not too sure. Yuck, that sucks to me. Let's keep digging," offered Reed.

After days of brainstorming, one morning, in a Eureka moment, Marc called out:

"Eh, Reed, I think I've got it!"

But before Marc could finish his sentence, Reed interrupted, jumping like a kid eager to know,

"What Whaaat? What you've got?"

"How about mail-order DVDs? You know I've done this before," reassured Marc with a victorious smile.

"Woohooo! Awesome! Man, this is cool. Let's get it done!" screamed Reed, not waiting for Marc's explanation.

Weeks later, the two pals got their brains together for their exciting new idea. Banking on Marc's experience in the mail-order business, in 1997, Netflix, a mail-order DVD venture, became a reality. Over the next two years, the two partners gathered a team of eight employees, and Hastings put up the seed capital of $2.5 million of his own money. Marc took the company's lead as the CEO, while Reed oversaw product development. Just five years after its inception, Netflix went public in 2002. Upon Reed's request, Marc was replaced in 1999 by Reed Hastings. Soon after, he left Netflix in 2003 to pursue other ventures.

What is the lesson here? Nokia died for lack of innovation in a nascent industry, while Netflix reengineered the rebirth of a dying industry.

From DVD rental, the venture entered the video streaming arena. The winning business model was revolutionary yet straightforward. The company saw the opportunity the Internet economy had created. In contrast to the old trend that focused on the sale and a rental fee per video, Netflix leveraged the growth of Internet users and modeled its offer accordingly. It saw the power of the subscription model. Banking on the growing number of households and businesses making Internet access part of their must-have utilities, the company applied the theory of large numbers.

Netflix kept things simple. With its 214 million monthly subscribers, even if the company charged an average of $10, it would earn a $2.14 billion monthly income, or around $26 billion yearly. *The subscription business model* made sense for the team because it kept things simple. Subscribers have unlimited access to hundreds of thousands of titles and TV shows anywhere, anytime, for less than the price of a meal. With this innovation, Netflix became like the Internet, present anywhere and everywhere you can access an Internet connection.

REED HASTINGS'S SMART MOVE AT BUILDING STRATEGIC ALLIANCES

Netflix did not just stop its reach within the US boundaries. When Netflix partnered with French CNRS scientists to compress its content, the company conquered the world. Smartly reinventing itself and maximizing profitability, Netflix entered the movie production business, controlling one of its largest cost centers. It also provided original content at the speed of light anywhere. In 2020, Netflix became a giant competing with Amazon, making Reed Hastings, a math scientist and a Stanford graduate, a $5-billion heavy tycoon with just one percent of the company stock ownership.

Despite losing 200,000 subscribers due to fee hikes, Netflix has grown in more than 200 countries, with over 221 million household and business subscribers worldwide as of April 2022. Its share price has skyrocketed, maximizing investors' portfolio value; however, Hastings knows he cannot slumber. He must be alert and continue innovating.

Fierce competition from Disney, Warner, Hulu, Apple TV, and Amazon Prime made Netflix's business harder in 2019. The company's stock price fell to $325 in 2019, but with the advent of COVID-19, the company stock experienced a surge to reach as high as $503 in December 2020. With a market capitalization of $267.49 billion in 2021, this quarter-of-a-century-old company uses its first-mover advantage to stay ahead of the game. Netflix is a win-win for all its stakeholders: it creates value for its customers, maximizes investors' wealth, and offers appealing career opportunities for its employees. You cannot beat that. Despite Netflix's growth, Hastings knows you cannot order success from the drive-thru. Learn to exercise patience.

SOICHIRO HONDA'S WAITING-ROOM MINDSET CREATED A GIANT ON THE ROAD

The greatest gift of success relies on the power of waiting. Any enterprise, be it human or spiritual, obeys the law of the cycle. Our lives, nature, the weather, the animal species, and elements of nature obey the law of growth. Even the grizzly bear starts as a cubby. The yearly seasons are evidence of the life cycle. Those who understand the principle of the waiting room are the resilient ones who succeed when everyone else has given up. Savvy investors live by the concept of buying, holding, and selling. Farmers know that the seed must be put into the ground, rotten, and produce the plant, the tree, the fruit, and the ripe fruit before it can be harvested.

When you hear Honda, what comes to mind? Honda Acura. Civic, or Prelude. Yet that was not always what made the Honda brand. Born in, the unorthodox, rebellious mechanic and car racer turned CEO only saw his company make cars for the last of his 84 years on this earth. Starting as Honda Research Institute, the company focused on manufacturing engines and motorcycles in the first 50 years of its existence. Though Honda loved racing cars, he did not enter the car industry until later in his life.

Any form of investment goes through a silent period of waiting. It takes a startup seven years to yield a substantial profit. Though Honda Soichiro had emptied all his savings and pawned his wife's jewelry, his company would still not show a promising future. A waiting room mindset helps you understand that you must observe a holding period before cashing in your blessing. Learn to wait even when you itch with ambition. Impatience can only frustrate you.

Our Lord Jesus Christ waited thirty years before fully engaged in his ministry. Patriarch Abraham did not mind waiting twenty-five years before welcoming the promised child, Isaac. The Israelites suffered over four hundred and thirty years in Egypt and forty in the desert before reaching Canaan, the Promised Land.

The ability to wait is the true character of maturity and endurance. Patience is unparalleled when it comes to building oneself up to the top.

PHENOMENAL ACHIEVERS KNOW HOW TO LEVERAGE THE POWER OF PEOPLE:

"Things do not make people. People make people."
— **Coach Greb**

Indeed, the self-made are people-made. When you hear Facebook, you think of Mark Zuckerberg. What about the other three classmates and his sister, Randi Zuckerberg, who ran the market development function of the start-up? When you hear Walmart, you think of Sam Walton. What about his brother, Bud, his wife Helen, and father-in-law, who loaned him the first $20,000 of the $25,000 seed capital?

When you hear Apple, you think of Steve Jobs; what about Steve Wozniak? When you hear Microsoft, you think of Bill Gates; what about Paul Allen, Steve Ballmer, and many others? A small idea started in 2004 as a hobby turned into a mega business that crosses international boundaries today. Marc Zuckerberg did not create Facebook alone. He would not have had the necessary funds if not for the seed investments from Peter Thiel's Sequoia Capital. How about Eduardo Saverin, Chris Hughes, Andrew

McCollum, and Dustin Moskovitz, Zuckerberg's Harvard roommates and the initial team that sacrificed brain cells and sweat?

Zuckerberg could not have built the multibillion-dollar empire without the courageous investors who risked their money. Today, Facebook is a multibillion-dollar giant because of a joint effort from everyone, but all we remember is the person who had the drive, the originator, and the point of reference. Reaching out to others is a tremendous strategic opportunity for entrepreneurs.

American entrepreneurs are successful because American investors have faith in their system. They brave all challenges and are not afraid to invest in ideas they view with immense potential. The nameless investors are the unsung heroes whose taste for adventure helped build America. The nation leads the world in inventions and innovations in most industries, from media to technology to science. The power of synergy works and benefits everyone, and no self-made person can do without it. The power of leverage assembled thirteen pals to create PayPal: everyone took the risk, pitched in his genius, sweated along, waited, and shared the pie when the PayPal mafia sold the company to eBay. A self-made is a network built.

Build your networks of social capital. What social organizations are you a part of? *It will be hard to achieve anything if you lack human connectedness.* When you are connected with the Source, it activates the human web to your advantage. You cannot meet the right people if you do not expose yourself to them. Fortunately, our information society has allowed you to socialize on a larger scale to find a niche of prospects for your millionaire idea.

Wealth-building is outsourced. You do not build your own wealth. *You hire people to do so for you. Have a pool of qualified professionals by your side.* You will seldom see self-made do their accounting or investment portfolio management. Is spending your valuable time behind your delivery truck's wheel more cost-effective? Wouldn't it make more sense to contract it out so you can focus your energy and time on working your system? Many self-employed struggle to grow their businesses because *they work in their systems instead of working the system.* In fact, many do not have a system.

Savvy entrepreneurs, conversely, work in the business for a while, then detach themselves to focus on *working* the business. Thus, they can focus on building relationships with different stakeholders. How will you see the strength or weakness of your business if it submerges you? How can you borrow more money, hire more qualified result producers, and exponentially grow your earnings if you are fettered to the business?

The self-made go way past the stage of self-employment. It is costly to be self-employed. You are limited and waste considerable time and money. If you are afraid of spending money on outsourcing some of the tasks that are not your core expertise or that only you can perform, do not try to do it all alone. It is a counter-productive scheme. I did not understand this when I started my company until I spent three years paying rent unnecessarily. "You have to spend money to make money," says the adage. I became a real business owner when I sacrificed the little bit left of my savings to hire the right people. I no longer had to concurrently be the consultant, sales agent, tech guy, customer service representative, and administrative assistant. I was free to focus on my expertise. That's how I went from a struggling entrepreneur to a thriving visionary.

Reject the "I-Me-and-Myself" business model. Outsourcing is appealing as it frees the visionary entrepreneur time and energy to focus on the *main thing*: playing the orchestra maestro. The secret of millionaire success is the extensive use of leverage: wealth-builders excel at accomplishing things through people. They hire a qualified pool of professionals at their beck and call. They do so through and throughout their wealth-building scheme.

Professional wealth-builders have a team approach to their daily dealings. They hire a trusted pool of people to whom they delegate. A typical circle of high-rolling superrich would look like the following list, but you will adapt it to what you can afford:

- Employees
- Managers
- Personal and administrative assistants
- Lawyers
- Bookkeepers and accountants
- Financial advisers
- Health and medical professionals
- Mentors and spiritual guides
- Bankers and fiduciary professionals
- Partners and associates
- Realtors
- Dedicated travel agents

- Insurance agents
- Lifestyle professionals
- Club member friends
- Household staff

To be able to outsource your wealth-building system, you must develop the art of people management and leadership: develop a high level of emotional intelligence.

PATRICK KING: EXCEPTIONAL ACHIEVERS RATE HIGH ON EMOTIONAL INTELLIGENCE AND THE LIKABILITY INDEX

How do you fare on the likeability index? People do business with people they like. People buy from people they like and trust. Companies hire consultants, service providers, and suppliers they like or do not hate. Being likable is essential to becoming self-made. If you want doors wide open, connect with people with many tentacles. Only your positive, selfless, and enthusiastic self can buy that.

How likable are you? How empathetic are you? Wealth-building, the business world, and life function as a web of relationships. *People, not things, are the spice of life.* To make money, you need no machines; you need people. To spend it, you need people. How unenchanting it would be to be popping a Dom Perignon Champagne in utter solitude! Having plenty of money but lacking the touch of people only makes you rich, not wealthy. You will fail if you cannot connect your revolutionary ideas with the right people. People are at the heart of your wealth-building scheme, and the ability to connect and maintain strong bonds is paramount. *Relationships are more important than knowledge, more important than money and status.* So, what does likability mean, why is it important, and how likable are you?

Views vary on the usability of likability. According to the *Merriam-Webster Dictionary*, "likability" is "having the qualities that bring about favorable regard." In his book *The Science of Likability: 27 Studies to Master Charisma, Attract Friends, Captivate People and Take Advantage of Human Psychology*, Patrick King explains how being likable can open doors to better friendships.

Perry Yeatman, CEO of Perry Yeatman Global Partners, disagrees. He believes it is not necessary to be liked as a leader. He argues, "*Looking at the* leaders *of Fortune 500 companies, you would not say they are likable, would you?"* Reportedly, Steve Jobs's employees disliked him because of his arrogance.

Your business is not about you. Whatever your view on likability, the wisdom is to ask yourself: "How does it hurt me to be courteous, genuine, respectful, caring, and honest? How could it hurt my business to be likable?" The greatest mistake uninspired or *rookie entrepreneurs* make is to think that the business is about them. No! Once you have started a business, you have taken the focus off yourself. You have signed up to pamper your patrons and pacify their tantrums. Some call it customer service and create a special department for it. Wrong. Customer Care is the heart of every business. It must be executed by every actor in your business, from the rank-and-file employee to the top executive.

Your leadership style will help you in or out of business. Business success is about leadership: building trusting and caring relationships with your three constituents: the Client, the Employee, and the Investor. Successful entrepreneurs take this seriously. They know, develop, and rehearse their leadership style. What are you, an autocratic, democratic, or charismatic leader? Does your leadership style coerce or empower? Are you a people magnet or a repulsive, cold-blooded stone hearted monster? Oprah Winfrey can teach you how to rally the whole universe by being genuine and relatable. Dale Carnegie believed the best way to win friends is to show genuine interest in people. Raising others is the easiest way to rise, which means being a *care-ismatic* leader:

> *Weak leaders overpower; strong leaders empower.*
> – Coach Greb

"

HOW OPRAH BECAME A SYMBOL OF HUMANISM: "LEARN TO CARE ABOUT PEOPLE"

"

Role models like Oprah serve as a source of inspiration for the power of goodness. Hence, many followers model their behaviors according to their values. Oprah has tremendously demonstrated how people should care about their fellow human beings. Consequently, she has become an unmatched icon of humanism.

As Dale Carnegie put it, to make friends - to conquer people's hearts, show a genuine interest in them. How did the poor, molested girl from Mississippi become a media mogul in America, straight from the deep South? How did she outperform any media anchor in American history, raking $315 million a year to come and feel people's pain, wipe their tears, and cry with them? You give me just $2000, and I will cry a bucket of tears with them.

Born Orpah Gail Winfrey in 1954 in Kosciusko, Mississippi, Oprah came to this earth to serve as a beacon of hope, to show what is possible when you are selfless, genuine, and caring. Oprah invested so much in philanthropy that Forbes Magazine named her the most influential American in 2012 and 2013. The Giving Back Foundation also acclaimed Oprah as the most generous person in 2008. She has donated to over fifty charities, foundations, and disaster funds. Oprah is a cheerful giver. She gave away over $1 billion, the equivalent of more than a third of her estimated net worth of $2.6 billion.

Oprah has become a cross-cultural phenomenon because she skillfully becomes a beacon of hope for many and a role model for others. Funny, scandal-free, and generous, Oprah attracts fans because of her humanism. She knows how to empathize with those in need. Oprah knows how to feel with her audience and continues to charm and inspire people from different races and cultures worldwide. God-fearing, she is what I call a perfect child of God. Oprah had the IQ (Intellectual Quotient), the right measure of intelligence, to get her feet into the media industry. Now, she has the EQ (Emotional Quotient), the measure of humanism, to maintain herself in leadership.

IQ or EQ? Your intellectual quotient (IQ) gets you the job, but your emotional quotient (EQ) brings you to the top of the ladder. Strong analytical skills are no longer enough. You need people skills to have people refer to the right tech offer. You must add emotional intelligence and social skills to help you transition into leadership positions. The following ten social skills will make you a successful leader, entrepreneur, and employee:

- Be empathetic and relatable.
- Be honest
- Be a good listener

- Be creative
- Submit to authority
- Be Inspiring
- Have a team spirit
- Be a leader and take initiatives

Be empathetic and relatable. Billionaire Warren Buffet lines up like everyone to get his hamburger and coke from his neighborhood MacDonald's. Most people we see as geniuses do not take themselves as seriously as we do. If it were not for their staff, celebrities would be more accessible than the clerks at the grocery store. Most successful people know where they came from and are not as transformed by money as they may seem. Google CEO Tim Cook lives a humble life and once said, *"I like to be reminded of where I came from and putting myself in modest surroundings helps me do that. Money is not a motivator for me."*

Most super-achievers are humble and down-to-earth. Azim Premji is India's tech tycoon and founder of Wipro, India's software giant. Azim, whose net worth was about $23 billion in 2018, prefers to live a simple life. He is not interested in wealth and glamor. In 2019, he donated over 75 percent of his wealth to charity. Azim is not alone. David Green of Hobby Lobby, Ingvar Kamprad of Ikea, and Ratan Tata of Tata Group are wealthy people who have chosen to live meekly. True wealth is not about money. It is about alleviating other people's suffering by giving them hope.

To be successful, you must be relatable. People must find you genuinely interested in them. What makes Oprah Winfrey so successful as a public figure? She is empathetic. She suffered early on and knows how to feel other people's pain. That is why her fan base is so large and diverse. For two decades, Oprah topped the most popular shows in the USA. According to data from the research group Nielsen, over 48 million people watch her shows weekly in 150 countries.

> ***LESSON LEARNED:*** *This chapter taught you the value of being transformed to express your uniqueness. Change is the mother of progress. Fear of change begets nothing but dullness that paves the way to a dying life. Isn't it absurd to blindly follow desire growth and at the same reject that which brings about it. Don't be afraid to try something that has never been done. Follow your whims and awake that sleeping giant within. Get out of Main Street. Trace your own My Street. Be you. Be unique and*

birth that baby within that will save the world. Trying to follow a pattern is like walking to the gulags of misery. Be different and preach it around you. Liberate the insanity within.

YOUR TURN -DAY 2: THE AUDACITY OF CHANGE

Self-Reflection: *What change have you been hesitating to make in your life or career? Identify it and consider why you've been hesitant.*

- What are some significant changes or transformations you have experienced in your life, and how did they impact your growth?
- Are you generally comfortable with embracing change, or do you tend to resist it?
- Can you identify a specific change or innovation that has had a profound influence on your life or industry?
- What motivates you to pursue change and take audacious steps toward your goals?

Application: Small Steps: *Break down a significant change you want to make into smaller, manageable steps. What's the first step you can take today?*

1. **Role Models:** Identify someone who has successfully navigated a major life change. Reach out to them for advice and insights.
2. **Action Plan:** Create a detailed action plan for the change you want to make, including timelines and milestones.
3. **Accountability:** Share your change goal with a friend or family member who can hold you accountable and offer support along the way.

THE AUDACITY OF PURPOSE

DARE TO SURRENDER TO YOUR ONE THING

"In Him also we have obtained an inheritance, being predestined according to the purpose of Him who works all things according to the counsel of His will."

– Ephesians 1:1

"The two most important days of your life are the day you were born and the day you find out why you were born."

– Mark Twain

The Audacity of Purpose

You've just been to an ocean of illustrations about the power of change and the courage it takes to implement change no matter how painful. The fundamental question one should pose is: to what extent should change be implemented and for what purpose? Change without a overarching purpose is anarchy; behind every action, there must be a meaningful reason. So, what is purpose and why does it matter? A contrasted overview of CNN's Star Chef Anthony Bourdain and Grameen Bank's Mohammad Hunus's lives will shed light on the power of purpose. Reading the lines below will teach you why *a life lived without a purpose is a life unlived.*

ANTHONY BOURDAIN: WHAT TOOK THE LIFE OF OUR BELOVED STAR?

> "No one pursued his purpose that failed, yet achieving a purpose is never a cakewalk. He who seeks wealth, fame, and fulfillment must seek to manifest his divine calling."
> *– Coach Greb*

FAMOUS, RICH, YET MISERABLE?

If you were like me and selectively watched a few shows from CNN between April 2013 and November 2018 and enjoyed good food, travel, and great laughter, you would have probably heard of Anthony Bourdain. A renowned chef who toured the world, Anthony traveled with his viewers around the globe, filming his love of tasting and appreciating world culture and cuisine. Though I do not watch much TV, *Parts Unknown* and *No Reservations* were my favorite documentary series. The show toured me around the world, broadening my view. I became a globetrotter, surfing the world, sitting in my living room. Anthony enjoyed his show, and so did his audience.

So, what took Anthony's Life? On the sunny morning of June 8, 2018, Anthony's shooting crew grew impatient as they waited in their hotel restaurant. Not seeing Anthony coming down for breakfast, the crew started all kinds of questions:

"Where is Anthony? Anybody saw Anthony? He is not picking up his phone," worried the crew leader.

"Still upstairs! Maybe he is having a good time, finishing up a nightly business," giggled one crew member.

"What's he doing? " asked another, annoyed by this long wait.

"What's taking him so long?" sighed another member.

"Why didn't he show up for breakfast? We have a long day ahead!" asked the leader who approached the hotel staff. This attitude is not typical of Anthony, wondered the concerned crew waiting for him at the restaurant of LeChambard Hotel in Alsace, France.

Anthony would never show up for breakfast. The hotel staff found Antony dead, hanging in his hotel room. But why? Why, Anthony?

Why did Anthony, who seemed happy and enjoyed life, take his own life? Did he even think of the poor eleven-year-old Ariane, his only child from his second marriage? When you have pursued life's trivialities and emptied the inner self of substance, there is nothing to fall back on when the going gets tough.

Celebrities operate under heavy and constant pressure in their line of work and generally suffer from depression. Many of them resort to such substances as cocaine and marijuana. Anthony hid behind the wall drugs but was rehabilitated. However, substance abuse was not Anthony's only addiction. He was addicted to love: the love of Asia Argento, a 43-year-old Italian actress and filmmaker, who drove the 61-year-old Anthony insane.

Anthony's life hinged on his love for Asia. His happiness only depended on the sole will of another human being, another uncertain, inconstant, feeble being. Many people's happiness depends on the external environment they have no control over. Many idyllic lovers keep dreaming, forgetting that sensual love is like chaff that will wither away over time. Unlike sacrificial love that never dies, erotic love is like a wave that can die down without warning or over time.

On the eve of his death, Anthony argued with Asia. When he saw a picture of Asia holding hands with another man, his world suddenly became somber, and his life unworthy of another breath. Under the influence of jealousy, Anthony thought the only choice was to end his life.

And yet, Anthony seemingly had it all: a good life, fame, a little bit of money, and many laughs. So, why did he go to such an extreme? The shocking news of Anthony's suicide was not only disheartening; it was awakening and sent me into a profound pondering moment.

Upon collecting myself, I decided to embark on a mission to decipher the true meaning of life and what indeed procures happiness and fulfillment. A quick panoramic view of our celebrity world glared at a pattern that caught my attention: **rich but unfulfilled**. How even more disheartening to realize that all the money people chase boils to not much.

What is the greatest challenge in our high-speed society running on steroids? We lack foundation. Most people load themselves up with stuff to fill the inner void, expecting to be fulfilled. In our "Stuff society, we lack a genuine connection to the foundation that makes us humans. A foundation is a paramount basis for our lives and any ground. A house cemented on a solid foundation is a house that will weather the storm. The hurricane can take the roof away, but the foundation remains untouched. The wall can break, but the foundation will dwell. On that foundation, you can rebuild.

No matter how blessed you are, there comes a time when you must be tested. What will you rely on when you lack the foundation? Many build their foundation on sand: their parchment, bank accounts, or connections; not bad for our materialistic society. Unfortunately, that is too shabby. That's why others depend on the Almighty, who owns the ground and holds the divine authority, powers, and blessing. When you build your foundation, you will raise pillars that sustain the whole edifice. These pillars must be firmly rooted into the foundation, or the entire structure will crumble at the whim of the feeble winds. Who is your source?

You are only as powerful as you are connected to the Source. The biggest mistake we all make is that we are told to believe "Thing Big," "Dream Big," "Set Big Goals," or "Here are the XYZ Magic Steps to Achieve your Purpose," as if those declarations or intentions can be achieved with a magic wand. No. Nobody can do these things unless he has received spiritual authority. Those declarations and teachings are devoid of power unless they connect with a redirection toward the divine. Unfortunately, the masses are told to believe that all you need is physical bodywork. Superachievers know that their power does not depend on their efforts. Many seek it in the occults circle; others seek in the one true God. Ask a phenomenal person, and you will understand that his power comes from a divine source.

Unlike the average person, superachievers value the divine more than they do themselves. They do not take their spiritual connectedness lightly because they know it is the source of their power. How was Samson able to singlehandedly defeat a whole army of Philistines? How was David, a shepherd boy, able to defeat Goliath, a revered giant threatening the Israelite army? When you are spiritually connected, you ignite personal inner power that makes you superhuman and gives you the authority to overcome any adversity.

PERSONAL POWER IS ROOTED IN SPIRITUAL AUTHORITY.

> SECRET CODE #3
> MASTER THE POWER OF SPIRITUAL AUTHORITY AND INFLUENCE.

No powerful leaders, preachers, CEOs, state people, artists, and athletes can be without a divine election. They may appear human, but deep inside, they have a spiritual force that transcends natural abilities. You can only perform at an average level unless you demonstrate that power. The great news is that we all can connect to the supernatural within; unfortunately, many either ignore or neglect it. No wonder 95 percent of people live an average life.

Genius Steve Jobs spent a year studying Zen Buddhism in India to develop spiritual power. Writer, business builder, and coach John Verwey believes living without spirituality is egotistical. He wrote that religion does not serve what Jesus taught. John built a business from $0 to $23 million using his spirituality-based coaching in just eighteen months. John believes that the teaching of Jesus was to help people, and he proudly said that many of the people he trained had become millionaires and billionaires. He declared, "*For me, 'spirituality' is everything from thoughts, ideas, emotions, feelings through to the 'life energy' that Jesus teaches us about."* He then adds, *"Religion' for me, is a useless, egotistical set of rituals directed towards idols by people who lack true faith, and so religion has no useful purpose in my life."*

Spiritual connectedness has nothing to do with being a part of the Sunday morning *Amen assembly*. People you will never see in the Sunday pews practice more of Jesus's teaching than the religious pals; they are real and not superficial with God. The size of your Bible has nothing to do with the size of your faith.

I was at church one Sunday morning, sitting beside an elderly lady with a supersized Bible. Her repeated Amen distracted me so much that I missed what the preacher said, so I asked her to help me complete my notes.

"What did he say?" I whispered. But looking the other way, the lady shrugged, saying, "I don't know. Everybody said amen, and so did I."

Spirituality or divine connectedness resides in your intimate relationship with the Higher Source.

Harness the power of connectedness. Do you know how great men and women get to accomplish uncommon achievements? They rely on God. He is the one who, in His secret wisdom, prepares such people to be mission-ready, whether they are aware of it or not. Inventions we see happen in human history stem from a divinely coordinated scheme. If you develop a sense of discernment, you will be able to understand that what happens in your life may have been divinely orchestrated. Hence, be comforted to realize that your life events will revolve around your mission, like it or not. Why do so many people struggle to make it into their destiny?

- They are too busy chasing the ephemeral.
- Those who want are afraid of inadequacy, so they run away.
- Some people fear human criticism more than God's wrath.
- They try to alter God's plan to fit their own agendas.
- They rely on their own strengths, resources, and abilities.
- They fail to give glory to the divine.

Like Solomon, those connected to the power of the Source marvel. These people have nothing special that sets them apart. They are everyday people like you and me. So, what makes them achieve outstanding accomplishments? Is it money, education, or family background? No! None of those. Superachievers have what most people lack: **spiritual authority**. What is spiritual authority?

Spiritual authority is the power of connectedness to the supernatural spiritual force that gives you unparalleled control to steer your life where it must be. It is the power to subdue life, order evil away, and activate God's will in your life in the face of adversity. It makes you act in the likeness of the Supreme God. It is the evidence of your connectedness and approval from the divine, for authority comes from above, as expressed in Romans 13:1, *"Let every soul be subject to the governing authorities. For there is no authority except from God, and the authorities that exist are appointed by God."*

It is a privilege to connect to the divine source. Those who fail to obey the laws of love and harmony are disconnected and thrown into the solitude of the orphan spirit to suffer a lack of direction and divine favor.

As a result, they will not experience the manifestation of divine intention. It takes insanity to follow God's plan for you and never expect humans to understand you. Despite their desire to unite with the divine, many fail miserably for the following ten reasons.

TEN REASONS PEOPLE FAIL TO REALIZE THEIR CALLING

1. Lack of clear providential purpose.
2. Lack of compelling reason (personal motivation).
3. Lack of a plan.
4. Lack of action.
5. Unwillingness to sacrifice.
6. Lack of faith and self-confidence.
7. Reliance solely on self.
8. Surrender to negativity.
9. Self-sabotage and overindulgence in premature self-gratification.
10. High dependency mentality.

TIP: *Your journey toward success will start when you stop blaming someone else for your shortcomings. Success will greet you when you courageously accept taking ownership of, repent, and make amends for your failures. If you continue to blame others, you will diverge the energy that could help. Instead, embrace life-changing opportunities ahead. STOP FAILING. START WINNING, starting today.*

LIVE A PURPOSE-DRIVEN LIFE SERVING GOD'S INTENTION

"A life given away for a good cause is a life lived. A life lived for self is a life unlived."

We can spend centuries debating the source of happiness in scientific findings. Human power lies in surrendering to the supreme purpose of life: to be content, live in the moment, and serve your neighbor's needs. That is finding your happiness in loving others.

The surge of happiness that comes with pursuing circumstances and acquiring material possessions can only be short-lived, as the sensation it provokes soon fades away and sends you back to your starting point, also known as your set point. Psychologists call it *Hedonic Adaptation or Hedonic Treadmill.* To dwell in a chronic state, you need to upgrade yourself to live within the divine self by showing the virtues of selfless and self-directed unconditional love manifested in the attituded below:

- Loving-kindness.
- A sense of contentment with one's life.
- Generosity and selflessness.
- Empathy.
- An attitude of service.
- Hope and expectation.
- Optimism and enthusiasm.
- Constant growth.
- A feeling of self-worth.
- Strides toward a larger goal.
- Self-belief and self-assurance.
- Connectedness to the divine.

MANIFEST THE "ONE-THING PRINCIPLE"

Ordinary people seek to build riches. Exceptional people live to build wealth.

– Coach Greb

A research article published in the 2014 issue of the Harvard Business Review revealed that business experts consider *"goals to be the key driver of exceptional performance."* It further noted that doctors find people with a clear purpose less prone to disease. Psychologists affirm that purpose is the pathway to greater well-being.

Surprisingly, among business executives who get paid tons of money to run large corporations, less than 20 percent have a keen sense of their life purpose. Really? I did not believe it at first, but it was true. Over 80 percent of those brilliant business gurus, strategists, and tycoons that everyone relies on to make critical decisions in those large companies have no idea of their calling. Eight out of ten geniuses trained in some of the most prestigious institutions, racking up billions of dollars for their investors, stakeholders, and themselves may look successful. Yet, they do not know if they are pursuing their life mission. They are clueless when it comes to their purpose. What does this tell you about your purpose? You do not get your "one thing" in a class or a coaching meeting. So, how do you find it? Sit tight and read on. Dr. Mohammad Hunus's story will teach you how to manifest the true meaning of your life here on earth.

DR. YUNUS: HOW ONE MAN'S $27 ACT OF SELFLESSNESS SAVES THOUSANDS OF WOMEN

Do not just be goal oriented. Be purpose driven. Setting goals without purpose is like walking in the desert without a compass.

— **Coach Greb**

When we question our lives and see so much poverty, we hold the poor accountable, arguing that they fail to do what it takes. The case may be valid in many instances, but in many others, poverty comes as an imposed form of controlling power over the powerless. In this case, whom do we call? How would you sit fed up with the rampant injustice and frustrated by your people's misery? People like Yunus cannot afford to watch like passive bystanders; they rise and say, "Enough is enough; I must do something, or these people will perish, even if this involves jeopardizing my welfare."

It takes an outrage to change the world. It takes a village to impact the world. It takes one uncommon human to drive change. It takes a sense of urgency to spearhead new inventions. A Fulbright scholar, Dr. Muhammad Yunus returned to Bangladesh, his home country, upon receiving his doctoral degree in economics from Vanderbilt University in 1969. He started teaching economics at the University of Chittagong, Bangladesh, near a village, which allowed him to witness something that would change his life forever. Unlike many scholars who would raise a wall between them and their people, regarding them as a nuisance, Dr. Hunus became an active local community member. As a concerned observer, Dr. Hunus saw how loan sharks exploited the poor villagers. He could not stand the exorbitant interest rates unscrupulous lenders practiced.

Women live in deep poverty, as is the custom in most nations, especially those with a solid religious iron hand, high masculinity dominance, and utter unconcern for human rights. Society treated them as outcasts in the generation of wealth. Frustrated by this utter exploitation and discrimination, Muhammad launched a community microfinance lending organization to loan money to women and the underserved population, thereby breaking one of the "social rules." The concept grew so popular that Dr. Yunus received the Ford Fund's support in 1996 and converted his microfinance organization into Grameen Bank, which means "Village Bank" in Bengali.

Through his business model, Dr. Muhammad Yunus, the university professor turned banker, loaned money to women in an unusual way – trust. Based on trust, as do credit card lenders in developed economies, Dr. Yunus, who adapted his idea from his research, believed that *the most efficient way to help people escape poverty is through charity and affordable loans that enable them to start their own ventures.*

A small idea that started as a loan of $27 to forty-two villagers to help them fight the 1974 famine in Bangladesh turned into a global phenomenon, reaching forty-three countries. Since its inception, Grameen Bank has been lending upward of $9 billion so that women can embrace entrepreneurship without being charged astronomical interest rates.

For the past four decades, Dr. Yunus's microfinance concept to help women in his small village has changed the lives of countless people on the planet. It has been implemented in the United States, Asia, Latin America, and Europe, and many more countries are signing up.

Grameen Bank added home loans, student loans, and even no-interest loans to homeless people to its portfolio to maximize its lending opportunities. With close to 99 percent repayment rates, Grameen Bank has something to teach traditional banks. Despite his engagement in seeing women thrive, Dr. Yunus says he owns nothing, as his clients own all the companies. He is a fulfilled recipient of numerous recognitions, including the Nobel Prize and awards from several global entities, such as the United States government, renowned universities, and leading organizations.

While several high-profile institutions praised Dr. Yunus's work, a few loud-voice critics questioned the efficiency of his model and Grameen Bank's lending practices. Some went as far as dismissing the sincerity of his intention. "How pathetic!" you might sigh. Never forget that you will not escape criticism no matter how well-intentioned your actions. However, criticism feels like a friendly hug if your purpose exceeds your personal goals. One should pose the critical question: *why do people do what they do?* The six essential questions will help you decipher your One-Thing, the reason God bothered to bring you to this earth.

SIX ESSENTIAL QUESTIONS TO DISCOVER YOUR PURPOSE

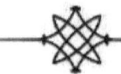

What if each person could find and pursue his calling? Would that be a utopia? Wouldn't that be paradisial since everyone would do God's will when surrendering to life's mission? Unfortunately, many of us will spend our journey never attempting to find our reason for living.

Yet, we cannot ignore the call of those who relentlessly and genuinely seek to find and devote themselves to manifesting their purpose. The following line will light up the path for you.

Where do we start with such a compelling task? We all make the mistake of rushing to seek outside what we seek. If you ask the wrong questions, you will always have the wrong answers to your issue. Below are the six essential questions that will help you find your purpose.

ESSENTIAL QUESTION # 1:
"WHO AM I ?"

"Definiteness of purpose is the starting point of all achievement."

– W. Clement Stone

As we delve into the most significant queries of existence, one fundamental question remains: what is the meaning of self? Who Am I? Many of us focus more on artifacts and externalities than on the core: not the things created but the creature's call to extend creation. Lost in pursuing materialism, we skip the self that makes everything possible. If I were created in the creator's image, I would be a creator. If I were made in the likeness of a person who owns all things, then I would have ownership rights over my surroundings. God is mighty, and so am I, endowed with controlling power to subdue life and be accountable to God for my neighbor's welfare.

Unfortunately, overwhelmed by the labeling scheme, we forget our original identity. So, we spend our lives searching for human labels, Doctor John Doe, MD, President X, General Y, XYZ, and CEO. The suffixes and prefixes result from human appraisal of our value or ranking, but that does not make us WHO we are. As a result, lost in the pursuit of name tags, we never get to meet ourselves and live the life we were sent for. Unless you discover your true, unique identity tattooed in your DNA, you will only wander from one title to another and no title at all… and what do you become when you are stripped of your title? Unfortunately, that's what we all crave: the perception we want to portray to humanity. The day you find who you are is when you will find the reason for being here on Planet Earth.

ESSENTIAL QUESTION # 2:
"WHY AM I HERE?"

"There is no greater gift you can give or receive than to honor your calling. It's why you were born. And how you become most truly alive."

– Oprah Winfrey

The next most compelling question is to ask the "Why Question." As I continued pondering the meaning of human life, I wondered: what is the purpose of life? What goal is worth pursuing? What am I on earth to accomplish? Those are the fundamental questions essential to any worthy pursuit. You should ask yourself the same existential questions: What goals lead to achieving your life purpose? In other words, what are you pursuing: riches, fame, recognition, or power? What is the cause worth fighting for? What wrong needs to be righted? What is burning inside of you? W. Clement Stone believes that "*Definiteness of purpose is the starting point of all achievement.*" What are you on earth to achieve?

GIVE YOUR LIFE AWAY FOR A MEANINGFUL, SELFLESS PURPOSE.

If you have a strong purpose in life, you don't have to be pushed. Your passion will drive you there."

— Roy T. Bennett.

A lot of people are seeking but will never find. They look in the wrong place. Many seek outside what is right within. Many are asking but will never get the right answer because they ask the wrong question. Countless people are marching through life but will never reach their destinations; they took the wrong roadmap. Some took shortcuts, others the broadest roads, and still, many did not even bother to look at the destination. They followed the direction everyone took or the one someone pointed them to. No wonder 95 percent of people on the planet are stuck, unchained, and unable to manifest their exponential potential.

Most people do not know why they are here, so they jump onto whatever is moving, hoping to get anywhere. Unsurprisingly, they are surprised the train is just riding along a Hedonic treadmill.

If you have enough audacity, do the following test next time you enter a crowd of friends or strangers. Pick a group of ten people or twenty if your boldness allows it, call yourself a researcher, and ask:

"Hi, Ma'am. I am doing a survey and would like to ask you one quick question. Please rate your happiness level on a scale from 1 to 10. Or can you say how satisfied you are with your life?"

You will be surprised that most people live average, unfulfilling lives. Many will have no clue and will give you a vague answer. Nine people out of ten will tell you, "Sometimes, happy, other times, not." Or they will answer: "Depends." The rude ones will ignore or welcome you with a "Do Not Bother Me smile or ask you to roll on.

I tried this test with my friend Ricky and his wife Helen when they came for dinner. I regretted the experience. It went on and on until the dinner table became a consultation room.

When I popped the question, Rick suddenly became calm and melancholy, so I asked: "What's the matter, Rick?"

He replied, "Man, I am stuck. I feel enchained."

Rick added with anger: "Coach, I hate my job. I can't stand it, but I do not know what to do. The pay is not bad, but I'm just not happy."

I asked, "What did you expect from the job?"

Rick mumbled, almost in tears, and the voice distorted out of a suppressed cry. "I just wanted to make money, care for my family, and enjoy life. Life's short, you know!"

Calming Rick down, I said: "Then you are on the right path. You are working for money."

When Rick understood my sarcasm, he asked, "What do you mean? I don't get it," almost sniffling and trying to hide a stubborn drop of tear that ran down his right cheek."

I replied:

Listen, Rick. You are not alone. Everyone who chases a career or money will always be empty at the end of the day.

Pursuing money or a career will drain life out of you. You can do better. You can see it for yourself.

It is a challenging yet lifesaving decision. I made mine years ago. I fired Corporate America years ago; I erased my name from any payroll roster, cut up credit cards, and tamed stress and anxiety. I am a fulfilled servant, committedly manifesting God's dream here on earth.

When Rick finally understood,

he asked, "Coach, how can I find a job that can make me happy."

I corrected him, saying to replace the words happy with fulfilled and *job* with *purpose*. Happiness is a short-lived emotion. Fulfillment, conversely, is the state of your soul when you have accomplished your life purpose.

I added that getting a job is like giving your blood to earn money to pay for your basic human needs of food, shelter, and maybe transportation. Nothing more.

When Rick got where I was going, he calmly asked, "Coach, how do I find my purpose?" I interjected: Rick, wait for the book. It will be out soon!

When I analyzed the poverty level, especially among Christians, I decided to check to understand what the self-made do right and what the poor do wrong. I decided to dig into the lives of inspiring superachievers and will tell you what I have learned. I spent countless sleepless nights reading, analyzing, and interrogating over 300 biographies of the world's prominent superachievers, start-up entrepreneurs, business leaders, frontier pioneers, and savvy wealth-builders. What I found is breathtaking yet amazingly simple.

Not the *What* or the *How* but the *Why*. I have reached one understanding worth mentioning: ***It is not what we do or how we do it, but most importantly, why we do what we do.*** Once I found that out, I discovered my eureka moment. I have realized that unless what you do has a profound meaning to you, you will only experience misery. It took me years of questioning to know what the heck I came to do in this life. This question is the most critical self-assessment that comes after you have bloated yourself with the pleasure of the flesh and still feel dissatisfied. I wrote a chapter on *Finding My Way* in another book, *Dreams Beyond the Oceans™*, to be released soon.

When I finally found the meaning of my work, my satisfaction went far beyond the pure financial compensation I derived from my employment. This satisfaction felt like a feeling that ran deep down in my heart and created a state of contentment no one else but I could understand.

ESSENTIAL QUESTION # 3:
"WHAT IS MY B.I.G (BOLD INSANE GOAL)?"

"The greatest tragedy is not death but life without purpose.
– Rick Warren

What do super-achievers have in common? Considering the selfless endeavors of the people who marked our time, I wondered what could have prompted people like Jesus to give their lives away for others. I wondered why Mother Teresa would rather live meekly to see others prosper. I asked why Martin Luther King had no fear of the bullets of the oppressor and ended up falling to one. I questioned the motives behind Gandhi's selfless life.

My quest for answers taught me the one thing great leaders have in common. What separated ancient Greek philosophers, French revolutionaries, Chinese teachers, English industrialists, American pioneers, and today's young technologists? They all lived to achieve one thing: *to fulfill their prophetic destiny and positively impact other people's lives.*

Each self-made resolves to uphold her unique challenge and urge to make a difference: to lay her stone in the edifice called life on earth. Some of these world-changers came from humble households, many from troubled youth and a dysfunctional upbringing. Andrew Carnegie, Dale Carnegie, Jack Canfield, Jack Ma, Michael Jordan, Mark Zuckerberg, Steve Forbes, and Steve Ballmer are prominent self-made people. None of them were born with silver spoons in their mouths. These superachievers rose from humble backgrounds to revolutionize the way we live today. They achieved monumental heights and added something to humanity; they changed the world with their **One Thing, The Big Idea**. These people devoted their lives obsessively to realizing their earthly mission for the sake of others.

> *The luckiest people are those who found out what they were called for early and lived to fulfill it. As you commit your life to raising others out of poverty, so will you rise to wealth.*
> **– Coach Greb**

How happy are you with your life? Are you satisfied with what you have accomplished? Do you see yourself on the path to your destiny? Are you on the proper course of the earthly mission? Can you, with certainty, argue that you know what you are supposed to do on this earth? Is there in your mind, soul, and spirit a cause worth fighting for that you see higher than self-gratification, and that success, money, fame, and power cannot bring? Do you see yourself as fulfilled? Can you state what your definite purpose is?

Do not confuse achieving personal goals with realizing life's purpose. Fulfilling your purpose is more than attaining personal, individualistic goals such as success, fame, power, and the accumulation of material possessions.

That is one of the most critical and challenging issues I have frequently confronted in my financial coaching sessions. Many of my clients are clueless and do not know their life purpose. Some people do not even bother to know it. One client even asked, "What does it matter if I make money and have a great career?" This client is not alone. Most people do not know their purpose, which explains why they live aimless, unfulfilling lives. So, I decided to devote a whole chapter to it because I was once one of them.

When my life went smoothly as the earth's pleasure surrounded me, I thought I had it all. When I looked at the cars in my driveway, a few dollar bills in the bank, and the mortgaged house, I thought I had achieved my life goals. Then, things changed drastically. As I matured spiritually, especially when the middle-age bell rang, I gradually lost the appetite for the stuff I had worked tooth and nail to build. I felt miserable and empty. I knew something more valuable was missing. As I went on a long journey of questioning, the answer trickled down drop by drop until I felt immersed in an anointed presence. Though dissatisfied with my job, my discontent went deeper until I could no longer stand it.

Your purpose is the realization of your earthly mission. What defines your purpose? You must see it as a selfless spiritual invitation to accomplish a missional endeavor that impacts the lives of others. It is a calling to revolutionize our world and expand our lives to new horizons.

Your purpose is the mission statement that defines what you are about. Corporate entities take acute care in creating a mission statement because it is the most defining trait of the business. It is the statement that contains the value statement of the whole organization and its people.

The purpose of our existence is to create value for the greater good. Each human being has the ability and the duty to transform ideas, talents, time, and treasure into wealth for the greater good and benefit of the majority. Patriarch Abraham was promised to be the father of many nations and his descendants to inherit the Promised Land. David risked his life fighting with the giant Goliath to defend Israel. We follow Jesus because he accepted being the sacrificial lamb that redeemed humanity. God immensely blessed Solomon with abundant wealth when the latter only asked for wisdom to rule the Israelites.

ESSENTIAL QUESTION #4: "WHAT IS THE BEST AND HIGHEST USE OF MY LIFE?"

Fulfillment does not come from rewards; it comes from achieving a purpose.

– Psalms 30:5

*E*ach human is endowed with the three Ts of life in one measure or another. *We all have access to T as in Time, T as in Talent, and T as in Treasure.* Those three gifts constitute the seeds we owe to put in the ground. Your harvest depends not on the quantity you have received but on how industriously you have used your seed to maximize the harvest. Do you know or remember the parable of the talents? You might check it out in Mathieu 25: 14-30. Jesus's parable is a parody of our society, and don't tell me life ain't fair.

Those who do not use their time wisely, waste their money, never think they have any talent and prefer to lay at anchor in other people's plantations will do so for eternity, for generations. No wonder the rich get richer and the poor, well, you get the idea.

As stewards, we have the fiduciary and spiritual obligation to use our gifts most efficiently and productively, and that's why we each have our specializations. Rabbi Daniel Lapin discusses this issue in his book *Business Secrets from the Bible*, where he debunks the intrigue of why the Jews are reported to be wealthy. He explains how each person in the Jewish community specializes in one area of need and becomes the go-to person, a mechanic or accountant. Lapin further suggests you are better off getting a specialist to mow your law instead of doing it yourself. Doing so liberates you to focus on your core expertise but also creates an income for the lawn specialist, thereby increasing the wealth of the community.

Each of us must operate in a way to spend our time serving others with the unique talent we are uniquely good at. Suppose you are a member of a village community; what would be the best and highest use of your time, serving as a bricklayer? No, even if you grew up around masons and can build castles, there are people better equipped than you, but when it comes to healing the sick and prescribing the right medicine, you have no match. What would you instead do?

Those who desire to live the most fulfilling life must learn to commit not to the pursuit of self-satisfaction but to using and honing their gift to the best and highest use unless they choose their careers, not out-calling. How do you achieve that?

"Surrender your whole being to Him to be used for righteous purposes" (Romans 6:13). When we study the lives of inspired wealth-builders such as Warren Buffett and Mark Zuckerberg, we realize they are not moved or transformed by money. Most game-changers are not motivated by money.

Building wealth is never the purpose of their lives; it is a byproduct and a reward.

Studying the lives of the super-achievers made me realize that despite the wealth they have amassed, they never tire or retire from working on their life's missions. Although Sam Walton had already achieved financial success and fame, he never retired from growing Walmart into a global giant. Super-billionaire Amancio Ortega never retired from building Zara, even in his eighties. When you see these people still working with their frail bodies due to the weight of age, you might wonder, *but they are already rich; what are they looking for?* The answer is that these people are not working to make more money.

The term *work* is inappropriate to describe what these super achievers do. They do not work. They are merely enjoying their passion. It is a game they enjoy, not for the money or the fame it brings, but because they enjoy and excel at what they do. John Rockefeller put it well when he argued, "*to get wealthy, have a purpose beyond getting wealthy.*" He added,

"I had no ambition to make a fortune. Mere money-making has never been my goal. I saw a marvelous future for our country, and I wanted to participate in the work of making our country great.

Everyone will answer his call. You might tell yourself, *"Why me? No, it can't be me! I don't have what it takes."* If you are reading this book, be assured, comforted, and certain that it is not by chance. If you came across this book, your life is about to take a new turn starting today. You are one of those few people called to do something about our greatest enemy: poverty.

You are more than what you think of yourself. Looking at your current situation, you might not believe you are worth anything, but remember that your reality does not determine your truth. As you read the Holy Scriptures, you learn about countless promises from God. Like the Israelites, you, too, were promised a life of abundance and prosperity. However, looking at your current life, you may wonder, "What am I still doing in the desert?" I thought the same thing when God called me to teach about poverty and wealth-building, and so did Moses when God called him to lead God's chosen people to the Promised Land. We all find excuses as we fear being inadequate. So, how do you discover one thing?

> **The secret to a successful, fulfilling, and joyful life is to find a cause you want to live for and commit your life to fight for it.**

— Coach Greb

ESSENTIAL QUESTION #:5
"WHAT ONE CAUSE WOULD I GIVE MY LIFE FOR?"

"The meaning of life is to find your gift. The purpose of life is to give it away."
— Pablo Picasso.

What is the one thing you could give up everything and focus on for the rest of your life? Who lived the most fulfilling life between Indira Gandhi, Martin Luther King, Mother Teresa, and our many billionaires from the Forbes list? The answer might sound easy, but it is not and should not be. How do we define fulfillment? Motivational writer, speaker, and trainer Tony Robbins once stated:

> *I have seen business moguls achieve their ultimate goals but still live in frustration, worry, and fear. What is preventing these successful people from being happy? The answer is that they have focused only on achievement and not fulfillment. Extraordinary accomplishment does not guarantee extraordinary joy, happiness, love, and a sense of meaning. These two skill sets feed off each other and make me believe that success without fulfillment is a failure.*

Fulfillment does not come from the external display of happiness and joy. It is the state of your soul. What do you think will bring you the utmost fulfillment? Find the one thing that will get you enjoyment by bringing joy to others.

Looking at the lives of great wealthy builders, you will see that these people sacrificed their lives to seek a better life for others. The Bible teaches us that *"He who loses his life will save it, and he who saves his life will lose it"* (Matthew 15:25). The reason for our existence is to be creators of solutions for others, using our God-given gifts because He made us in His likeness. Only when you love your neighbors will you serve as the conduit of infinite possibilities for their benefit. In that case, you become a steward, not the creator. As a conduit, God uses your God-given abilities to inspire you to design, devise, and direct the implementation of solutions to human challenges. As such, you are obsessed with the one thing you believe will improve the lives of others.

You were created to bring about a new way of thinking and doing, no matter how tiny. Our individual efforts amount to the ocean of infiniteness called abundance - the essence of life itself. The value of life is measured on the quality and magnitude of the causes it is devoted to fighting for. We live to engage in the pursuit of happiness for others, to make wrongs right, to advocate for the weak, to empower the feeble, and to preserve lives. Ultimately, we are to live according to God's manifested will: to be bearers of fruit, the calling He prepared us to, as His workmanship so vividly stated in Ephesians 2:10. *"For we are His workmanship, created in Christ Jesus for good works, which God prepared beforehand that we should walk in them."*

WHAT IS THE ONE THING THAT OBSESSES YOU?

Unless an idea fires you up, you will not have the stamina to charge forward. What are your interests, passions, and hobbies? Is there one thing that occupies your attention? What do you spend the most enjoyable moments of your days on? What do you enjoy doing? Beyond the call of duty, what is your center of interest in life? The degree of positive obsession is what drives you to success. When you have given your all and worked diligently, relentlessly, and intensively and devoted 80 percent or more of your time, energy, and resources, there is no reason you will not succeed. Forcefulness is the art of success, for, as writer Terry Orlick puts it,

"The heart of human excellence often begins to beat when you *discover a pursuit that absorbs you*, frees you, challenges you, or gives you a sense of meaning, joy, or passion."

ESSENTIAL QUESTION #6: "WHAT IS THE ONE THING I AM UNIQUELY GOOD AT?"

> *"As each one has received a gift, minister it to one another as good stewards of the manifold grace of God. If anyone speaks, let him speak as the oracles of God. If anyone ministers, let him do it as with the ability which God supplies, that in all things God may be glorified through Jesus Christ, to whom belong the glory and the dominion forever and ever. Amen."*
> — 1 Peter 10-11

You build wealth by exercising your **dominant talent** and realizing your purpose through your unique gift, your distinct advantage. You achieve purpose through your God-given abilities. During my coaching sessions, I asked my students, "What is your gift?" I am often amazed at the answers I hear. One would have thought a question like this would be a piece of cake. But no. They answer, "Well, I have too many gifts," or "I do not know what I am uniquely good at." You cannot see and pursue your purpose if you cannot find your unique gift.

The short answer is that you must first understand that you may be wired to do several things, but *only one gift will be used* for your life purpose. Your unique gift is also known as your **dominant skill** or talent. Instead of weeding through the myriad of talents, you need only focus on the one that gives you a *distinctive advantage*: the ability to do anything better than anyone else.

Your gift will make way for you. African American lawyer Barack Obama made history by becoming President Obama because of his unique gift of electrifying speeches. Oprah Winfrey became the highest-paid media mogul because of her unique gift of touching people. Joan Rowling's remarkable writing gift once earned her a ticket into the billionaire club. King Solomon's unmatched wisdom made him the richest man on earth in biblical times. Nerdy Marc Zuckerberg, Elon Musk, and Steve Jobs are examples of people who transformed our world and their lives through their unique gifts, not because of education, jobs, or family.

Only one gift per purpose. You may be good at playing golf, writing, singing, speaking, or acting, but you must identify the skill for which you are exceptionally talented. Michael Jordan and Michael Jackson were respectively gifted with unprecedented movements in the performance of their talents. Who can do the air spin better than Michael Jordan? He built a fortune from Nike's Air Jordan. Who can do a moonwalk better than Michael Jackson? That robotic movement made him unforgettable in the minds of adults and children.

Once you have identified your gift, hone it and build an occupation around it. It will be the one through which you can solve other people's problems, create value, and significantly contribute to society. Nothing else will fulfill you more than using your inborn talent to serve your life purpose. The most challenging exercise for many is finding their unique talent. Below are five essential questions that will help you identify yours.

A SIMPLE EXERCISE TO FIND YOUR DOMINANT SKILL

1. What is the one thing I can effortlessly do without formal training?
2. What is the one thing my conscience says I am gifted for?
3. What is the one thing I was good at and enjoyed doing as a child or teenager?
4. What is the one thing people say I am good at?
5. What is the one thing most of my interest, passion, and activities gravitate around, such as painting, sports, leading a group, working with people or gadgets, selling something, helping people, playing the hero or the boss, or advocating for the less fortunate?

SIX STEPS TO SURRENDER TO YOUR DIVINE NATURE

Where will you find your unique gift? You do not need formal training or copying other people's talents. You need to connect to the Source that gives it to you and build on it and from it.

STEP 1. FIND YOUR ONE SOURCE OF STRENGTH

Inspired wealth-builders understand the power of the mighty hand of God. And they value and seek to abide by it obediently. They accept finding the true meaning of their lives to be wealth-builders in God's kingdom. In other words, they agree to commit their existence to a cause that extends far beyond material possessions, money, fame, and earthly power. Wealth is more than money. It is life itself as God intended it to be for His heirs, for His plan is to prosper you, as stated in Jeremiah 29:11: *"For I know the thoughts that I think toward you, says the LORD, thoughts of peace and not of evil, to give you a future and a hope."*

STEP 2. MANIFEST SELF-REALIZATION AND EFFORTLESS SURRENDER

The attainment of purpose is accomplished through the process of self-realization and effortless surrender.

You may not understand this process through rational thinking, for this is performed in the spiritual realm, the higher order of life. You must submit to a total surrender to the Almighty and make sure your intellect and ego are not in the way of your attainment.

The attainment of purpose is accomplished through the process of self-realization and effortless surrender. It is not an end but a journey on which each of us is called to deliver a message of hope. It is a call of duty to perform the actions that open the gates of endless possibilities. It is an opportunity to show a genuine interest that extends human life beyond belief. It is a charitable duty to find joy in creating joy in others' lives.

Connecting to the spirit requires full concentration in a propitious environment where the spirit can brood. You can sit quietly in silence or be in contact with Mother Nature. It would help if you stayed away from spiritual pollution and human distraction.

STEP 3. ALIGN WITH THE SOURCE OF TRUE WEALTH

How do you connect to the source of *Spiritual Wealth and Abundance?* You will fly if you act like the eagle and put yourself in the wind's course. Your

Life Path is your providential calling; it is your earthly mission. An assignment is never for the sake of the messenger but rather for the sake of the sender. So, if God is your sender, the task is never intended for you.

Focus your life on building wealth, not amassing riches. Do you prefer riches or wealth? Everyone can become rich, not wealthy. People become rich by all means, legal or illegal, crooked or straight, but God only gives wealth. This is the fundamental difference between those who enjoy total peace in wealth and those who must live in riches with their eyes on their shoulders.

How do you define and measure wealth? Many people have a blurred understanding of what constitutes wealth. It is noteworthy to differentiate economic wealth from spiritual wealth. **Spiritual wealth** is complete access to a life of abundance and fulfillment. It includes peace of mind and sound health of mind and body. Spiritual wealth is a liability-free type of wealth. No one else has a claim over it except the Giver Himself.

In contrast, **economic wealth** includes intangible assets, such as goodwill, patents, and royalties, as well as tangible ownership in the form of cars, money, stocks, bonds, jets, boats, business interests, and real properties. Some people have negative wealth, and others have positive wealth. Economic wealth is measured in terms of **net worth**, the value of your assets free and clear of external claims. This obeys the accounting account principle that contends that your wealth is obtained by subtracting what you owe others from all your assets. Some people owe more than they own: they have **negative wealth**. True wealth resides in growth for that which does not grow dies. If your wealth is not growing, it is doomed to die and was not wealth after all. True wealth crosses multiple generations, for a just man knows to leave an inheritance to his children's children (Proverbs 13:22).

That should not be that hard. If you work hard and save your money the way the gurus advise, by age 100, you could probably make it into the millionaire club. Why then break a leg dumping beautiful lives in the pursuit of riches when you can have both money and wealth serving your purpose on earth? However, despite those two broad definitions, wealth is more than material, monetary possessions. It is fulfillment itself, the expected state of living. In this sense, being wealthy is being able to afford what money cannot buy. Wealth is a state of contentment as divinely prescribed and is defined based on people's values.

People strive for happiness when they can thrive in fulfillment. Riches bring happiness, an ephemeral feeling of joy conditioned by externality. On the other hand, fulfillment is created by wealth, not a feeling but the state of your soul when you have accomplished your duty and are achieving your purpose with the divine. It is the blessing of the LORD that enriches for He adds no sorrow with it (Proverbs 10:22). A friend of mine is thriving professionally, but his wife and only son kids are bedridden with chronic diseases; my cousin makes a ton of money but must constantly be on the road and can never find time to enjoy life with his family. My mentor's career is soaring, but he feels lost emotionally. He has no one to share his joy with. Many people are rich but have lost contact with God and live in spiritual solitude. Others are submerged in material possessions but are spiritually hacked and shackled by guilt, remorse, resentment, and fear. There are eight types of wealth measures based on these values: spiritual, psychological, financial, social, intellectual, physical, emotional, and relational wealth.

STEP 4. RELEASE THE INFINITE INTELLIGENCE, NOT YOUR RATIONAL MIND

God is spirit. No one has ever seen Him, not even Moses, Abraham, or Joshua, who had a chance to speak to Him frequently. He is ever-present in you yet eternally invisible to the naked eye. To connect, you cannot do so through the physical body only. All three parts of your being must be tuned: your spirit, body, and mind. For example, some people say they feel the presence of the Holy Spirit through a sensation of heat or any other. You may feel His presence through physical visitation and manifestation or through a stranger who comes to accomplish a given deed, such as revealing something to you and disappearing. Some people say they feel the holy presence in different forms: a sensation, a voice, a dove, a light, or an image.

STEP 5. PRACTICE A WELL-STRUCTURED MEDITATION

The power of meditation is underrated. What made Steve Jobs build one of the world's largest companies? Where do America's most prominent CEOs and superachievers get their strength from? From actor and ex-governor Arnold Schwarzenegger to super-achievers, all recognize that meditation is the key to success. Many say they meditate daily, even if for just ten minutes. The benefit of meditation is unlimited and proven to the point that many large companies like Amazon and Apple have included meditation in their employee training.

Experts say meditation marvels at boosting your brain power, body cell rejuvenation, cognitive abilities, and mental toughness. Meditation gives you grit, one of the most potent ingredients of success. It is believed to prolong your life and help you heal your body. It gives you focus, energy, and stamina.

True connectedness to the divine is triggered through deep meditation through which you can hear the voice of God. When you do, surrender, block all sources of distraction, and release yourself to total spiritual governance. Refrain from interference with your human reasoning.

Productive meditation must occur in total silence. Depending on your lifestyle and preference, you can do this exercise in the wee hours of the morning when silence is at its height. You can do the activity in a quiet room between 3:00 a.m. and 5:00 a.m.

Talk to God and listen to his reply before you move on. We often see ourselves as part of a system that must act according to mechanical design. The truth is that we are spiritual beings that are only functioning in a physical body. Hence, the dominant part of our nature is our spirit, which connects with the Spirit of God. Spiritual wisdom transcends human intelligence, and the only way to access spiritual enlightenment is to connect to your divine being through prayer and meditation. What sets Jesus apart as superhuman? What sets the great monks apart? How do you acquire the sixth sense, the Spirit that transcends all beings? You do that through meditation.

STEP 6. STOP PRAYING; START PRAISING

Prayer and praise are a form of meditation. They are powerful because they reunite you with yourself and the divine. You cannot enjoy meditation and shy away from prayer and praise. Where do you gain the strength that keeps you going? We pray to praise and petition the divine for our livelihood and the sake of others. Positive declarations are a form of prayer. Prayer is an inward communication with the soul to cleanse and align it with divine purpose. Mahatma Gandhi believes that

> *"There is an eternal struggle raging in man's breast between the powers of darkness and light, and who has not the sheet anchor of prayer to rely*

upon will be a victim to the powers of darkness. The man of the prayer will be at peace with himself and with the whole world, the man who goes about the affairs of the world without a prayerful heart will be miserable and will make the world also miserable."

We all have a divinely designed, funded, and orchestrated purpose. Those who find and surrender to theirs will eat the fruit. Finding your purpose should not be that hard. Surrender to your divine nature; Achieving your life calling should not be a challenge either; surrender to the inner voice that loves and calls you to liberate your best self, not for a piece of silver, but the foundry of gold.

> ***LESSON LEARNED:*** *What lesson did God teach me in those few lines? Do not fret, I will always be with you. As long as you dwell under the protection of God, surely you will experience trials, but he will deliver you from them all. Even when you walk with God, you will go through the shadow of death, but God will always raise a table in front of your adversity to show that the victory is always on side. That is what gives the immigrant that I am the fortitude mindset. I know troubles will come my way, but I am also sure I will win over them all. Joshua won almost all of his battles because God was with him in all of them.*

YOUR TURN – DAY 3: THE AUDACITY OF PURPOSE

Self-Reflection: *Have you clearly defined your life's purpose or overarching goals, and if so, how have they influenced your decisions and actions?*

- What aspects of your current activities and commitments align with your sense of purpose, and what may need adjustment?
- Can you think of individuals or role models who have lived with a strong sense of purpose and left a lasting legacy?
- How does a sense of purpose impact one's audacity and willingness to pursue ambitious dreams?

Application: *What change can you make to identify and work on your life purpose, committing time, effort, and resources?*

1. **Purpose Discovery:** Take time to reflect on your life's purpose. What activities or causes make you feel most fulfilled?
2. **Alignment:** Evaluate your current activities and commitments. Are they aligned with your purpose? If not, how can you realign them?
3. **Impact Assessment:** Consider the impact you want to have on the world. What steps can you take to move closer to that vision?
4. **Daily Intentions:** Set daily intentions that align with your purpose. How can you make each day meaningful?
5. **Inspiring Figures:** Research individuals who have lived with a strong sense of purpose. What lessons can you learn from their lives?

THE AUDACITY OF IMAGINATION

DARE TO SEE THE INVISIBLE

> *"And he has filled him with the Spirit of God, with skill, with intelligence, with knowledge, and with all craftsmanship, to devise artistic designs, to work in gold and silver and bronze."*
>
> — Exodus 35:31-32 ESV

How do great men, leaders, and visionaries accomplish a great purpose? How would the general go to the battleground without a strategy? How would the architect launch the groundwork of an edifice without a blueprint? Many people err in setting big goals without an underlying purpose; others want to embark on their life calling without a vision. Vision, imagination, and the ability to see the invisible is the true expression of connectedness to the divine, without which people will perish.

Self-made like Bill Gates and many other visionary leaders are distinguished by their visionary leadership.

THE GRAND VISION THAT MADE BILL A BILLIONAIRE

Bill Gates's business acumen and genius have often been celebrated, making his ascension to billionaire status look smooth. But that's far from it. Although he lacked nothing during childhood, William Gates did not just run into wealth. Bill Gates Sr. was a wealthy Seattle lawyer, but Gates Jr. was born to build his wealth.

> *"Every great advance in science has issued from a new audacity of imagination."*
>
> *– John Dewey*

Though a little nerdy, William had skills and a passion for computers at a young age. He sought every opportunity to be in contact with one. Bill's love for computers made him what he is today: a shrewd businessperson.

Moreover, at an early age, Bill demonstrated the skills of a strategic, daring, creative, combative, and competitive visionary leader. His interest in computers grew multifold when he started middle school at Lakeside Preparatory School in 1967 at age 13. The exclusive, private school gave students access to the new equipment it had received as a gift. Bill fell in love with the machine and spent most of his time in the computer lab.

Because of his talent and eagerness to learn, the school administration asked Bill to write a scheduling program for the whole school. That was a lifetime opportunity to hone his skills, Bill thought. He spent long hours enjoying his new assignment.

At Lakeside, Bill Gates befriended Paul Allen, two years older than he, and another geek who shared his passion for the machine. With his new friend, Bill regained a dose of enchantment and did all he could to have the opportunity to use the computer. In the 1970s, computers were so expensive that people could only afford the shared time. The Lakeside Mothers' Club had purchased a computer that was not a local machine like the one we have today. It was a teletype machine that only offered remote access to a computer time-sharing machine. The school's mothers' club could not afford to buy an actual computer; the price was prohibitive. Access to the machine was restricted, a remote privilege for many students. Still, Bill and Allen maneuvered through mischief and influence to have their chance around the device. The two pals created a programming club and played the role of experts.

With much excitement in their new roles as the bosses of the Lakeside Programming Group, Bill and Allen would use this opportunity to explore and work on their passion; that was the beginning of a lifetime partnership and the launch of an aggressive business venture, Microsoft, the follower of the defunct Traf-o-data.

SECRET CODE #4
Connect with the source of revelation and enlightened wisdom.

"No power can match the ability to see the invisible."
— **Coach Greb**

How do you ensure you do not fail at acting on your vision? Without a vision, you cannot accomplish anything. Yet, we fail to act on our vision and miss our life calling altogether.

> *"Visionary people are common people courageous enough to carry the torch through the unknown."*
> **– Coach Greb**

THE TWENTY-TWO POWER HABITS OF SELF-MADE SUPERACHIEVERS

What sets great leaders apart? Every leadership authority comes from above, writes Apostle Paul in Romans 13:1."

> *Let every soul be subject to the governing authorities. For there is no authority except God, and the authorities that exist are appointed by God."*
> **– Roman 13:1**

1. CONNECT WITH THE SOURCE OF INSPIRED WISDOM

As you learn more about the self-made, you will not miss the striking difference between those who build riches from doing what everyone does and those whom God inspires to invent technologies yet unknown to humans. A lawyer, a medical doctor, a hairdresser, and a plumber do not create anything new. Yet, with focus and diligence, they can build massive wealth. On the other hand, you have *inspired wealthy builders* who are recipients of a divine vision we call imagination or *inspired wisdom.*

Inspired wisdom is a revelation made only to the beholder to know how a particular concept, process, or product works. If the beholder believes in revelation and pursues its realization, he will invent a new product that will amaze the world; if he does not, the idea will die. God uses human intelligence to further Creation. Creation only happened once when Divine

Intelligence birthed all matter into existence. Everything is just an alloy of what all exists. No new matter is created.

The Wright Brothers knew that the idea of building an airplane could only come from a higher force, a supernatural source. Some call it the universe, God, Source, or any name that fits their culture.

How do you go from a nobody to a self-made? How do you go from an impoverished immigrant to billionaire Jack Koum, inventor of WhatsApp? *A divine blessing does not come as logs of gold.* Your divine blessing comes in the form of a vision or an idea. God will not just pour money into your bank account. He will inspire you with a golden idea to create something that can benefit others and reward you. What made Jeff Bezos a billionaire? A golden vision. How did Garrett Camp and Travis Kalanick, the founders of Uber, get so wealthy? A golden idea. A small inspiration. A small faith. A small act of obedience.

When you browse the Forbes list, you will notice that billionaires are ordinary people inspired by a vision that became the gold that turned their lives around. Pay close attention to the voice that is talking to you repeatedly. That thin voice that you call little might be the inspiration to change your life and the lives of many others.

2. BE OBSESSED WITH AN INSANE IMAGINATION

Can you imagine what our world would have been like without the power of imagination? Physicist Albert Einstein once said: "Imagination is more important than knowledge, for knowledge is limited, whereas imagination embraces the entire world, stimulating progress, giving birth to evolution."

For British playwright George Bernard Shaw, *imagination is the beginning of creation.* You imagine what you desire, you will see what you imagine, and at last, you create what you will." American writer Alice Walker believes, "If you fall in love with the imagination, you understand it is a free spirit. It will go anywhere, and it can do anything."

To me, imagination is the picture of life on a postcard. Yet imagination cannot lift itself. **Curiosity is the mother of imagination and creativity.** Bill Gates never stops learning. An avid learner, Bill's curiosity is one of the driving forces behind his creative genius. As a passionate reader, Bill has an impressive home library. He reads over fifty books a year. He never misses an opportunity to read and carries books in his duffel bag wherever he goes.

The extent of your curiosity will determine the magnitude of what your mind can create. Your ability to think big depends on your ability to stretch your mind through search and discovery. As simple as it may seem, the power of creativity lies between the lines of a book.

3. ELEVATE YOUR CURIOSITY WITH READING

Reading is the dividing line between poverty and wealth. A United States Department of Education and the National Institute for Literacy study reports that over thirty million - nearly 20 percent - of high school graduates cannot read. Close to two in ten American adults cannot read or write. Over 21 percent of adults read or write at only a fifth-grade level.

A 2018 New York Times report indicated that the "education gap between the rich and the poor is widening." The article further noted that only five percent of Americans aged 25 to 35 whose parents did not finish high school have a college degree. In affluent homes, children have a higher literacy rate than in more modest households. The study argues that reading is the top activity of super achievers. According to CNBC, most wealth builders read an average of two books monthly. Bill Gates reads an average of fifty books annually in the billionaire world, and Warren Buffett spends over 80 percent of his time reading. The article advises reading at least seven or more books yearly because reading increases your chances of becoming wealthy by over 120 percent.

Author Tim Corley spent five years studying people's habits relative to wealth. In his book *The Daily Success Habits of Wealthy Individuals*, he studied 233 wealthy and 128 low-income people. The study revealed that rich people watch less television, with less than 67 percent spending time in front of the screen. In contrast, only 27 percent of poor people forgo TV time.

4. DEVELOP A GROWTH MINDSET

A visionary leader never stops learning. A more meaningful choice to rally successful followers is to teach them to become better leaders than you are. A creative person knows how to inspire and empower. To influence people, you need to be able to tout their emotions. Charismatic leaders make their followers enter the surreal world, the land of fantasy, the uncommon, the unthinkable.

The most powerful way to become a better person is to find ways to empower others to become better versions of themselves. A visionary is someone who can see the invisible. *You cannot become a visionary if you cannot stretch your mind's capacity.* Though Bill did not complete college, he was awarded several honorary doctoral degrees by institutions, such as Harvard, because he knew the value of learning. He trained himself to become a better communicator and public speaker. While known for his hard skills, Bill did not neglect to hone his emotional intelligence and managed to develop better people skills. Bill believes his success is grounded in maximizing what he excels at while reducing his weaknesses. He calls it a **growth mindset:** the power of stretching your imagination.

5. BE ENLIGHTED: DEVELOP HINDSIGHT, INSIGHT, FORESIGHT AND OVERSIGHT

A leader must have **hindsight**, the ability to predict the future. Why did the two entrepreneurs choose to launch a software company instead of a hardware company, computer hardware being popular at the time? Bill and Paul accurately predicted the future boom of the software industry. At the inception of their partnership, the two geniuses banked on what I call the **power of information**. They knew where to get the information critical to decision-making.

You are a seer. You cannot call yourself a visionary if you cannot see yourself as a prophet, a seer capable of seeing the invisible. You must have the *foresight* to capture a glimpse of your future life: a picture of yourself surrounded by wealth. You must see yourself as a millionaire living the wealthy lifestyle you desire. Learn to speak wealth into your life, think wealth into your mind, and act rich in your daily dealings. Bill "Trey" Gates prophesied that he would be a millionaire at age 30; he became a billionaire at age 31. The future will be what you instruct her to, and Jim Carrey's success story is my exhibit B.

Debuting his struggling acting career in the 1970s, Canadian comedian Jim Carrey had the nerve to write himself a $10 million check and postdated it. When asked about it later in his successful career, Jim replied: *"I wrote myself a check for $10 million for 'acting services rendered,' and I gave myself five* years ... or three years maybe. I dated it Thanksgiving 1995, and I put it in my wallet, and I kept it there, and it deteriorated and deteriorated. But then, just before Thanksgiving 1995, I found out that I was going to make $10 million on Dumb and Dumber." Ironically, the actor put that check in his father's pocket in his coffin. Jim probably thought his father might need it to bribe the angels to let him into heaven or maybe buy himself some supplies—just a thought.

As insane as Jim Carrey's action may appear, one can learn the power of visualization here: you call into existence your expectation. Regardless of where you are now, you must create and call your future into reality with precisely what you desire. Jim was nothing but a broke, struggling actor who was still at the bottom of the hill. But through the power of visualization, Jim Carrey projected with precision. He ordered from the universe what he wanted to see in his career. He visualized playing significant parts in blockbuster movies and being praised for his performance.

"Life will only deliver to your doors what you order through the power of words and the mind. Do not toy with what you say or think." Coach Greb

A visionary must have **oversight** over his vision. You cannot just passively be walking with it. You must control, talk to, and do everything to bring it to life. Many motivational speakers encourage something called a vision board. It is a board on which you will pin a physical picture of your goals: your dream Ferrari, mansion, jet, or million-dollar check. Frequently, looking at the vision board reminds you of your goals.

6. EXERCISE A KEEN SENSE OF RISK TOLERANCE

He who takes a chance at life is not the one taking risks; the one who dares not try has risked all his opportunities for upward mobility.

– Coach Greb

A visionary leader must embrace the concept of risk when you are a pioneer leading a new path. You have to be ready to take risks, and Bill Gates took a considerable risk. First, gambling with his future, Gates decided to drop out of the prestigious Harvard University to create a company in an industry just at its inception. He found something worth doing and was ready to use the best of his abilities. At the start of Microsoft, he and his partner Paul Allen took a considerable gamble, promising to deliver an application that would operate on the Altair machine. Gates and Allen knew that they did not have such software. However, the two pals -took two months to create an application that worked perfectly.

In another instance, Gates pre-sold the QDOS (Quick & Dirty Operating System) to then-computer industry leader IBM, which would run on computers made by IBM. At the time of the proposal, the two entrepreneurs knew well that they did not have such software ready. Upon securing the contract, Bill purchased the software from Tim Patterson of Seattle Computer Group for $50,000. He then renamed it MS-DOS (Microsoft Disk Operating System). He brought it to IBM as if Microsoft were the developer.

A risk-averse person will waste his time asking unproductive questions, such as, "What if it does not work?" This behavior can only make you waste time and miss out on opportunities. Instead of dwelling on the problem, visionary leaders work at finding the solution by asking, "Where is the solution?" not "What is the perfect solution?" There will never be a perfect solution. You will find your answer by walking on fire.

As you browse the life of visionaries, you will discover something: superachievers are *ordinary people who do ordinary things extraordinarily*. Bill Gates's life story will teach you one or two things about visionary leadership. Below are five key traits that define Bill as a businessperson.

FIVE CORE SKILLS THAT CHARACTERIZE BILL GATES

- He has a competitive, combative, and shrewd strategic entrepreneurial mind.
- Bill is a farsighted leader who likes to challenge himself and others.
- He is a logical, critical, and objective thinker.
- Bill is passionate and only focuses on what he knows best.
- He is a genius with a curious mind thriving on discoveries.

Bill is the kind of person who likes to take a step-by-step approach to business ideas. Like his friend Warren Buffett, Bill only focuses on what he knows best. He carries this passion for reading in whatever he does. Bill created an environment that promoted employee creativity in the company. Most of all, When Bill went into business, he never doubted what he set his mind to. He knew no matter how things played out, they would end in his favor. That is called *audacity of self-belief*, a concept I will discuss in the following chapter.

7. SURRENDER TO YOUR VISION IN OBEDIENCE

Wealth comes in the form of a vision, a small idea that must be believed in to bear its fruit.

– Coach Greb

Faith in your vision does not blow trumpets or sound alarms. Yet, it can change the wealth of nations. Steve Jobs's ideas of the graphic user interface, the point-and-click technology, the iPhone, and the iPad demonstrate how one person's insane obsession can alter how the world communicates. Such approaches have revolutionized our world.

Every idea is a million-dollar idea. Why do we often underestimate our inspiration? We shouldn't. We should treasure our vision, protect it, and commit ourselves to its manifestation. Imagination builds human progress, and ideas are the sources of wealth. Microsoft is a product of ideas materialized. Bill and Allen saw they could deliver superior value by supplying a product that could help the world of computers. Likewise, Howard's crazy and stupid craving for coffee has become a lifestyle in America and worldwide.

> ## HOWARD SHULTZ'S FIGHT OVER STARBUCKS: *"YOU WILL GET IT IF YOU REALLY WANT."*

You must fight to see your dream come true. Having great insight is the fun part. Who does not like daydreaming? Execution is the real battle, which is why many ideas are dying in the confines of corporate cubicles - in the heads of geniuses who are too afraid to leap out of faith.

Do you like drinking coffee? Not the one you consume in your living room, but the one you chat over while discussing business with your client somewhere amid the aroma of a freshly brewed espresso. Starbucks is a household name for fast food, especially coffee. You may not be familiar with the man and the story behind it, so here you go.

Howard Shultz, who did not invent Starbucks, turned the original idea into a lifestyle millions of people worldwide enjoy daily. Howard's biography reads that upon returning from a visit to Milan, Italy, he was obsessed with a novel idea of consuming coffee in America. As the marketing director of Starbucks, he tried to convince the company owners Jerry Baldwin and Gordon Bowker about the kind of coffee bar he had experienced in Milan.

As fate would have it, the owners of Starbucks, who had no plans of running their business beyond selling coffee beans, rejected Howard's idea. Frustrated, Howard left Starbucks, created his coffee shop in 1986, and gave it an Italian name, *Il Giornale,* after a Milanese daily newspaper. Convinced of the future of his new venture, Howard took huge risks, raising money and opening his first shop in an expensive building in downtown Seattle, Washington.

Howard hired a team of dedicated staff with whom he started brewing and offering fresh coffee, other beverages, and Italian delicacies at Il Giornale. Howard successfully communicated and shared his passion for providing his customers with the enjoyable experience of drinking coffee as a new lifestyle, as he saw it in Milan, Italy. Convinced and enthusiastic about his newfound love, Howard shared his vision of Il Giornale, a contagious passion, through the company mission statement. Determined to make the new company the world's best coffee company, Howard galvanized his team with a powerful mission statement still available on Starbucks's news website:

> *Il Giornale will strive to be the best coffee company on earth. We will offer superior office coffee and related that will help our customers start and continue their workday. We are genuinely interested in educating our customers and will not compromise our ethics or integrity in the name of profit... Our coffee bars will change the way people perceive the beverage, and we will build into each Il Giornale coffee bar a level of quality, performance, and value that will earn respect and loyalty of our customers.*
> *"Onward."*
>
> **– Howard Shultz**

As Kathleen Elkins of CNBC's Make It reported, shortly after the opening of Il Giornale, the owners of Starbucks made an irresistible offer to Howard. He could buy six stores for $ 3.8 million, which he did not have. Excitedly, Howard launched a capital campaign to find investors. Midway, he received a call from owner Gordon Bowker informing him that Jerry Baldwin, the co-owner, had a change of mind and was outbidding Howard.

8. BE PREPARED TO FACE THE UNEXPECTED

> *A mind marred in vandalism and baseness has no room for great thoughts.*
>
> **– Coach Greb**

Train your mind to stride forward. Howard, who was midway ready, needed luck. Here is when you learn the value of people. When confronted with this ordeal, you tell your ego to shut up and be humble enough to let someone help you. Here is where you understand why you should never burn bridges. Long-lasting friendships can come in handy, and quite often, they do. Here is when you need God's helping hand to do the miracle and be wise enough to let your guardian angel come to defend your cause. Howard had not one, but two.

Howard went on to explain his ordeal to his well-connected lawyer friend. To succeed in this life, you must learn the art of building and maintaining influential relationships. *Your net worth is a function of your network.* A great visionary excels at that. Attorney Scott Greenberg introduced Howard to the father of Bill Gates, a wealthy Seattle lawyer with power in the city. Infuriated, Bill Gates Sr. took Howard's cause personally. He met with Bowker, threatening and asking him to withdraw his bid, which he did.

You will often win the fight you do not seek as fate comes to help you. Like any success story, yours will take twists and turns, adding spice. Today, the Starbucks coffee chain is a world giant with operations spanning over six continents, grossing close to $36 billion from 38,038 stores in 80 countries in 2023, as reported by statista.com. Howard Shultz's vision paid off; he is a Forbes list billionaire, boasting $3.7 billion in 2024.

9. RISE TO THE FIGHT: YOUR BLESSING WILL NOT GO UNCONTESTED:

Be prepared to face all types of opposition as soon as you prepare to rise. However, don't fret. When you surrender to the divine power, there is no opposition you cannot overcome because the LORD is always with the righteous (Psalms 37:39-40). He gives the ability to conquer adversity. However, *those* who knowingly engage in treachery will not go unpunished and will pay their debt to the last penny (Matthew 5:26).

Several competitors sued Microsoft for becoming too powerful and threatening healthy competition. The company did not shy away from using its position to cross many lines and bully other companies. In business, your quick wit can get you in trouble when it becomes a nuisance to others, especially when they can build a case against you.

Being honest and fair can help, but your growth can sometimes threaten your competition, which will try to bar you from becoming too powerful. Microsoft suffered several adversities in its rise to market leadership. First, Apple accused Microsoft of stealing its graphical user interface (GUI). Then, IBM sued Microsoft and received a settlement for shortcomings in its business dealings.

YOUR VISION WILL BE CHALLENGED

Every good intention will have a set of opposition. Trust in your Superior Power to give you victory.

– **Coach Greb**

You should not be dismayed in front of adversity; you should trust not in your ability but in the power of He who sends you the vision. Nehemiah trusted the power of God, who sent him to rebuild the fallen walls of Jerusalem amid opposition from the local leaders. Nobody can stop or prevent God's plan.

When evil governors Sanballat, Tobia, and Geshem reignited their historical enmity to prevent rebuilding the city walls, they all failed. Nehemiah empowered his people to finish the work within fifty days. God will always stand behind his promise and work. Working on God's calling, you will meet adversity but always win over any form of hurdle. When you see that all you do crumbles, stop and ask: "Is God in what I am doing?" And when you realize that God is not with you, what do you do?

Jesus relied on the strength of He who sent him and did not do his own will, but the will of He who sent him (John 5:30). What gave shepherd boy David the strength to dare the Philistine giant so bravely?

When David courageously dared and sent Goliath to his grave, he trusted not himself but God. He confidently declared, "This day, the LORD will deliver you into my hand, and I will strike your head from you. And I will give the carcasses of the host of the Philistines this day to the fowl of the air and the wild beast of the earth." (1 Samuel 17:46).

10. HOLD YOURSELF TO HIGH STANDARDS: LIVE BY A STRICT CODE OF INTEGRITY

Trust is like the breath of life. Once you lose it, you cannot get it back. Above all else, toil to preserve your public image.
— **Coach Greb**

Dishonesty will catch up with you. Undercutting competitors and cheating the government, the customers, and employees are practices that blemish the stature of business genius. The way some rich act is one of the reasons the average person tends to despise them. Not one company but a horde of competitors complained of Microsoft's dishonest business practices. Between 1994 and 1997, Bill Gates's image took a hit. Some news media even reported that he created the Bill and Melinda Gates Foundation in 2000 to restore his reputation.

First, IBM, which allowed Microsoft to become an actual company, was left in the dust when Bill Gates undercut it on the OS/2 project. In 1989, the two companies agreed to create OS/2 (Operation System 2), an operating system that would work on a PC (personal computer). Disregarding its agreement with IBM, Microsoft developed Windows, cutting IBM off. The company then forced all PC brands, such as Gateway and IBM, to include Windows as their default operating system.

Reportedly, Bill Gates pressured IBM to force other companies to support Windows. The Federal Trade Commission (FTC) investigated Microsoft based on complaints from its rivals. James Barksdale, CEO of the defunct Internet browser Netscape, and many other business leaders filed lawsuits against Microsoft. They argued that Microsoft forced computer makers to include its web browser - Internet Explorer - on every computer that used Microsoft's Windows applications. The FTC investigated Microsoft and threatened to split the company because of an antitrust law violation.

As a result of the company's unethical practices and the antitrust lawsuit launched in 1995 and concluded in 2000, Bill Gates's Microsoft spent close to $3.6 billion in settlements. With Microsoft's colossal cash chest, this may sound like a penny in a bucket, but the message resounded loud enough. According to the New York Times, the company paid $1.6 billion to rival Sun Microsystem in 2004, $775 million to IBM, $150 million to Gateway Computers, and $750 million to America Online in 2003. In 2007, on the same grounds of antitrust law violation, a class action ruling by the Iowa Supreme Court caused Microsoft to yank a $175 million check from its fat checkbook to appease consumers and businesses who had had enough of Microsoft's bullying. The long ledger of payees is unending.

With Edge, Microsoft's new browser, complaints are already fusing against malware software that maliciously forces users to buy some software. Dozens of complaints from enraged Edge users on several Internet forums started fusing when Edge replaced Internet Explorer, some arguing that Edge fraudulently captured and sent customer data to its browser server.

I bet the whole universe will soon have its payday n Microsoft's books. I am sure Bill Gates will not mind pleading guilty if he can gain from his unlawful practices.

In the world of technology, where people steal other people's ideas left and right, being sued is like brushing your teeth. In expectation of more suits, Microsoft has set up a lawsuit reserve. The Department of Justice's ruling to split Microsoft into two companies - to reduce its power - was overturned by President Bush in 2002.

Besides the temptation of bowing to malice for some, a visionary leader must have an imagination of gigantic magnitude.

11. THINKING SMALL IS A TRAGEDY.

Thinking small and failing to act on a vision is a tragedy and a lousy outlook on life. What if French military engineer Nicolas-Joseph Cugnot suffered from intellectual myopia and thought that building a car from the steam-engine technology was too unrealistic? Had he had a shrunk view on life, he would have never been able to build the first automobile in 1769. Likewise, the Wright brothers, Orville and Wilbur, did not believe that making a machine that could defy the law of gravity was a far-fetched fantasy.

For Elon Musk, sending people to the moon is no longer a childish dream. It is something that he has done so numerous times with his commercial shuttle, SpaceX. Any creative endeavor aims to create solutions to human challenges and push the horizon.

As such, a vision must add value to people's lives. Hence, an idea becomes a philanthropic endeavor to bring value, no matter how tiny it may seem. Thanks to other visionaries who added to the original idea, most inventions were small additions that later became leading innovations. Against all beliefs, Thomas Edison was not the originator of the incandescent light; English physicist Sir J.W. Starr preceded him.

Apple did not create cellular phone technology. Motorola engineer Martin Cooper and his team spearheaded this invention in the 1970s before Apple even eyed the cell phone industry. Upon releasing the first iPhone in 2007, Steve Jobs announced that the existing smartphones were good but complicated for the average person to use. He wanted to make phone use user-friendly and integrated. Has he succeeded in doing so? What do you think?

12. DEMONSTRATE YOUR WORTH TO HUMANITY

Your net worth is the result of your net contribution. We live in an efficient world that will determine your worth based on your contribution to society.

How do you create value? You can only create value if you have value.; therefore, investing in yourself is the first step toward building wealth. Every idea is a big idea. Before you dismiss any idea, find out what it offers: does it have the potential to add value? When Tim Berners-Lee invented the World Wide Web, who knew it would create a new type of economy? Today, the Internet has snatched thousands of millionaires and billionaires out of the jaws of poverty. If you have an idea, love it enough to pursue it.

Vision gives you the authority to build a better world. Bill Gates and his partners have revolutionized how we use computers by promoting Windows and Microsoft Office Suite. Computers in their various forms have become pervasive in our lives, creating a digital economic platform accessible at the click of a mouse or the swipe of a screen. No industry has produced more wealth than the high-tech industry. How are these people able to create so much value and wealth?

Visionaries are people with ambitions of an enormous magnitude. They wholeheartedly commit to solving human problems in an industry they love. Look at any great fortune builder, whether it be Carnegie, Ford, or Gates, and you will find that the source of their vast accomplishment was a problem solved.

13. STRIVE TO ACHIEVE PHENOMENAL HEIGHTS

Creativity frees you from the shackles of poverty and turns you into a mastermind. Vision sets people apart and turns them into legends whose accomplishments we tell from generation to generation. Vision sets great leaders and entrepreneurs apart.

If your imagination is not insane, it is not worth pursuing. Creativity enables you to launch your own SpaceX like Elon Musk and send people to the moon. Insane imagination can drive you to design a colossal machine to float in the air, as did the Wright brothers with the airplane. What do you see in your vision? If your idea is not wild enough to stun humanity, it has not been revealed to you yet.

A creative mind is like a child flying a kite. When released, the kite can go far from the child's expectations, running beyond his reach, his horizon. If your imagination cannot consume and lose you, it will never impact anyone. Innovation starts with one individual, flies into the sky's limitlessness, and lands on unsuspected grounds. Likewise, a technology created in a US-based Bell Lab can swim through the ocean to find itself in Germany or Japan. True imagination reveals the unique, phenomenal character of the dreamer.

In the arena of creativity, you must learn that *being good is not enough; being great is common, but being phenomenal is what is worth pursuing*. How far do you stretch your horizon, or how connected are you to your missional journey? What is the purpose of science, engineering, entrepreneurship, and innovation, and why do we invest tons of money in medical research if not to give humans the tools to dig out from the vast universe the solution to human challenges and uncover the limitless possibilities?

Creative minds are ordinary people with ridiculous ideas that defy the status quo. When Bill was a child, his parents feared he would be a loner. There was nothing special about this nerd in his young years beside his gift for numbers. Topping the SAT (Scholastic Aptitude Test - College Admission Test) with 1590 out of 1600, Bill was already a genius; he had a gift that never departed from him.

Where others see roadblocks, a creative mind always finds a way. Creative freedom distinguishes leaders from followers; it separates legends from everyday people. Creativity separates geniuses who build wealth for themselves from those who create wealth for others. It delineates overcomers who subdue life from those who subject themselves to life's whims.

Bill Gates had already set out to be a business genius from his early childhood. How many fifteen-year-old kids can earn a $20,000 profit with their own venture? Bill Gates and Paul Allen made that with their first venture - Traf-o-Data - a company that tracked traffic data in Seattle, Washington, in 1970.

14. SET OUT TO PROVE NAYSAYERS WRONG

One typical attitude is that most people you approach with your novel idea will be skeptical. Even trusted media and scientists would dismiss brilliant ideas. Throughout history, people have continued turning revolutionary ideas down. In 1632, the Catholic Church persecuted Italian Astronomer Galileo de Galilei for claiming that the earth was not the center of the universe. In 1986, over two hundred investors laughed at Howard Schultz's idea of the coffee shop Starbucks.

In the late 1990s, over thirty investors turned Alibaba's founder into a joke. Graham Bell's telephone was called a toy in 1876; Henry Ford's automobile idea was ridiculed when he started his company in the early 1900s. Today, it is unthinkable for most families to spend the night without sitting in front of the TV set. Most households in America have more television sets than people. Yet, Scottish inventor John Logie Baird's idea was turned into mockery when he invented the television in 1927.

When Motorola engineer Martin Cooper pioneered the cellular phone, he and the company doubted this would get anywhere. If the creators had listened to railleries, inventions such as the TV, the automobile, the telephone, the airplane, online shopping, and electricity would have been thrown in the trash and forgotten.

The Wright Brothers of North Carolina, who built the airplane, must have been insane to think that a massive load of zinc could fly in the air, disrespecting the law of gravity. Scottish inventor Alexander Graham Bell was called insane when he dared to think that he could communicate sound over distance through telephone lines. What about the man who believed he could create light from an incandescent light bulb?

Thomas Edison's idea of the incandescent light bulb and the alternating current was initially laughed at, and so were many brilliant ideas that revolutionized how we live today. Most of these visionary ideas were considered flops by those who had the first chance to weigh in on them. Indeed, the people who made significant differences in our lives started with a ridiculous idea they only believed in.

Creativity is the blessing bestowed upon everyone regardless of educational background, social status, and national origin. Each person receives a vision in various measures. Only those who act upon theirs see the fruit of it.

15. ACCEPT THAT PEOPLE WILL NOT BELIEVE IN YOUR VISION

Do not be surprised if nobody believes in your vision. It is not uncommon for people to dismiss ideas they are not familiar with. Nobody knew anything about operating software when introducing Windows software, so very few believed it could work. Bill Gates, the great communicator, went on a world tour to convince skeptical companies to adopt Windows software as the most revolutionary innovation of the time. Windows became the most widely used software globally a few years later, bringing Microsoft billions of dollars in revenue from worldwide sales.

Visionaries frequently suffer rejection in the initial phase of their ideas. As we read the story of a biblical figure named Noah, we learn one valuable lesson: pay no mind to raillery. In His fury against man's sin, God instructed Noah - the man God found sinless - to build a boat that would house the chosen species. God planned to cause a destructive flood to wipe all living creatures off the earth except those on the ark. As Noah started building the boat, he asked his neighbors to repent of their sins, but they took him for a joke and had a good laugh. When all inhabitants of the earth perished in the 40-day flood, Noah was the one who had the last laugh.

16. LEARN THE ART OF COMMUNICATION: VISIONARY LEADERS ARE FARSIGHTED LONERS

The genius of today was a fool at some point in his past. Being a leader is traveling a lonely road.

– Coach Greb

Most visionaries have come up with ideas people never imagined and are generally treated as nonconformists and often written off as crazy, nerdy, or irrational. A vision is a spiritual manifestation of connectedness. Until it becomes a visible reality, the vision will be explicit only to the beholder. The beholder sees the realized state of things in the vision, including the roadmap, outcomes, and possible rewards that others do not apprehend. An idea is visible only to the beholder, whose task is to share it with others because they cannot see it until it is realized.

Astute visionary leaders excel at the art of communication. Life and success are all about communication. If you are deficient in communication, you can quickly learn it. You will need it to play offense and defense in the business world. Learn to build powerful alliances and find the right investors, stakeholders, benefactors, and beneficiaries. American entrepreneurs dominate the world because of their unmatched gift of communication.

Our ideas often die because of the reactions of the people we trust the most. Being a pioneer demands more than just being a seer; you must be a persuasive communicator and a wise owl capable of exercising indulgence, patience, and self-restraint.

17. APPLY WISDOM, PATIENCE, AND DISCRETION

"For patience and fortitude conquer all things."
— **Ralph Waldo Emerson**

People you share your vision with may not be on the same level as you, which can be a source of frustration in many instances. Those surrounding you may not believe in your vision, understand it, or be excited about it.

Do not be shocked when your idea is the subject of jokes, and no one believes in it. The secret is to guard your vision against shortsighted and small-minded people. Only share your vision with people you have prayerfully identified as positive contributors to its manifestation. Visionaries are wise with their tongue, "For *whoever guards his mouth and tongue keeps his soul from troubles*" (Proverbs 21:23).

What happened to the projects you talked about so much? They never got started, and do you know why? You thought you were doing the right thing by telling everyone you trust. Do yourself a big favor: guard your mouth. You are only drawing people's wrath on you. Joseph's example speaks to this reality. Why did biblical figure Joseph's brothers sell him to Egyptian merchants and tell their father Jacob that wolves killed his favorite son? When Joseph shared the vision of his bright future with them, his brothers, including the firstborn, Reuben, became jealous.

Envy and jealousy are uncontrollable forces that make people commit atrocious crimes. As someone said, *"Keep your money, your wife, and your dreams from anyone,"* even people you think you trust because they could steal or bust it.

Your loving spouse, best friends forever, dedicated teachers, friendly coworkers, caring parents, or competing siblings are not always a reliable source of support for your million-dollar inspiration. These people are naysayers who can only block you from realizing your dream in their vast majority. Love them enough to keep your vision from them.

Jesus was rejected by those who knew Him as a child. They did not believe that the carpenter's son could suddenly call Himself the son of the living God and do miracles. Jesus performed forty miracles and healing in many lands, such as Capernaum. But in his hometown of Nazareth, where he grew up, he barely performed any miracles apart from a few healings. You can rarely be a prophet among your people, as reported in the Gospel of Matthew in Jesus's own words:

"A prophet is not without honor except in his own country and his own house." (Matthew 13:57), and Matthew added, *"Now He did not do many mighty works there because of their unbelief."* (Matthew 13:58)

18. PROTECT YOUR VISION. IT IS A PREGNANCY

Visionary wealth-builders believe they are enlightened with a burning fire they will allow no one to steal from them.
— **Coach Greb**

Would you trust anyone to touch your belly with your precious baby in the womb? Pregnant mothers are particularly protective and would not let a stranger dare draw near them, let alone touch that sweet and fragile little thing inside them. To every mother, no baby is more beautiful than her own. Likewise, visionaries protect their baby in the womb and are not dissuaded by naysayers. So, do not tell your best friends forever the next time you have your killer idea. They will only tell you what they see: the silly, nerdy, and crazy individual you are today, not the genius within. They will only view you from their limited sight. After weeding out naysayers, you must be able to distinguish distraction from inspiration.

19. LEARN TO WEED OUT DISTRACTORS

Have discernment to discriminate distractors from real vision. An inspired and experienced smith distinguishes solid gold from plated gold.
— **Coach Greb**

How many business ideas have you had in your life so far? Each day, you get a myriad of ideas flowing through your mind. While science has not yet provided the exact number of thoughts we produce each day, among which are business ideas, some people range between 20,000 and 70,000. How do you sort out the distractions that aim to derail you from your actual goal path? How many new business ideas did you receive when you started a new project? I succumbed to so much distraction until I surrendered to the power of focus. Renowned evangelical preacher and radio host Charles S. Swindoll believes we need discernment in what we see, hear, and think.

How can you weed out distractions? Remember, you must only pursue the idea attached to your calling. *God will only stand behind his promise and the endeavor that serves His interest.* If you are distracted by some funny project that has nothing to do with your divinely designed life path, be ready to welcome frustrations over frustrations. With discernment, you can differentiate a divine vision from distraction. You can quickly identify distractions by their fruit:

- Ideas that only magnify how much money you can make for yourself are distractions.
- Ideas that do not consider your passion, skills, and interests are distractions.
- Concepts that focus on the short-term more than the long-term are distractions.

Every day, you receive countless ideas, but not all are your life-purpose ideas. You need to seek **enlightened wisdom** through prayer and meditation to identify the ones that come from the source of divine inspiration.

20. LAY OUT THE VISIONARY BLUEPRINT FOR YOUR PURPOSE

When God enlightened Moses to build the Tabernacle, he was very precise. He gave Moses clear instructions on how He expected him to build the Tabernacle. If God is the one who gives us visions to do remarkable things, He cannot do so ambiguously. You should be wary if you are still debating what to do with your life or are fuzzy about a vision.

A vague idea that overwhelms you with worry does not come from God. Divine enlightenment comes with joy, peace, and excitement, for *"the blessing of the LORD makes one rich, and He adds no sorrow with it"* (Proverbs 10:22). What makes a dream or a vision exciting? It is a vision's clarity. God is a God of clarity. The Source of Infinite Intelligence will never send you a confusing and ambiguous concept. If you have a vision that worries you and appears confusing, it is not from God. God transmits his mission to us through a clear vision in the form of a night or daydream, inner voice, or inspiration that most of us call an idea.

All the great men whom God used to carry great missions received grand visions from the power of the angel of the LORD, who appeared to them to instruct them on their tasks. The angel of the LORD visited Gideon in a dream to go and fight for Israel. Joshua received a preview of the victory when God clearly instructed him on how the children of Israel should behave in Jericho as God himself prepared to deliver the city in their hands. Daniel, Moses, and David received clear directions for their missions. A vision is the road map to accomplishing a task.

21. BE A WAY MAKER WHERE THERE IS NO WAY

A visionary leader is a pioneer. Sometimes, you may be overwhelmed by a novel idea and not trust your ability to bring it to life. Nehemiah faced formidable opposition when he decided to rebuild the fallen walls of Jerusalem. The endeavors would have failed without divine inspiration. As a visionary leader, Nehemiah skillfully learned to pave the way by successfully rallying the king of Babylon, the people of Jerusalem, and others to support his efforts in building the wall. He avoided the trap set up by the ruler of Jerusalem. He empowered his people to participate willingly in rebuilding the fallen wall. Your vision will suffer physical, verbal, visible, and invisible attacks.

22. DUMP YOUR PLAN B. IT WILL KILL PLAN A

If you care enough for and believe in the beauty of your vision, you will conquer it.

– **Coach Greb**

Stick to the original vision. Things will not go right. Many of your plans will not work the way you expect them to. Many people change lanes when things get tough; don't. God stretches His mighty hands to empower those who dare to hang on. The book of 2 Chronicles 15:7 reads, *"But as for you, be strong and do not give up, for your work will be rewarded."* Repeatedly, the Bible teaches about the value of persistence and patience, virtues fading away in our "microwave" society. We want what we want right now. When their expectations take time, some people downgrade their standards and settle for whatever life throws their way.

Lowering your standards is an excellent way to forgo excellence and the opportunity to achieve greatness. Courage, persistence, and resilience are the ultimate expressions of your integrity. Achieving success is overcoming hurdles, which come in packs, just like a conveyor belt spilling out one problem after another. Many will settle for mediocrity instead of pushing for the excellence they aim for. The word "try" should not be part of the vocabulary of superachievers. Superachievers do not try things. They commit to engage in result-oriented endeavors, expect to succeed, and are prepared to learn from setbacks as another step toward success.

> ***LESSON LEARNED:*** *Imagination is the mother of science and progress. If you can see it in your mind, you can create it. This chapter illustrates how audacious individuals have harnessed their creative and imaginative powers to envision and realize groundbreaking innovations and projects. This chapter challenges you to unlock your own imagination, sparking audacious ideas that can change the world.*

In this chapter, you learn about the power of imagination in the spiritual realm, also known as inspired wisdom or vision. Without vision, the people perish, says the Holy Book. What each person realizes in the physical world is already built in the spiritual realm. Your mind becomes the depository of all your physical realizations. Your mind controls and directs your body to act one way or another. Your mind creates the energy you need to charge forward. Vision is generated in your spirit and manifested in your mind. Every idea stems from spiritual insight and becomes intellectually conceptualized before being physically displayed. Imagination or Vision is the blueprint for the manifestation of your divine purpose.

YOUR TURN – DAY 4:
THE AUDACITY OF IMAGINATION

Self-Reflection: *When was the last time you allowed yourself to explore your imagination and creative ideas freely?*

- How do you typically approach problem-solving and innovation in your personal or professional life?
- Are there specific areas where you feel my imagination is underutilized or constrained?
- Can you recall instances where imaginative thinking led to groundbreaking discoveries or solutions?

Application: *Set aside time for creative brainstorming sessions. What audacious ideas can you generate in your field or personal life?*

1. **Visualize Success:** Close your eyes and vividly imagine the successful realization of an audacious idea. How does it feel, look, and sound?
2. **Creative Prompts:** Seek out creative prompts, such as writing prompts or artistic challenges, to exercise your imagination regularly.
3. **Cross-Disciplinary Learning:** Explore fields and industries outside your own for fresh perspectives and ideas.
4. **Collaboration:** Connect with creative individuals who can inspire and collaborate with you on audacious projects.

THE AUDACITY OF EXPECTATION

BELIEVE IT.
CREATE IT.

> *"Trust in the LORD with all your heart and lean not on your own understanding; in all your ways, submit to him, and he will make your paths straight."*
> — Proverbs 3:6
>
> *"In order to win, you must expect to win."*
> — Richard Bach

As you read in the previous chapter, imagination is the mother of entrepreneurial endeavors and the heart of human progress. Yet, dreams and creativity alone cannot lift themselves. They must be sustained and honed by an unwavering load of faith, endurance, and expectation. Expectation is the engine that makes you stick around in a dead marriage, a dead-end job, a failing venture, a stressful work environment, a barren dream, or a rescue mission.

What happens when you chase someone who snatched your wallet? What do you do when the lad runs faster than you? If you believe you can catch him, you will pursue him, won't you? The moment you have lost hope, you will stop all actions. The same happens for a rescue mission and anything we do in life. Many fail just a few shots away from victory because they give up too soon, while a tiny few, iron-made like Elon Musk, boldly march forward amidst fire, insults, and raillery. What sets them apart?

ELON MUSK: A LEGEND OF AUDACITY. A DEMONSTRATION OF SELF-POWER

Winston Churchill believed that *if you are unsure of a course of action, do not attempt it. Your doubts and hesitations will infect your execution. Timidity is dangerous."*

Success takes time to cook. How much do you challenge yourself? How far can you go? How long can you wait? When do you know it is time to call it quits? How much are you willing to sacrifice? Success likes to be courted to see how far you can go. Sometimes, it will play the trickster and hide from you. What do you do? If you believe you can catch it, you will pursue it. Why, then, do people stop chasing the object of their desire? Either the desire is not obsessive enough, or the lack of self-belief is too formidable.

> *Failure only starts when you abandon and stop the pursuit; otherwise, all other attempts are just myriad ways to find the right way. That is why they are called trials, not failures.*
> — **Coach Greb**

What if fear did not exist in our lives? Would the world still be the same if it were free of fear? Self-doubt is a potent agent of failure. Because of your background, experience, perception, or the environment in which you grew up or were exposed, you may find it difficult to accept that you are worth anything. Maybe you still vividly remember classmates and siblings' name-calling when you were young. The humiliating events of your childhood affected your self-esteem in one way or another, making it impossible for you to see value in yourself. The reminiscence of those adverse situations thwarted your self-confidence and blurred the vision of the genius within. Let go of the past that kills your present and aborts your future. You now have the power to reject any self-defeating beliefs that ruin your chance at greatness, but you can't do it alone.

The mission you are called onto is not yours, so do not worry when and how it will be accomplished. God has promised to be behind His words, His promise. You will only fail when you detach yourself from God and try to walk and do it alone.

You are more victorious than you think, and Elon Musk's story you are about to read will prove it. As you will soon discover, Elon Musk belongs to a breed of humans who know how to build themselves up from their adversities.

Elon Musk has been forged by adversity and vowed to defy Planet Mars. He believes cruising onto the red planet should be like making a trip to Disneyland.

You will only see what you magnify. Expect greatness, and it will show up. What do you see in your rearview mirrors? What do you see through the front windshield? Life's failures and tribulations may cast a gloomy reality on your future and abilities. You may think you deserve nothing and indulge in negativity about yourself. You must quit now! You have the inner power that nobody can take away from you. Your nature comes back, again and again, to lift you when you feel beaten. Your task is to return within and touch the divine self to identify, hone, and utilize your inner power, gifts, or talents.

> SECRET CODE #5
> DEVELOP AN ATTITUDE OF IRRATIONAL EXPECTATIONS.

"Faith sees the invisible, believes the unbelievable, and receives the impossible.

– Corrie ten Boom

Insanely successful game-changers know how to emerge from darkness to glory. Like Elon Musk, we all have our dark years. During my years of hardship, which I have come to call the years of formatting, I felt as if I had never known what happiness was. All the pleasures of life had left me. I was continually failing, even at minor tasks. I was in a constant state of fear and blamed myself for not obeying God enough.

From an upbeat and optimistic person, I could not believe what I had become. I could not bear to overhear myself uttering demeaning and self-defeating thoughts and words that send you nowhere but to the abyss. People who knew me and used to call my enthusiasm contagious positivity could not understand. My wife even called me antipathetic and anti-social. I lost my youthly face and smile, an appearance that shocks many people when I tell them my age.

For many years, though I was past middle age, I still had a radiant, childish face because I enjoyed laughing and being around people who loved laughing. But all that radiance had left me. I spent two years in this shack right after my father's passing. I was overwhelmed by fear: the fear of death, the fear of losing, the fear of failing; those fears made room for all sorts of negative imagination, dreams, and attitudes. That was when I discovered the creative power of negative thinking. This experience blatantly illustrated the so-called **law of attraction**; as writer Rhonda Byrne put it, **"Thoughts are more powerful than action."**

Gradually, ordeal after ordeal, I uncovered the one thing that changed my life forever. What was it? How hard was it? Many times, we complicate our own lives when things are so simple. All I had to do was change my mental reaction to life. After losing my father, I shut myself down and changed my lenses. Instead of focusing on what I desired, I started looking for things I did not want.

The constant state of fear made me expect nothing but the things I dreaded the most, which haunted my sleep and dreams. I expected nothing but the worst until I fell on an online video that taught me about reframing your mindset. After many unsuccessful practices, I started gaining more confidence in myself. I gradually shifted my outlook on life after reading the stories of people who went through the abyss, emerged back up, and soared. One such person is Elon Musk.

TWELVE MANIFESTATIONS OF THE ATTITUDE OF EXPECTATION

"Whatever we expect with confidence becomes our own self-fulfilling prophecy."

— **Brian Tracy**

If you can believe it, you can create it. Life will deliver at your door your most dominant expectation. Among the many entrepreneurs I have studied, people of high quality and accomplishment, none has fascinated me more than the daring Elon Musk. Elon Musk is an iron built. He was born to defy common sense. When he embarked on his prosperous entrepreneurial career, Elon faced life's tribulations. I am surprised he kept his dark hair. President Obama got his painted gray after eight short years in the White House. I guess the White House rhymes with gray hair or maybe white.

No setback was strong enough to deter the audacious entrepreneur. His companies took time to yield dividends when SpaceX and Tesla Motors flapped their wings of despair. When Tesla demanded a fresh cash boost, Elon did not think twice about infusing an extra $40 million of his own money into the venture. That same Tesla company made him the wealthiest man on the planet.

Elon believed in his project so much that nothing could stop him. After experiencing a period of turbulence, Elon began to see his fate smile at him. The three companies are now growing and bringing their tenacious founder serious dividends. If you would like to learn more about Elon, here we go.

1. SET OUT TO IMPACT THE WORLD

"Leadership is the capacity to translate vision into reality."
– Warren Bennis

Some people were born to change the world, others to follow it. The story of Elon Musk is one of the most inspiring legends for those who want to pursue their passion and start building wealth from scratch. The life story of Elon Musk is a cocktail of visionary leadership, uncommon sense, utter audacity, resilience, determination, stubbornness, sacrifice, and faith. Today, the co-founder, CEO, and founding partner of Tesla Motors, SpaceX, Solar City, Starling, and The Boring Company has emerged from the storms and is now hailed to the podium of the great among the great.

After weathering many storms, Elon Musk can take a break and look to the horizon. He has courageously proved countless times that nothing can stop the rise of a burning hunger for innovation. Smiling and confident, despite the many uncertainties, opportunities, and setbacks he faces as a parallel entrepreneur, Elon is looking forward to unexplored grounds. How does he concurrently spearhead innovation in three unrelated industries: solar energy, space exploration, and renewable energy?

2. TRACE YOUR OWN LANE: BE THE EXCEPTION, NOT THE EXPECTATION

Sometimes called a dreamer, Elon Musk is an idealist who wants to change the world by conquering planet Mars while powering planet Earth with renewable energy. One question you may ask is, "Who is this nerdy lad who defies the limitlessness of the universe?"

Create your own path. Elon Reeve Musk was born on June 19, 1971, in Pretoria, South Africa, to a wealthy South African Engineer and a Canadian mother, once a Cover Girl magazine model. I now understand why he is called a dreamer. Early in his childhood, Elon's daydreaming attitude worried his parents and caregivers, who feared something might be wrong with his hearing. No, nothing was wrong with him. The boy was born a dreamer, and the parents did not know their child was already surfing space, sometimes on Mars, the moon, or, shall I say, snooping around the earth. Elon wants to accomplish what no ordinary person has achieved. At 12, he announced that he was not just another kid. He is the man who is planning to change it. As soon as Elon entered puberty, he entered the den of those who control the world. Like Bill Gates, Elon sold his first software, Blastar, right before adolescence.

Force your destiny. Like the biblical prodigal son, young Elon Musk, who has nothing to envy King Solomon's sons. He left his father's sumptuous mansion to emigrate from South Africa to avoid being drafted into the army. At age 17, Elon and his brother Kimbal landed in Canada, their mother Maye Musk's country of origin. After three short years in Canada, Elon moved to the United States to attend the University of Pennsylvania. Bookish Elon was not content with earning just one degree. He got two: one Bachelor of Science in economics and a second Bachelor of Arts in physics. Superachievers are people who go the extra mile; they reach beyond the horizon of the average person.

Despite being born in a foreign land, Elon Musk has never found an excuse to think of himself as a foreigner and create the mental block as many foreign-born American citizens would. Upon graduating from the prestigious Wharton Business School at the University of Pennsylvania with a dual degree in economics and physics, Elon moved to Silicon Valley to experiment with what being a genius was all about.

3. LEVERAGE THE GIFT WITHIN

"True genius lies not in doing extraordinary things, but in doing ordinary things extraordinarily well."
— **Major General Louis H. Wilson**

Geniuses peep into the future before everyone else. Like Jeff Bezos, who left D.E. Shaw to create Amazon, Bill Gates, who dropped out of Harvard to pursue the dream of Microsoft, Elon said his farewells to the prestigious Stanford University just two days after starting a Ph.D. program in physics and material science. He smelled the Internet boom and thought he could create his own lane on the Internet superhighway. When rejected for a job with Netscape, Elon knew he would make a way where there was no way.

Charge forward like a bull. At 23, partnering with younger brother Kimbal, Elon tapped into his programming skills - honed since the age of twelve - to create Zip2. This online directory helped businesses promote themselves online. The two brothers pitched to family friend Gregory Kouri to launch their first company. This Lebanese real estate investor funded Zip2 and PayPal.

4. BUILD A SHIELD AROUND YOUR FORTRESS

Find ways to hedge against adverse take-over of your idea. When Zip2 started growing, venture capitalist Mor Davidow, who invested in the venture, replaced Elon with a more mature leader. Young Elon swallowed his pride and anger when he was demoted as CEO and replaced by Rich Sorkin because the board considered him unqualified to run such a large organization.

Learn to turn every stone. When Compaq Computers bought Zip2 in 1999, Elon sold his shares and used his proceeds to invest in X.com, the first online FDIC-insured bank. X.com merged with rival Confinity to become PayPal in 2001. With the PayPal Mafia, a group of thirteen business geniuses who each created their own million and billion-dollar ventures, Elon Musk built PayPal into a company that gave cold sweat to online giant eBay.

Know when to call it quits. The team worked tirelessly to raise PayPal to control most of the online payment transactions, beating eBay's system, even if the latter eventually ended up acquiring PayPal. The young company suffered internal strife, and the co-founders disagreed on the company's direction. In 2002, rival eBay acquired PayPal after it went public. Elon was once again demoted as CEO.

"Not again!" you might sigh, "Poor Elon."

"Enough. I'm out of here!" Elon made up his mind.

Why stick around a culture that fails to meet your vision? One would wonder.

Someone rightfully said,

"I'd rather be where I am celebrated, not where I am tolerated," and I couldn't agree more.

Elon did not wait too long to cash his $165 million stakes and move to larger projects. Having explored the idea of buying a lot on Mars for quite some time, in 2003, Elon decided to create SpaceX, his own *ultimate flying machine,* so he didn't have to beg Jeff Bezoz, his fierce rival, to give him a lift on his Blue Origin.

"Why Mars?" you might wonder.

Why Mars? At least the Martians will give you some respect, I guess.

5. SET BOLD, INSANE GOALS AND STICK TO THEM.

World changers like Elon Musk dream B.I.G. They have Bold, Insane Goals. No, I meant phenomenal people dream crazy dreams.

Upon cashing in his stake in PayPal, Elon put up $100 million to create SpaceX Space Exploration Technologies. Elon had a vivid interest in renewable energy. He also wanted to create a greenhouse on Mars and make commercial space flight to Mars efficient and affordable. In the meantime, leaving PayPal with a fat checkbook, Elon was approached by the co-founders of Tesla, Martin Eberhard and Marc Tarpenning. The two founders wanted to build the electric car, following the dream of inventor Nikola Tesla. Elon, who dreamed of renewable energy, invested $6.5 million in 2004, became the majority owner, and later took up the CEO seat in 2008.

In 2006, Elon invested $10 million to co-found Solar City and let his first cousins Lyndon and Peter Rive run it while he retained the role of chairman. Solar City was a success, becoming the largest solar panel installer in the USA until 2015. Solar City was acquired in 2016 as Tesla Energy amid a storm of lawsuits from Tesla investors who charged Elon with buying a limping company. Adversities come in conveyor belts but will feel like a sauna bath if you develop grit and learn to weather them. They bear the seed of innovation and opportunities. Elon Musk never runs away from them, and neither should you.

Learn to leverage every adversity. Being demoted from PayPal with plenty of cash was a goldmine for Elon. He did not sit around to fuss because creative geniuses do not sit around to mourn their demises. They move on to bigger and better things. Elon became a serial entrepreneur with the resources to do so. Resilient Elon turned every challenge into a stepping stone to higher and better grounds.

Be the one even when the sky is falling on you. If it has never been done, "Be the One" to pioneer it. Elon faced multiple setbacks in his personal life. He lost his first child, his marriage broke apart, and during his darkest moments, he became the joke of the media, some calling him "a dreamer."

The business media fiercely criticized Elon for his insanity. No one gave him a chance or believed he could surprise the planet as he now did.

Despite it all, Elon never shied away from stepping onto the uncharted ground. Elon is an insightful innovator who wants to revolutionize space exploration, clean energy, and solar energy.

Savor the fruit of tenacity. Elon invested every penny in three companies that took time to bring the expected dividends. SpaceX experienced three launch failures before it could become a success. Tesla Motor dove its nose in the sand, demanding an infusion of new cash. The board and investors were reluctant to pitch in, so Elon reached into his pocket to boost the company. Elon invested over $180 million of his own money in his three ventures. He did not leave a penny for rent – while he amassed millions, Elon did not care about owning a home. That was not on his list of priorities. "Insane!" some would say. "Weird," others will chime in. That is what focused entrepreneurs do: they care less about their self-gratification than the health of the *babies* they are birthing.

Committed to seeing his venture succeed, Elon emptied his coffers to save Tesla Motors. Today, Tesla is a robust machine on the road, ready to match up with any vehicle. In 2017, Tesla left General Motors in the dust, surpassing one of the grandpas of carmakers in America. Tesla shares soared to 695 percent at the close of 2020, bloating Elon Musk's wealth six-fold.

Ranked 35th on the Forbes List, Elon Musk surpassed Jeff Bezos in January 2021 as the world's wealthiest man with a treasure chest of over $126 billion, close to a $100 billion payday in less than a year. Tesla's rapid growth thrust Elon Musk into the first-row seats. In 2022, Elon's wealth skyrocketed to $249 billion, distancing himself from Bezos by a wide margin just shy of $60 billion. Who makes over $200 billion in less than two years? Those who do not run after money let money flow to them like a magic wand. Elon wants to help our planet and contribute to the advancement of humanity. He does not care about money. As a millionaire, he did not care about buying a house. He rented his dwelling. As a billionaire, he is not impressed by mansions. He decided to let go of all the homes he owned. Maybe he is not interested in life on Earth after all he's doing to create life on Mars.

The universal law of harmony. The universe will bless whatever you choose to do as long as it is aligned with the universal law of harmony. When it sees your determination, it sends you an army of angels. Our universe is efficient. It will empower whatever you resolutely subject yourself to. Whatever you decide, the universe will obey and manifest.

The future is shining bright for Elon Musk. His revolutionary ideas and drive to conquer the unthinkable won him billion-dollar contracts from the United States NASA, and the Russian Government. In 2019, the Chinese government gave Tesla Motor the green light to make cars in China, a win-win deal. Opening a $2 billion Tesla factory in Shanghai aimed to cut the car price for Chinese consumers in half while pouring more cash into Elon's coffers: doing good and being paid for, *the essence of business.*

6. START FROM THE END

Take bold steps to the finish line. What matters is not where you start but where you end. Often, the true definition of *entrepreneurship* is misconstrued. Entrepreneurship is the ability to carry your vision boldly and resiliently through opposition, setbacks, and roadblocks. Dreaming but failing to take bold steps will make you spin your wheels. Put your faith to the test. Christian Nestell Bovee, the author of "*Intuitions and Summaries of Thought* and *Thoughts, Feelings and Fancies,* believes that "The method of the enterprising is to plan with audacity and execute with vigor. There is a difference between wishful thinking and active faith. Wishful thinking waits for the ship to come in; active faith moves the waters. The stories of people who believed in themselves and triumphed over adversity are familiar.

Move the frontier. We will never tire of recounting the epic stories of the pioneers who overcame the new frontier of the West and those who broke the barriers of racial, gender, and age discrimination. Many who overcame poverty and seemingly impregnable challenges are heroes whose tales are inspiring examples in our coaching sessions. They are references that help us train a new breed of pioneers whose role is to take the torch and run with it to victory. These stories set benchmarks we can all use to mirror the effectiveness of our own endeavors: "Could you try and be a little like Elon Musk, who was undeterred by huge setbacks, or like Jack Ma of Alibaba, who gave rejection a new meaning?"

Have an unshakable faith in your dream. What is the common denominator of these American pioneers? They hold to their dreams and trust in the American system as the land of opportunity. The pioneers who braved the sea, the distance, the physical threats from enemies, and the unforgiving weather had good reasons to give up. But no. They triumphed over adversities, losing precious lives at sea and in battle as they waged wars to conquer lands and force their freedom.

7. TRUST THE SOURCE

> *Self-confidence or self-belief not grounded in the faith in the divine, the supernatural, is like a flower that will wither with the wind.*
>
> **– Coach Greb**

How does the power of expectation correlate with the law of divine reward? Expecting is believing in the certainty of a forthcoming reality, living in the supernatural, and trusting in Divine Sovereignty: **Trust God, have faith, and believe in yourself.**

What prompted one man like Elon Musk to engage in space exploration, something mighty nations like the United States and the Soviet Union have been competing on?

Audacity gets you beyond the horizon. Elon's audacity goes beyond common understanding. That is what happens when you have an unshakable belief. When you expect, the universe can do nothing but deliver. The law of expectation perfectly mirrors the famous law of attraction. You will receive what you expect; life will throw smallness to your door if you expect small things. If you expect great things, greatness will run after you. You will not rise above your expectations of yourself. As bestselling author Brian Tracy believes, *"Positive expectations are the mark of the superior personality."*

Expect the manifestation of God's glory. Expectation builds on faith, a frame of mind unshattered by storms or uncertainties. It is surrendering all to the divine and trusting His intention to make our expectations come to pass. You must have faith and trust God to deliver on his promise; if He did it yesterday, He would do it again this time. Why did David take a chance fighting with Goliath, who defeated the whole Israelite army? David experienced God's power when God delivered ferocious animals into his hands as a young shepherd. It only made sense to expect God to defeat Goliath,

Stay obedient and committed. Inspired wealth-builders do three things: they obediently commit themselves to God; they trust Him and expect His blessing; they use God's direction industriously to build wealth. Successful entrepreneurs work and expect their recompense from what most call the universe. Being obedient is trusting in God's ability, love, and promise. In a word, it is honoring God in all things.

8. HARNESS THE POWER OF COMMITTEDNESS

Faith in the Superior Power gives you self-confidence, self-assurance, and self-esteem. Self-confidence pushes you to be committed and determined to succeed. Determination and commitment are the key character traits of a successful person. You must be dedicated to your mission, goals, values, words, and relationships regardless of weather, time, season, or challenges. Phenomenal people are those who remain faithful irrespective of the scope of the tribulation. Jesus could have abandoned and found a good excuse and accused the Jews he had come to save as people with stiff necks (Acts 7:51) and thrown in the towel.

Without faith, self-belief, and commitment, you will hardly accomplish anything, not with God or anyone. Moses clearly expressed the importance of commitment in the Book of Law when he wrote:

> *If a man vows a vow to the Lord or swears an oath to bind himself by a pledge, he shall not break his word. He shall do according to all that proceeds out of his mouth* **(Numbers 30:2).**

Commitment is an engagement to accomplish a given task or assignment and force oneself not to breach it even if the condition involves pain, discomfort, and loss, or even if our own gain is no longer at stake. Committing yourself to your spouse is out of love, but when you surrender to God, it is our trust. Commitment implies trust. You trust the other party to fulfill her share of the obligation. Elon Musk never quits - because he has committed to seeing his ideas succeed.

Self-confidence is the fuel that ignites your gut, empowers your bones, releases your feet to jump forth, and prompts you to enchain adversity bravely. Self-belief gives you the boldness to subdue life. It fiercely propels you to the frontline to fearlessly order your heart's desires like a teenager in love.

9. BE UNYIELDING AND MARCH FORWARD THROUGH THE GATES OF STRONGHOLDS

You will never rise above the belief you have of yourself.

Know and believe in your worth. Most people do not act upon their vision because they do not believe in the God-given talents that lie dormant inside of them. You have a skill, something that makes you unique. Despite negative perceptions, self-saboteurs must understand that something positive is worth discovering in each person.

God will never give you a task for which he did not prepare you. You are more than you think you are. Rise above your present or past to project yourself into the future. Your past does not necessarily birth your present, nor does your present beget your future. You must learn to recognize what holds you back, know your worth, and put it to work.

How do you explain that someone like Jim Carrey grew up in poverty and is swimming in riches today? How was he able to snatch himself out of the jaws of poverty? What about famed billionaire movie producer Tyler Perry, once homelessly parading Atlanta streets and headed towards the desolate abyss of suffering? How did Tyler maneuver to escape the iceberg of poverty that has stalled many into the womb of misery? How do you feel when you see your name on an exit of the streets that was once your bedroom? Go to Atlanta, and you will witness how funny life can be. I laughed when I came across the exit sign off Georgia Route 166 that reads, "Tyler Perry Studios."

Be courageous. *Worries about the future can only kill tomorrow's opportunities in the womb.* "*Which of you by worrying can add one cubit to his stature?*" asked the Gospel of Matthew in chapter 6, verse 27. Worry is the anticipation of woes and the emptying of tomorrow's magic. Dutch church watchwoman and writer Corrie ten Boom put it so clearly when she argued, "*Worrying is carrying tomorrow's load with today's strength- carrying two days at once. It is moving into tomorrow ahead of time. Worrying doesn't empty tomorrow of its sorrow; it empties today of its strength.*"

10. LEARN TO TAME YOUR FEARS. FRIGHTEN YOUR FEARS BY THE POWER OF SELF-BELIEF

"I can do all things through Christ who strengthens me."
— **Philippians 4:13**

Never let fear close doors to you. Fear is one of the most manipulative and destructive enemies for any human being, visionary entrepreneurs, and wealth-builders. No matter how strong, everyone faces some form of fear. Some may fear heights, thunder, darkness, ghosts, spiders, or roaches. Others may fear the police, the idea of death, or anything.

Fear is a paralyzing, imaginary force. Your fear is a projected idea of an adverse experience that sends negative mental signals to your brain. Initially developing as a psychological dysfunction, fear can culminate into a spiritual, paralyzing force. In a dreadful situation, you lose your sense of rationality and physical energy. You become easy prey to the danger at hand. Multiple champion boxer Mohamed Ali had one successful boxing strategy: he would psychologically beat his opponent before they met in the ring. He would insult, demean, and anger his adversary before and during the fight. His strategy of demeaning and putting fear in the opponent served him well. Mohamed Ali won fifty-six fights; thirty-seven were knockouts. He only lost five fights out of the sixty-one matches of his brilliant twenty-year boxing career.

Fear is often a controlling tool, especially for entities that seek absolute power over their subjects. Selling the idea of a looming doom does nothing but send the unsuspecting citizens as weak lambs in the hands of protective leaders, government, or system. Many nations continue creating uncertainty, fear, and panic to infuse the need for a powerful government. We have seen that during wars, pandemics, or crises.

Fear causes failures because it weakens your defensive and offensive abilities. When overwhelmed by fear, you lose all senses, including common sense, making costly, often deadly mistakes. According to Indian Jogi teacher Jaggi Vasudev Sadh guru,

> *Fear is simply because you are not living with life, you are living in your mind. Your fear is always about what's going to happen next. That means your fear is always about that which does not exist. If your fear is about*

the nonexistent, your fear is a hundred percent imaginary. If you are suffering the non-existential, we call that insanity.

11. BECOME AN EXPERT AT FAILING.

Unlike audacious people like Elon Musk, those afraid of failing prefer never to try. Great ideas never become a reality because the bearers are paralyzed by fear. As commonly said, the graveyard is the richest place on earth because of the countless geniuses who went to their graves without ever accomplishing their marvels.

Fear of failure is an excuse for those not undertaking their brilliant ideas. These people's great ideas go to their graves with them. Many are afraid of the risk of entering the reality of the unknown. According to research in Business Insider Australia, Asians top the list, with 50 percent of respondents arguing that the fear of failure is why they do not want to start a business. Europeans follow them at 41 percent. In Oceania, including Australia, that number falls to 39 percent. In comparison, only 29 percent of Americans can forgo the opportunity to create wealth because of fear. Americans, in the majority, are risk-takers and born entrepreneurs.

So, what happens when you surrender to the fear of failing? You stay idle and don't do anything. Fear eats up your life. Can you count how many opportunities you have missed because of fear?

Failure is the first step to success. Expect it. Some people say failure is not an option. No, failure is the first option; you must acknowledge that failing is the first step and the first thing to expect at the top of your list on your rise to success. Those haunted by the idea of failure never try. The medal goes to the person who has failed while trying. What merit goes to a man who has never tried?

12: STICK TO YOUR VALUES

Self-confidence yields bold integrity. An inspired wealth-builder does not try to cut corners, hurt, or cheat someone. Those who do pay the price. How many lawsuits have been filed against Facebook and its founder, Mark Zuckerberg? Large corporations rating themselves too *big-to-sue* do not hesitate to bend the rules to indulge in illegal, illicit, and unethical practices to steer the advantage in their favor, especially when dealing with the little guy.

" WHO STOLE THE FACEBOOK IDEA? "

In the 1980s, Apple accused Bill Gates of allegedly "stealing" its Graphic User Interface to create Microsoft's Windows platform, which brought the company billions of dollars and made its founder the first tech billionaire. In 2004, three Harvard students, Indian-born Divya Narendra and twin brothers Cameron Winklevoss and Tyler Winklevoss, sued Mark Zuckerberg for stealing their idea to create Thefacebook, the forbearer of Facebook. The trio argued that Divya Narendra, the originator of the Harvard Connection ConnectU, invited the two brothers to join his coding team as partners. In turn, the brothers introduced freshman Zuckerberg, who had coding skills, to Divya. Instead of receiving monetary compensation for his work, Zuckerberg said he preferred to join the team and contribute sweat. Zuckerberg was granted full privilege and access to the codes. Instead of developing the ConnectU network, Mark Zuckerberg secretly created his own platform. He avoided meeting his pals and gave bogus excuses.

On February 4, 2004, to the greatest surprise of the partners, Mark Zuckerberg unveiled Thefacebook.com. The team quickly sued, but the lengthy litigation could not block Facebook from growing. That case was settled in 2008, four years later. Though the three plaintiffs accepted a $65 million settlement in 2009 and small ownership of Facebook, the two brothers were unsatisfied and unsuccessfully sued Zuckerberg for more reparation.

Today, Mark Zuckerberg has faced numerous litigations for unethical business practices, which, to some extent, tarnished the image of the visionary. Accused of abusing user privacy for gain, Facebook is one of the top twenty most hated companies in America. Despite Facebook's strong cash position, the platform's future can be in grave danger of losing ground when a more revolutionary giant thrusts a novel ideal to compete with it.

As you noted through this chapter, the law of expectation can empower you to manifest what you want to see in your life. Believing is seeing, for all that is created stems from a firm belief. You can recreate yourself in newness if you think you can.

> ***LESSON LEARNED:*** *You've just explored the power of expectation in achieving audacious goals. Positive thinking, high expectations, and self-belief are the gateway to superior accomplishments. Leaning on the examples of Elon Musk and many other legends, you, too, can practice how expecting success can lead to remarkable outcomes, thereby setting audacious expectations for yourself.*

YOUR TURN – DAY 5: THE AUDACITY OF EXPECTATION

Self-Reflection: *What are your expectations regarding success, both in your personal and professional pursuits?*

- Have you ever witnessed the power of positive thinking and high expectations in achieving remarkable results?
- Do you tend to set high expectations for yourself and believe in your ability to meet them?
- How can you cultivate a mindset of audacious expectation in your life?

Application: *Develop a list of positive affirmations related to your goals. Repeat them daily to boost your expectations.*

1. **Visualization:** Visualize yourself achieving your audacious goals in detail. How does this practice affect your mindset?
2. **Setting High Standards:** Reevaluate your expectations for yourself. Are they high enough? If not, raise the bar.
3. **Mentorship:** Seek out a mentor who can help you set and meet higher expectations in your chosen area of focus.
4. **Goal Tracking:** Create a system for tracking your progress toward your audacious goals. Regularly review and adjust your expectations based on your progress.

THE AUDACITY OF SACRIFICE

FOR EVERY HARVEST, THERE IS A SEED.

"Dreams do come true if only we wish hard enough. You can have anything in life if you will sacrifice everything else for it."

– J.M. Barrie

Expectation is not just idly sitting and waiting for a paternalistic hand to come and hand out the desire of your wishes to you. No! Expectation is unwavering active faith. It is the ability to contain one's cravings and indulgences and walk along the painful avenue of self-depravation, self-denial, separation, and detachment and *letting go to be able to go.* Expectation is not sitting around and waiting for your ship to come in; it is taking chances, throwing yourself into the waters, and swimming to it. Amazon's Jeff Bezos epitomizes what letting go is all about.

DARE TO QUIT LIKE JEFF BEZOS

I have often been frustrated with some youngsters who believe life can run smoothly without bumpers. When I remind them of what sacrifice their mother and I had to endure to get where we are today, they jokingly rebut, "Dad, that was your time." Alarmingly, this thought is typical among our younger generations. I wonder what good parenting we've done. We have sent the wrong message to our kids, telling them they can have anything without effort. I fear what will come of them and invite each parent to read and share the following words with their children: *"There is always a price for the prize. For every harvest, there is a seed."*

> ### SECRET CODE #6
> **LIVE BY A SPIRIT OF RADICAL SELF-DENIAL AND FORCEFULNESS**

Life demands sacrifice. We should teach our youth to do away with the free-lunch mentality. As a former high school teacher, I witnessed our children's behavior in the cafeteria with much awe. After finishing their meal, they leave their trash on the tray for the custodians to pick up, and nobody finds that scandalizing. I do. The way we handle them teaches them they can get everything for free. Many grow up with an entitlement mindset, so they may expect a handout and never fend for themselves. Our children get free transportation, free food, free books, free education, and free time. No wonder many students expect free grades at the end of the semester or school year.

Education is not about theories but about teaching life skills our youth lack. Every harvest must have a seed, and the self-made can prove it. American pioneers did give their blood for this country, and Virginia Governor Patrick Henry will not tell otherwise.

THE PRICE OF FREEDOM: "GIVE ME POVERTY OR GIVE ME WEALTH"

Accept to pay the price for the prize. "Give me liberty or give me death," hammered Patrick Henry in his speech at the Second Virginia Convention in March of 1776 to urge the Virginians to send troops to fight in the Revolutionary War against Britain. That speech galvanized so many who enlisted to join the fight for independence. The men who built America had the power to overcome adversity. What would have come of the United States if men like Patrick Henry had not risen to say enough is enough and offered their lives in exchange for freedom? That famous speech encouraged the colonists to rise out of fear and seize their freedom with the rifle's power. Imagine how much more freedom you could have if you told life, "Give me poverty or wealth." Billionaire Jeffrey Preston Jorgensen did when he chose the liberty of a wild open garage over the slavery of a sumptuous office.

> *Every success is a story of sacrifice. Fools run away from sacrifice; the wise run into it.*
>
> — **Coach Greb**

The first lesson of success is called **sacrifice**: *giving up something of value now in return for something of a higher value at some uncertain date.* After I had drilled this concept so much, my Sunday school Bible scholars became experts at it. Even my six-year-old David and other kids say it with closed eyes. You cannot welcome success from the comfort of your gated palace. Every successful person knows that you cannot win if you do not take risks. Risk-taking is one - if not the major - driving force of successful entrepreneurs.

The word *entrepreneur means undertaking and engaging in something challenging and risky*. Who are you to turn down prestigious Intel and Bell Labs jobs to join some uncertain launch of a start-up venture named Fitel that ultimately went bust? How dare you fire your boss, pleading with you to stay on the job while others beg them to keep them on?

The story of the man who threw away the rationed gold to create his own foundry, building a powerhouse from a tiny dose of inspiration, will get you to understand that you must give away something of value to get something of higher value. Learn to forgo short-term gain for lifetime abundance. The story you will soon read is about a man who was not born with a silver spoon in his mouth; he was the silver spoon itself, worth a mountain of gold today. Here is what you may not know about Jeff Bezos, founder and CEO of Amazon.

The world's second-richest man emerged from a humble background. Jeffrey Preston Jorgensen was born on January 12, 1964, to Jacklyn Gise, a teenage high school student, and Ted Jorgensen. His father, who barely participated in raising him, never knew he had a son who would soon be one of the wealthiest people on earth; Jeff was raised to face life. Adopted by stepfather Miguel Bezos, a Cuban immigrant who married his mother when he was just one, Jeff learned the power of delayed gratification early on. Miguel's attitude as an overcomer taught little Jeffrey how to punch life in the eyes. Every success story is a labyrinth of uncertainties and aha moments.

YOUR GOLD WILL NOT BE DELIVERED INTO YOUR GATED PALACE

How could a sixteen-year-old teenager migrate to an unknown land whose language he could not speak and whose culture he had no idea of? Fleeing the 1962 insurrection in Cuba, Miguel Bezos entered the USA as a refugee, leaving his parents behind. Upon graduating high school, Bezos started college and met Jacklyn Gise, a high school student he married soon after. In 1968, already married to Jacklyn Jeff's mother, Miguel finished his Bachelor of Science in Mathematics and Computer Science from the University of Albuquerque, New Mexico.

He adopted and treated Jeffrey as his own son and gave him his last name, Bezos. Miguel cared for Jeff and taught him the virtues of hard work. In fact, Miguel is the unsung hero behind Amazon.

Jacky and Miguel's faith in their son's stupid idea made the family multibillionaires. Miguel and Jacky did not think twice when they emptied their coffer to serve as Amazon's first *angel investors*, providing the initial seed capital of $245,573 for a six percent stake.

SUPER-ACHIEVERS VALUE THE POWER OF MENTORSHIP

Bill Gates said that Warren Buffet is the one who. Mark Zuckerberg points to Steve Jobs as his mentor. Millionaire motivational speaker Tony Robbins proudly declared that he was a student of Jim Rohne. Biblical figure Peter was a disciple of Jesus. Every good leader is a good follower. People who made phenomenal contributions are conscientious about their own gifts yet humble and wise enough to let some teach them.

The richest man in Babylon did not just become rich overnight. Miich. The story is that the young man approached the richest and asked him to teach him how he became wealthy.

Trying to apply the teaching, he made his own mistake but returned to his Master to correct his errors and learn more. As a result of his diligence and humility, the rich let him manage his own estate, as his own son had no interest in doing so. Eventually, the learner became so rich his friend became envious of him. This teaches the value of humility and mentorship.

Before becoming a dog, learn to be an underdog. Samuel served Eli before becoming a mighty prophet. Miguel Bezos and Grandpa Gise became the mirror through which Jeff will trace the trails of his career and life.

Our self-made were molded by someone in authority at some point in their lives. Stepfather Bezos and Grandfather Gise molded Jeff's attitude toward hard work. Unlike many youngsters today, Jeff learned to be of use from childhood through his teenage years and did not mind getting dirty. Grandpa Preston Gise taught Jeff the taste of responsibility, castrating bulls and repairing mills during summer.

Under Miguel's apprenticeship, Jeff manipulated tools, read graphs, was introduced to technology, and learned to look at life through *self-madeship*. With Miguel's job with Exxon, the family moved quite often, which exposed Jeff to more opportunities to meet different people and landscapes, shaping his character and view on life.

Children copy what they see in the people surrounding them. Paul Jobs, Steve Jobs's adoptive, was a man *"with genius in his hands,"* as Steve affectionately referred to him. His handy work with cars and electronics sparked the boy's imagination and interest in electronics. Likewise, Miguel Bezos, known for hard work, surfed the corporate ladder in various companies and positions to become a Product Manager at Banker's Trust. Steve Jobs's adoptive father introduced Steve to electronics. Jeff Bezos taught him the magic of working hard to get what he wanted from Miguel. Practicing the art of hard knocks on his grandparents' farm, Jeff quickly learned the virtue of hard work, even as a toddler.

Industry leaders are not formed by school education; they are only discovered. Growing up, Jeff already developed the character of a go-getter. In high school, he founded his first company, the Dream Institute, a summer school program for elementary school students. As I wrote, successful people start early in life to demonstrate their ability to lead change. Upon graduating valedictorian from Miami Palmetto High School, Jeff pursued a computer science and electrical engineering degree at Princeton University.

At Princeton, Jeff did not just focus on education. He exposed himself to extra-curricular activities, including computer science, space exploration, and programming. He became the President of Princeton's Students for the Exploration and Development of Space. Jeff even developed a computer program for IBM and traveled as far as Norway for a summer internship.

Authentic learning happens beyond the classroom. Students should understand that the classroom curriculum rarely teaches exemplary character, taps into their passion, and hones essential life skills. That is not the purpose of school. We often mistakenly expect the school to provide education, meals, transportation, and character education. What are parents for, then?

My passion for entrepreneurship did not come from the classroom curriculum. It came from my extracurricular activities. I did not develop my leadership and social skills from my academic class.

Success is not about the parchments on the wall but about the brain's circuitry. Jeff had the brain to succeed in any field and the drive to land the best and most lucrative job on Wall Street. After turning down jobs with Intel and Bell Labs in 1990, Jeff landed at hedge funds firm D.E. Shaw. Though the position, sumptuous office, salary, and perks were enticing, they did not impress free-spirited Jeffrey.

Jeff did not stick around to become Shaw's indentured worker.

He decided to make his pathway and quickly worked his way up to become Senior Vice President of the company. Jeff ran the options trading group and was subsequently in charge of finding Internet-based opportunities, which would open his exit door. CEO David Shaw was picky when hiring his employees. Eventually, like PayPal, the firm produced four billionaires, including the founder and Jeff. That is to show the caliber of the staff and the opportunities ahead for Jeff at D.E. Shaw and Co. Today, David is a wealthy man with a net worth of $6.5 billion, which is only 20 times less than Jeff's. Not too bad.

Jeff had a spark for an online shopping business in his new role. Just four short years at D.E. Shaw, Jeff stole two golden eggs from Professor David Shaw and ran off to Seattle, Washington. One was a young research associate named Mackenzie Scott Tuttle, whom Jeff had interviewed for the job and married years later while still working at D.E. Shaw. The other was a billion-dollar jackpot ridiculous idea of selling books online.

Upon studying the potential of the e-commerce business, Jeff quickly understood that giving sweat to swell another person's pocket was a less appealing approach to making a living. He set sail to pursue his vision and never looked back. Unlike several bright minds baited with a high salary, bonus, and perks, Jeff made a bold decision. He elected not to lie at anchor to sip the luxury of an executive suite. Do you know what would have come of him if Jeff had stayed on? I don't think his name would have been noticed or mentioned in this book or any book.

Jeff would have been a microscopic dot only visible to himself like so many nameless cubicle or glass office renters. Jeff was itching to get off the payroll at 30 after just eight years on Wall Street. Emboldened by what he had read about the future of the Internet, Jeff packed up and did not look back. He had decided to put his landmark on the Internet superhighway, as he mentioned in his commencement speech at his alma mater:

> *"I came across the fact that Web usage was growing at 2,300% per year. I'd never seen or heard of anything that grew that fast, and the idea of building an online bookstore with millions of titles--was very exciting to me,"*

In 1994, Jeff called it quits, sacrificing his lucrative vice president job at investment banking firm D. E. Shaw and Co. He decided to take a chance with Amazon, a strange idea in a nascent industry back then. Like any success story, Jeff's did not start in the skyscrapers of Seattle, Washington, but from his garage, with five employees.

Jeff had a brain and a plan. Wait! Jeff did not just leave on a whim; he had a plan and an insight. What product would have a continually growing market that would be quickly sold to anyone, anywhere, have a low shipping cost, and still yield a substantial margin? Guess. Guess again. Ask Jeff if you can't find it.

In business, quick wit trumps money and knowledge. Wise Jeff had his eureka moment: selling books online. Jeff initially named his *baby* Cadabra but changed the name to Amazon to match his idea of an exotic, unique business type. Like most success stories, Amazon started as a garage venture to become the world's largest e-commerce retailer giant today, bringing its founder over $478 billion in 2021 from a mere $1 billion in 1998.

START WITH A GARAGE MINDSET

> *A garage mindset liberates the creative beast within, gives you the license to become a potter to mold your insanity, and unleashes your imagination to run wild in the confines of yourself without external pressure... to birth the next big thing.*
> **– Coach Greb**

Like any self-made, Jeff had a **garage mindset.** How can a tiny garage idea turn someone into one of the world's wealthiest people? What do you know about garage venture stories? Let us pause to learn about them. Maybe they can inspire you. Garages must have some magic. I even started my business in my garage. Do you want me to tell you about the **garage mindset**?

What is a garage if not a workshop, a place with tools, a wide-open space offering unlimited opportunities to liberate your mind's whim and hone your insanity to invent, design, and build prototypes? The garage's openness with a high ceiling conveys to the entrepreneur the impression of limitlessness that only the sky is the limit.

A garage is ideal for a young inventor to exercise his creative genius. He finds the freedom to try to make products, start, break, and start over. The garage allows you to get dirty, sweat, work long hours, and try new ways without anyone noticing. You are confined away from the gazing eyes of critics. The garage gives you the chance to have privacy and hide your mistakes from the judging world. You can act like scientist Victor Frankenstein and make a monstrous creature that threatens people in the streets. Alternatively, you can follow in the footsteps of Steve Jobs, the designer of the Macintosh computer, an ingenious product that enhanced people's lives. The setting of a garage startup is humbling because it focuses not on you but on the idea, the concept.

The added benefit of garage startups is that you have no overheads, pressure, or deadlines. The parts you use are mostly cheap, and you can work if you want and make as many mistakes as your nerves can handle. Only you are in charge. You can start when you please or stop when you deem it convenient. Starting in his garage, British entrepreneur Sir James Dyson made over 5100 prototypes of his popular bagless vacuum cleaner. He lived from his wife's teacher salary before the idea took off. Several ventures that began in a garage, a dorm, or a basement have become legends of success. Here are some examples that will probably inspire you. According to data compiled by Business Insider, the leading companies below started not behind glass doors but in humbling settings:

- Steve Jobs and Steve Wozniak started Apple in a garage.
- Larry Page and Serge Bring started Google in a garage.
- Jeff Bezos launched Amazon in a garage.
- Michael Dell started Dell Computers in his college dorm.
- Mark Zuckerberg launched Facebook in his college dorm.
- Bill Gates and Paul Allen began Microsoft in a garage.
- Kimbal and Elon Musk made their office their bedroom.

And not to forget that I started Greb & Co. Ventures in my garage. What is the point of this remark? Wealth-builders are wise and humble, even if you see them living in mansions today. They did not rush to the glass windows, the sumptuous offices, or where they are today. Most of our success stories had humble beginnings. Jeff Bezos had a tiny, silly idea: an online bookstore. "What a dumb idea?" I bet naysayers told him. Jeff had a personal motive. What motivated him? He did not want to be remorseful after he let opportunities slide through his fingers, and here is what he said:

> *"I don't want to be 80 years old and in a quiet moment of reflection, thinking back over my life and cataloging a bunch of major regrets."*

Jeff and Makenzie Bezos took a chance and had no fear of failing. Now, let me ask you: what is more regrettable: the chance you took or the opportunity you did not take?

Speaking to a group of kids and teenagers at my Sunday Bible Scholar's Academy, I often tell my students: do what you must and let the chips fall where they may. So, last time I tested their understanding, asking,

Who do you think is the real failure: he who failed trying, or he who failed to try? The room sounded like thunder. **"The one who failed to try," they replied in unison.** After two years of molding them, the youngsters have learned to anticipate my intentions.

Makenzie Scott Bezos, Jeff's ex-wife, and business partner, must have been insane to let her husband leave a secure executive position to start a bookstore online, not even a clothing store, but a bookstore. In general, the people closest to us are the ones who empower or keep us away from manifesting our calling. In my soon-to-be-released book The Power of Two, I discuss how a small "Go, Honey! You can do it" fires up the spouse to ride like a horse on steroids. Conversely, a "Why don't you just quit?" from your most significant other can only turn off your engine.

HASTE NOT TO OPEN YOUR GATES TO ANYONE WHO KNOCKS. CAREFULLY PROBE EACH GUEST.

Sometimes, unknowingly and with genuinely good intentions, your family can be the source of a hindrance. As an illustration, an overprotective family would engage in the scenario below as Jeff approaches Mackenzie with his idea of quitting D.E. Shaw to start a venture.

A wise, caring spouse would have asked, "Humm! Honey, are you sure?" and in an aside, not trying to frustrate her husband, she would have sighed, "How many people read that much? LORD, help us."

How about Daddy Miguel Bezos, who didn't have a second thought when asked to break the bank and yank out a $300,000 log of gold to invest in Abracadabra, the original name idea of Amazon? Common sense would have questioned, "Has the whole family gone mad or what?"

"This sounds like a spell," the Pastor's wife would utter in a breath of despair.

"Yes, let's pray for Little Jeffrey's soul."

"The devil has gotten him confused," would the man of God add and probably organize a night vigil for poor Jeffrey.

Jeffrey's stepsister Cristina would not have it. She would call Mackenzie and give her a life sermon, accusing her of being an accomplice in letting her husband throw away her father's life savings to support Jeff's "stupid idea."

And don't forget Grandma Mattie Louise, the family-wise owl. I bet she was not in the loop because she would have interceded to "save" Little Jeffrey from his insanity. A good Grandma doesn't sit around and mourn. She prays. Discreetly.

For forty days and forty nights, Grandma Mattie would have fasted herself thin and pleaded the good Lord day and night:

"LORD Almighty, I plead for my grandchild. My Little Jeffrey has gone mad. First, he threw away the prestigious job you gave him. Now, he and his wife are about to throw their parents' savings away to start some kind of business called cadaver, I overheard them say."

And what do you think the good Lord would have replied,

"I hear you, Woman, but I warn you; get out of the boy's calling."

Jeff's brother Mark and relatives left and right, would have pressed upon Mackenzie to bring her husband to reason:

"Talk to your husband. Don't let him throw away Daddy's money as you guys did your job," a caring sister-in-law Christiana Bezos might advocate for the whole family.

I bet Mackenzie Scott probably was prepared to lend a deaf ear to the counsel of the fly-by-night wise owls and any form of raillery, had they surfaced. The previous enactment of the typical family attitude is why bright ideas die. As I look at it, every successful person pursuing his divinely designed course of life receives supernatural favor, a sprinkle of sheer luck to win over the bad guys, just like the hero, who rarely dies.

She did not just cook dinner, wash clothes, and care for the kids. She committed herself to the venture, being an active part of the business. Mackenzie took care of business planning, shipping, and anything that could help make the new venture successful. Eventually, her waiting-room mentality paid off. With a four percent stake in Amazon, her $43 billion vault positions her at the top of the Forbes list's world's self-made female billionaire and fourth wealthiest woman.

Highly involved in philanthropy, Mackenzie deserves her wealth because she agreed to sow the seed of wealth early on. You may not know that while her seed grew, Mackenzie Scott moaned, cried, laughed, worried, hoped, and expected. She worked hard side-by-side with Jeff, focusing on shipping, account management, business planning, and more. Mackenzie was committed to the venture and ready to suffer the consequences should the venture go bust.

The couple took a considerable risk, abandoning their lucrative careers simultaneously to enter the unknown realm. A commonsense attitude would have been, "Honey, you go ahead with the venture while I keep my job, just in case." Indeed, just in case, an utter demonstration of fear. A wise alternative to "I don't trust myself, God, and my calling." That is the shared wisdom of ordinary people: "Don't put all your eggs in the same basket." You will be surprised how some people's eggs are so secure they never hatch.

Entrepreneurs do not hold on to one or two eggs. If they break one, they just get another one. Risk-averseness is a poverty mentality: hold onto your little one, for a bird in the hand is worth two in the tree. How will you ever score a goal to win if your entire game is about defense, not offense? The fear of losing the little you have is why the middle class is flattening. Why do you think Elon Musk decided to forgo earning a Ph.D. from Stanford University? Creative geniuses are not short of ideas; they do not fear losing one opportunity because they will always find a way where there is no way. Elon Musk had agreed to sacrifice a Stanford University Ph.D. to launch a company that made him a millionaire and paved the road to wealth and success. What could he do with a Ph.D.?

Jeff made a bold decision and never looked back. What was the opportunity cost of Jeff's choosing to keep a lucrative job at someone else's company? In life, you must learn that often, you need to let go to get more.

Life is a dynamic labyrinth of choices. Every day, you make over 35,000 choices. Some are hard choices; others are as easy as picking food or clothes. Every day, you make decisions that make you lose something; every day, you make choices that make you gain something. You cannot thrive at playing it safe and expect substantial gain. The gain is in the risk you take. As King Solomon puts it so well, *"Cast your bread upon the waters, for you will find it after many days. Give a serving to seven and eight, for you do not know what evil will be on the earth"* (Ecclesiastes 11:1).

Like Jeff Bezos, our world superachievers made their way to reach heights they never fathomed. Do not worry if your beginning looks awkward and challenging; what truly matters is how things end. If you started a venture and seem lost and feel like throwing in the sponge, I encourage you to hang on. Success is the birthchild of resilience, as you will read in Colonel Sanders's story below.

We delight in the success stories of people who changed our world. I enjoy reading the stories of self-made millionaires, where the protagonist wins against all the odds to build a thriving company we all come to admire. *How do you build the world's second-largest food chain?* Is it luck, inspiration, perspiration, resilience, determination, or a combination of all the above?

YES, YOU STILL CAN, COLONEL: HARLAND SANDERS AND THE MAKING OF KFC

How did the tiny idea of Colonel Sanders become a global giant?

Colonel Harland Sanders, not a real colonel by profession, was like you and me, a man whose life had taken on many journeys of trial and error, doing all kinds of odd jobs. Until he turned sixty, Colonel Sanders, the founder of Kentucky Fried Chicken (KFC), recognized today as the world's second-largest fast-food chain, never thought his tiny idea would produce a world giant. After his father's death, Harland had to grow up at age twelve.

> *If you are staying in motion, you will undoubtedly provoke your luck. You do not know what opportunities lie ahead."*

– Coach Greb

For many years, he had to hustle doing any job to support his mother and siblings. He did many jobs: steamer, laborer, lawyer, insurance salesman, secretary, and entrepreneur, among many others. One of those odd jobs sent him to work at a gas station. As fate would have it, here is when the real story begins.

> *If you are staying in motion, you will undoubtedly provoke your luck. You do not know what opportunities lie ahead.*
> – Coach Greb

Life took Colonel Sander on a long journey of twists and turns. Unlike many young entrepreneurs who demand success in the fast lane, Sanders befriended patience, which lent him a hand through thirty-five years until he became an icon and franchised KFC at sixty-two.

YOU CANNOT "HAVE IT YOUR WAY RIGHT AWAY" ALL THE WAY.

You are probably familiar with the famous slogan from Burger King, "Your way, right away!". In our fast-paced environment, people are victims of unnecessary urgency. We drive fast; we expect everything to be delivered fast, and Amazon is king in this arena. With Prime membership, my daughter orders stuff today and sees it at the door the next day. How couldn't Bezos be the second richest man on Earth if his company could deliver to your door what you want when you want? We want everything to fall in our laps.

You could even order your own machine to spoon-feed you if you think lifting the spoon to your mouth keeps you from catering to other urgent businesses, such as watching your best show. In Japan, having a toilet wipe you is no longer science fiction. How much does it cost?

There is a cost for a society running in the fast lane. Humans have become so obsessed with speed that they are ready to give their lives away if you can serve them fast food, fast money, fast everything. People even marry fast. They meet on Monday, marry on Friday, and divorce on Sunday, right before church; why not while we are at it? Today, with Uber, everyone can order his personal chauffeur and have it his way right away. If I wake up and feel like driving a Mercedes 450 SL in the afternoon, I can surprise my whole family right before dinner. Who cares if I cannot afford it? When the bus takes a little too long to come, many people take an Uber, or when the light takes two seconds too long, you will see grandpas at the crossroads throw tantrums, blow the horn, and show you the middle finger.

The mentality of and the convenience of "fast-everything" comes with a price: missed opportunities, diverted wealth, jeopardized health, and a total sense of dependency. As a result, young entrepreneurs miss the opportunities that patience brings.

What was Sanders searching for as he launched a national tour to promote his mother's magic recipe? What kept him focused? Why waste these long years? Building a solid business takes time. The large companies that control our economies did not start one or two decades prior. Many of them have hundreds of years behind them. America's third-largest bank, Wells Fargo, began in March 1852. Bank of America traces its roots digging in its 240 years of existence, while McDonald's opened its doors over 65 years ago. When did Colonel Sanders create KFC?

Just get started and let fate do the rest. Harland Sanders, named Kentucky Colonel by Kentucky Governor Ruby Laffoon for his popular chicken meal, began at a Shell gas station he was renting back in 1930. He had not even started including his magic fried chicken recipe that year. Harland served his first finger-linking meals from the gas station to the hungry truckers.

Life is not a straight road. You do not know what lies ahead, around the corner. After so many odd jobs, Sanders had settled into the food business. There he had it. His brilliant idea: food. He had a *Eureka* moment. The meal he served got so popular that he closed the gas station for a full restaurant, and from there, fate took over. Pay heed to the dumbest ideas! They could be the trigger to your destiny. So, food it shall be! Sanders had made up his mind: to cook meals using the recipe his mother had taught him.

The bone thrown at you could be the finger-licking recipe for your million-dollar fortune. At an early age, with his mother away at work, Sanders had to learn to cook for his siblings. So, the boy grew up with the gift of making delicious meals. Hence, when it came to cooking meals for sale, coming up with an eleven-herb and seven-spice recipe was not as hard as the algebra class that made him end school in grade seven.

In the school of life, you do not quit; you do your best because you do not control the future, and many things are out of your control. When he shut down the pumps at the gas station to focus on the restaurant that had become popular, an unexpected blow came to hit the dream of hopeful Sanders. As we say, when life throws lemons at you, make lemonade with them.

An entrepreneur does not stay beaten on the ground. The rebuilding of the road rerouted the traffic over seven miles away from Sanders's restaurant, taking away the roadsters who were his main customers. What would he do next? Sanders and his wife Claudia took this blow as an opportunity to hit the road with their chicken cooking recipe to restaurants around the region, asking them to try his magic recipe.

Look beyond the surface. You might find gold where you did not expect. People fear setting their feet beyond their comfort zone or physical boundaries. Colonel Sanders found that he could sell the recipe to regional restaurants. He and Claudia tirelessly toured as many restaurants as they could. What do you think happened? Over 1,009 restaurants rejected Sanders's recipe, his mother's magic formula! What would he do next? Give up? No! Quitting is not on the menu. It is not an option for superachievers. Nothing was formidable enough to stay in the way of the resilient entrepreneur's determination who believed in his product's quality. So, he went on to meet setbacks, rejections, and discouragement.

I do not know who would be crowned king: Thomas Edison with his 10,000 "steps" to create the incandescent light bulb or Colonel Sanders with his 1,009 rejections of his magic recipe? Colonel Sanders went on, relentless and resilient, like a bull in a torero arena, to charge forward to success. His resilience is a vibrant application of the philosophy of success:

> *"If you have tried, tried, and tried, success has no other choice but to give in."*
>
> **– Coach Greb**

Learn to navigate the twists and turns of life. Sanders's vision of service could be summed up in the following words: *do not focus on money; do not spare any effort to serve quality.* Twenty-two years after serving his first meal at the gas station, Sanders eventually opened his first Kentucky Fried Chicken in 1952. Sanders launched a campaign to market his famous chicken to franchises that could carry on with his tradition of quality the way it was to be. At age 66, Sanders and Claudia, his new wife, did not tire from crisscrossing highways and roadways to find restaurants that would use his recipes, even if that meant receiving a mere four cents per chicken sold.

You do not know where your blessing hand will come from, but surely it will come. In 1964, Colonel Sanders met with and sold his franchise to entrepreneurs John C. Massey and John Y. Brown, Jr., the son of Kentucky Congressman J. Y. Brown, Sr., for $2 million, $16 million today. Sanders could not resist the offer, especially with his advanced age. He would receive an annual income of $40,000, the equivalent of almost $400,000 in 2024. On top of that, Sanders would sit on the company's board and act as its ambassador.

Years after being eventually acquired by Yum! Brands, KFC has evolved into the flagship market leader it is today. No one can tell with or without the original recipe. The formula for the pressure-fried chicken marinated in eleven herbs and seven spices has been kept secret. A tiny, silly idea that emerged from the brain of a hungry sixty-year-old man from a small city has evolved into the world's second-largest fast-food chain. KFC fed billions of hungry mouths at 29,000 locations in 147 countries around a gigantic globe in 2024.

Wealth is built on ideas; no idea is too tiny, dumb, or silly. The seed of your success is within. Look at your talent, ideas, innate skills, interests, hunger, and passion.

TEN CHALLENGES EVERY SELF-MADE WILL FACE

Behind great success, there is a great challenge. There *is no sacrifice without bloodshed.* Life is about making choices. Every day, we make myriads of decisions. Some we like, others we do not. To lose weight, for example, you must be tough to resist all the temptations. Athletes must undergo strenuous mental and physical training to win the Olympic medal. Learn to befriend challenges, and you will never feel their presence.

WHAT YOU DIDN'T KNOW ABOUT CHALLENGES

By our nature of despising pain, we are often more inclined to run away from challenges than to face them. If you do, you are only human, but you could become super-human by identifying them, facing, questioning, and overcoming them; you have the power to triumph over any challenge. Superachievers do.

CHALLENGE #1: YOU WILL NEVER STOP FACING CHALLENGES. LEARN TO SOLVE THEM

As we journey through life, we face issues of all magnitude. Some are straightforward, others complicated. We solve people's problems; we deal with our own challenges and help people solve theirs. No matter the size of the issues, they all come to test us, toughen us up, give us skills to solve more problems, and teach other people how to solve problems. Ultimately, challenges are the tests that promote us to the next grade.

All problems have the same patterns. They come with their solutions and have known and unknown variables. If you focus not on the problem's complexity but on finding the answers, you will solve it. You will identify the known and the unknown. Usually, the set of known variables will make you discover the unknown. I remember the favorite saying of my high school math teacher, *"When you have a problem to solve, look for the solution nowhere else but in the problem itself."* As I grew up and experienced many life challenges, I agree with Monsieur Bernard, my tenth-grade math teacher.

Life is about solving problems. Businesses, organizations, people, and governments find and avail solutions to human challenges. Either they have all the pieces for the puzzle, and all they need is to put them together, or someone somewhere may have the parts they need. Or better yet, they are called to create those missing pieces. That is what life is all about: finding, creating, and availing the missing parts. The skills you need include searching, asking, manipulating, connecting, trying, and trying some more until you get it together. So, what should you know about challenges?

- Behind every challenge is an opportunity yet to be discovered.
- Challenges are not here to stay.
- Every challenge has a message for you.
- Every challenge comes with its own solution.

- Every challenge has a weakness.
- Challenges are testing moments.
- Challenges turn you into a problem-solver.
- Challenges turn you into a wise teacher.
- Challenges boost your confidence and groom you for victory.
- You are stronger by the sum of your challenges.

CHALLENGE #2: YOU WILL MAKE HARD, UNPOPULAR DECISIONS

While we admire Steve Jobs for his impact on the smartphone industry, he was not such an agreeable lad. In his career as an entrepreneur and business leader, Jobs made bold decisions that brought him wrath. He engaged in several unpopular actions that got him crossed with his board. Many do not understand how one gets fired by the guy you hired. The truth is that Steve conflicted with former Pepsi Vice President John Scully, whom he had hired to run Apple. Jobs was more like a coach to his people, so enamored with his baby, Apple, he would fight tooth and nail to protect it. What do you know about coaches? They may appear harsh, but they are the makers of a champion. Despite his lovingkindness, Jesus did not hesitate to rebuke his disciples or anyone crossing the line. Apostle Peter can write a library on this side of Jesus's character.

CHALLENGE #3: YOU MAY HAVE TO SACRIFICE YOUR TREASURED POSSESSIONS

You cannot receive without giving up or going away from something that costs you. When Soichiro Honda, the father of Honda Motor Co., wanted to start the Honda Motor Research Institute, he had to empty his savings and pawn his wife's jewelry. He did not mind sleeping at his workshop, sacrificing valuable time he could have spent with his family. Repeatedly, many entrepreneurs have had to sacrifice their most prized treasures to invest in their ventures. To become a wealth builder, you must practice the **principle of detachment**, the ability to trade off something you dearly value to acquire something of higher value.

To launch Apple Computers, both Steve Wozniak and Steve Jobs gave away their most prized possessions at the time. In 1976, the two partners had to start with what they had. Steve Jobs sold his cherished VW car for $200, and Steve Wozniak, his treasured super HP calculator for $500. It was not until 1977 that the two dreamers received a form of funding. Apple received a $250,000 loan guarantee from Mike Markkula, who became the company's second CEO in 1981. Before that, Steve had already made one bold decision; *you cannot expect to reach exceptional heights without personal effort and sacrifice.*

CHALLENGE #4: YOU WILL HAVE TO DO SOMETHING YOU HATE TO DO

To get your muscles in shape for the Olympic medal, you will need to strain them. The poor stay poor because they believe they do not have what it takes to accomplish something beyond their misery and, therefore, do not expect to be called upon to fulfill anything. Doing so is an expression of utter ungratefulness to God.

Unlike Mark Zuckerberg, who decided to run his company even though he was only 21, Jobs agreed to let go of the CEO position to Michael Scott, Apple's first CEO, in 1977. Sometimes, you must agree to let go to get more. Which sensible investor would invest in a company run by a 21-year-old hippie? It was an intelligent mover like many other concessions Steve made.

The law of sowing and reaping. "You reap what you sow." How many times have you heard this +? Apostle Paul, addressing the Galatians, puts it even better when he writes in Galatians 6:7, *"Do not be deceived, God is not mocked; for whatever a man sows, that he will also reap."* You cannot escape the consequences of your actions. You may reap more or less than you sow. The actual idea behind the statement is that nothing comes to you unless you do something. It is the law of deserving. You cannot expect to reap what you have not sown.

Every promise comes with a challenge. With the demise of Saul, David became the king of Israel by order of the LORD. David was a man after the heart of God, as stated in Samuel 13:14, which reads, "... *The LORD hath sought him a man after his own heart."* Yet, David had one of the most challenging ascendancies to the throne. David's psalms are very explicit about the wars, the challenges, the hurdles, and the enemies he had to face. Even though David had received the promise, he did not just wait for it to fall into his lap. He, not God, had to be on the battlefront to face his adversaries, but God was the one who gave him the victories. He was the one who exercised his hands to the battle; acknowledging God's works, David gave thanks, saying, *"He teaches my hands to make war so that my arms can bend a bow of bronze."* (Psalm 18:34).

CHALLENGE #5: YOU MUST BE SELECTIVE: SEVER UNPRODUCTIVE RELATIONSHIPS

> *"And if your right hand causes you to sin, cut it off and cast it from you; for it is more profitable for you that one of your members perish than for your whole body to be cast into hell."*
> **– Matthew 5:30**

In 1996, when Steve Jobs returned to Apple after selling Next to the company, he did what King David had ordered his successor, son King Solomon, to do: clean the house.

First, Steve was deeply concerned about Apple's dismal operation. The company was in shambles. The board and Gil Amelio, the then-CEO, were crossed. Using the argument of unproductivity, Steve, who only had one share in Apple, convinced the board to fire the CEO and proposed himself as his replacement. But the surprise did not stop there.

As soon as he took the reins of Apple, Steve Jobs fired the whole board and replaced them with those who could understand his new vision: to rid Apple of all products that dragged it down. It focused on four core products and hired top managers to keep quitting top designers to stay on.

Yesterday is gone. You've got to move on. You cannot want to build up and still be weighed down by unproductive relationships, including your old, nostalgic self stuck in the past. Wealth-builders surround themselves with like-minded people because *greatness and baseness cannot travel on the same boat.* The boat will sink.

In the biblical story of Jonah, we learn that the curse on Jonah caused the ship he was on to sink (Jonah 1:6-26). But the captain sailed home safely when he threw Jonah into the sea. God could not bless Abraham with Lot in his company (Genesis 13:5-23).

Some people cannot be in your company while God is trying to bless you. Do not reject your old friends. Let them understand that your priorities have changed. Do not forget them when you do get your million dollars. When it comes to wealth-building, you cannot be too emotional. You see why wealthy people sometimes tend to appear "heartless." You will not go anywhere if you are too emotional with your money. You may have to hurt somebody's feelings trying to be truthful to yourself. Legendary investor Warren Buffet - affectionately known as the Oracle of Omaha - believes that *if you cannot control your emotions, you cannot control your money.*

People who do not participate in your rise and cannot enjoy your success but come to mourn with you are people you want to avoid. Relationships are essential to human life and should not be taken lightly, yet who you surround yourself with will determine how fast you reach your goals—one good friend is worth a truckload of good-for-nothing pals.

CHALLENGE #6: YOU WILL HAVE TO LET GO EVEN WHEN IT HURTS

Is it more productive to keep hate in your heart? What profit is there in bearing coal in your heart again while you can release yourself and the other person and have both of you share the dividends of forgiveness?

Steve buried the hatchet with Microsoft to focus on promoting his company. He then agreed to run Microsoft's Explorer on the Macintosh. No one ignores the contention between Apple and Microsoft, the latter accused of stealing the former's GUI, graphic user interface, technology, and the point-and-click software that made computers so user-friendly. After many unproductive battles, Steve Jobs told his team and fans to bury the hatchet with Microsoft.

Like resentment, many other ill emotions can only bar you from success as the conditions and vibrations they create hinder the manifestation of goodness. Below are some of the most common self-defeating feelings and emotions you will work to stray from:

- Fear
- Rancor and resentment
- Jealousy and envy
- Guilt
- Greed
- Pride

Often, to see the greatness or the ugliness you are covered with, you must objectively look at yourself in the mirror and see who is really in the way of your ascension.

You have a nature that affects who you really are. Accept the truth and work at making amends. If you do not like the man or the woman you see in the mirror, forgive him or her. The following strongholds will go away by *the power of forgiveness*.

LEARN TO FIGHT YOUR SIX DEADLY MONSTERS

"Holding on to anger is like grasping a hot coal with the intent of throwing it at someone; you are the one getting burned."
— Gautam Buddha

Do not let the ugliness of your heart lock you up. There are six deadly monsters that cause you to fail: Pride, resentment, envy, fear, guilt, and hate. If you never got a chance to read the Bible, I encourage you to do so or read any holy book that teaches you the virtue of life. As a believer, I spend a lot of time reading and meditating on the Bible, and I now understand that all warnings are not just spiritual; they are real.

I now understand why the Bible summons us to forgive, have no fear, repent, and love others. It is for your own benefit, more so for you than others. Why? Why must you forgive? Why must you not covet other people's properties, and why must you not keep guilt in your heart? As you may already know or will soon discover, these feelings and emotions keep you captive, ruin your relationships, block you from success, and destroy your physical, spiritual, and emotional health. The many diseases we see in our societies are the result of these feelings and emotions.

Swallow your Pride. One of the deadliest monsters is a the origin of wars, sabotage, political bickering, and the inability to repent is pride. Steve Jobs, returning to Apple had no choice but to swallow his pride and accept Microsoft's investment of $150 million even though the company had over $1.2 billion in cash reserve. The move was working evidence of burying the hatch since the two companies signed other deals: Internet Explorer would run on Mac computer and a version of Microsoft office would be designed or Mac users, which meant that all the decade-long lawsuits and feud would come to an end.

Resentment *creates bitterness that holds you captive.* Resentment stems from unforgiving a wrong that was done to you or to a loved one. What pain keeps pinching your heart? Did you vow to never forgive your parents who told you that you were an unwanted child? Are you still angry at your father or mother for abandoning you or your family? Did you vow to pay back the guardians who abused you?

Did your spouse hurt you, have an affair, and leave you with the kids? Are you still angry at your boss for being unfair when firing you at the time you direly needed the income? Was someone you helped in times of need ungrateful and showed unconcernedness when you needed help? Did a partner embezzle the funds of your joint venture? Did someone trick you with a bogus business offer and stole from you? Did someone you deeply trusted betray you? Did you pay the price of your life because someone falsely accused you? Were you discriminated against because you are or look different? If you are still angry, you are just human, and you are not alone. Did you get to know Mandela?

Nelson Mandela spent over a quarter of a century in a tiny jail cell for defending his people's rights in South Africa, but when he was released, he praised forgiveness. He did not seek to retaliate against the white leaders when he was made president of his country. Nelson Mandela entered the Wall of Fame of history because of his greatness of heart and ability to let go. The force to forgive sets legends apart, for it is easier to bear resentment than to let it go. Indeed, forgiving is a win-win engagement, for it liberates the forgiver and releases the forgiven.

Billionaire Oprah Winfrey was sexually molested when she was a young girl; Steve Jobs was given up for adoption; Joseph, Egyptian Pharaoh's Prime Minister, was sold by his own brothers. But what did those people do? They forgave, rose to highness, and became legends. Joseph did not retaliate when his brother came to Egypt to beg for food. He treated them with kindness, like family. Jesus's suffering on the cross forgave his persecutors when he said,

"Father, forgive them for they do not know what they do." (Luke 23:34)

The power that lies in forgiving is paramount, and it takes people with character to practice it. Forgiving is reaching God's likeness, the ultimate nature of the divine human. Unforgiveness is at the origin of many modern-day deadliest sicknesses, including heart diseases. If you want to add years to your life, you must forgive.

Bearing grudges is like holding the other person and yourself captive. In this state, unless you are liberated by freeing the person from your heart, you are blocking your own way to freedom, peace, happiness, holiness, and wholesomeness, all that opens the gates to success. That is why the Holy book advises,

> *"For if you forgive men their trespasses, your heavenly Father will also forgive you. But if you do not forgive men their trespasses, neither will your Father forgive your trespasses." (Matthew 6;14-15)*

Another ill-feeling that blocks your way is guilt. **Guilt is an orphan spirit.** Like resentment, the feeling of guilt wipes away your ability to expect and puts you in a position of an orphan spirit. Guilt results from a wrong you did and for which you become remorseful. Guilt can be painful as it leads to depression, anxiety, insomnia, and loss of appetite. It annihilates decision-making abilities. Under constant depression, life becomes dull and not worth living, magnifying nothing but negativity - a good pal of poverty and suicidal intentions.

Self-forgiveness and repentance are the remedies of guilt. David, who cherished his relationship with God, did no lock himself in the bunker of guilt when he committed one of the most atrocious crimes. Trying to hide his mischief, David ordered the killing in battle of Uriah, one of his most loyal soldiers. He then took his wife Bathsheba and had Solomon with her.

When David's realized that his sin had been revealed and how angry God was with him, he couldn't believe the magnitude of the demise his lust could cause him. Instead of hiding the way Adam and Eve did, David went before the LORD to cry bitterly. He did not dwell on his wrongdoing like most kings of his time. He confessed and repented over his only sin that begot other sins, asking for God's forgiveness when he wrote Psalm 51 that reads in verses 1-3:

> *Have mercy upon me, O God,*
> *According to Your lovingkindness;*
> *According to the multitude of Your tender mercies,*
> *Blot out my transgressions.*
> *Wash me thoroughly from my iniquity,*
> *And cleanse me from my sin.*

> *For I acknowledge my transgressions,*
> *And my sin is always before me.*

David acknowledged that he was born in sin, thereby underlining the human frailties and the need for God's intervention to make him stronger. Only those in whom dwells the spirit of God are capable of such """. No worldly leader would mark a pause and ponder the effect of their bestiality and cruelty.

You need to forgive yourself, ask the person you wronged to forgive you, then ask God to forgive you. You will be liberated and free to focus on producing good fruit. Beside guilt, as we already mentioned in a preceding chapter, fear is a feeling. Be reminded that your repentance would have no value if you only repented before God. Indeed, you transgressed divine principle, but the person who suffered your wrongdoing is the one to forgive you. So, you need to go to that person and genuinely acknowledge your sin against her and vow never to do it ever again.

The Bible is clear about this. If you come to give your offering and know that your sister has something against you, go to the person to forgive her or ask for forgiveness; only then can God accept your offering. God will not accept offering from your hands until you have made peace with the person you wronged. David could not make it up to Uriah, who was dead. Though he was a brave soldier who killed his "1000' in battle, David rebuked Joab, his army general, for killing Saul's army general Abner, who he called a good man. David was a fair King who forbade his army from taking innocent lives. Indeed, had David guarded his heart against the lust of the eyes that coveted Bathsheba, a married woman, he would not have ordered the murder of Uriah and would have been a sinless man. Why did David have his loyal soldier killed? He feared the latter would discover his affair with his wife. Trying to cover up his sin, David committed an even more atrocious crime: killing the man who defends your throne.

To arrive at this mischief, David lied to the soldier he sent, betrayed a loyal soldier, and concealed his murder from the prophet who communicated God's intentions to his kingdom. One sin led to another until as you will discover in reading the scriptures, a curse came onto David's kingdom and caused its demise and affected the reigns thereafter. His son committed incest with his sister, which led a brother to kill a brother. Then David's son Absalom went into his concubines. Had David not been a man in favor with God, he would have been overthrown by his own son who conspired with David's trusted general. The sin did not go unpunished and frustrated David's reign: it caused what I call the Davidian curse that went from David to his son Solomon: lust destroyed a divine promise to never lack a Davidian on the throne of Juda.

Fear *is a weapon that debilitates and casts darkness around you.* It can stem from the feeling of inadequacy ingrained in low self-esteem and lack of faith. Also, some people develop the fear of failing and losing, failing at business, losing your money, your possession, relationship, position, or reputation. This is one of the biggest that threaten wealth-builders who think they are too big to fail again. Managing poverty is indeed much less cumbersome than managing wealth and reputation.

How did the now jailed investment firm executive Bernard Madoff live his nearly thirty years of Ponzi scheme estimated at $64 billion? Between the 1980s and 2008, close to five thousand investors trusted Bernie with their money until the connive was busted in late 2008. Pleading guilty on eleven counts of felony, Bernie Madoff must have felt terrible or maybe not. I wonder how he managed to earn a night's sleep with a fraud of this magnitude. I bet he was in constant fear, spending his days thinking of the days the scheme would be discovered.

This is another form of fear that is caused by hidden secret sins. When you have a skeleton in the closet and fear it being revealed, you can hurt your body and mind. It is generally the ordeal of those who commit sins or crimes such as embezzlement, defrauding the system, committing murder, lying under oath, or cheating on their spouse. Know this: one way or another, the body in the closet will stink someday, and someone will smell it. No crime goes unpunished, not even on this earth.

My word of wisdom is for you to live a life of integrity and honesty. You can build wealth by being honest. When the fear of losing it all preoccupies your mind, how can you be productive as a visionary person? Confide to God and, if possible, a trained counselor who will not throw your case in the streets. Sharing and searching for wisdom from a compassionate person can liberate you. NEVER share your deep secret with anyone who can blackmail you or use it against you, even with people you trust today. What about envy? Which of the two more significantly blocks your way to success: fear or envy?

Envy *is a manifestation of ungratefulness.* Have you ever been envious of someone? How did you feel? How did you hide your feeling of jealousy so the other person did not feel your shameful behavior? Envy is the worst feeling because you cannot control it. It is the reason the evil spirit is fighting a deadly battle against God's children. It calls for other crimes such as hypocrisy, lies, cover-ups, betrayal, disloyalty, treason, slander, and murder.

Envy comes from a lack of gratitude, a feeling of insecurity and hopelessness, and fighting it demands a great deal of effort. You can start by practicing gratitude. Instead of looking at what is on other people's plates, you could be focusing on finding out and maximizing your unique skills and individual strengths. You could approach and ask the person whom you envy to tell you how they made it. Uncontrolled envy ultimately leads to hate.

Hate *keeps the angel of prosperity away from you.* The spirit of hatred and prosperity cannot cohabitate. You have probably wondered why all your efforts amount to nothing. Maybe you need to look inside. The spirit of God that attracts and gives wealth cannot reside in a soiled dwelling. The most dangerous feeling is hatred.

In the late 1990s, when designer Tommy Hilfiger was trying to put his mark on the map of design clothing, he was accused of uttering racial slurs against Blacks and Asians, allegedly saying that those two races were not the intended targets of his brand. The issue became a hot topic on media, including the Oprah Winfrey show.

That was a big gamble because Hilfiger knew that it was thanks to the endorsement of hip-hop artists such as Snoop Dog that his brand took off, not the one percent he initially targeted as customers for his line. Despite strong public relations intervention and denial of such doing, that could have hurt his booming business. As for the truth that never came out, it lies somewhere between God, Hilfiger himself, and those who allegedly tried to smear his name. No matter what, a businessperson, especially a celebrity, must weigh his words because you can hurt your business. Even though Hilfiger bragged that his sales doubled that same year, you can't but wonder how much sales could have been made if the incident had not happened.

Hate does not have its place in the heart of he who seeks favor and blessing from all sources to build his empire. I do not think that Apple was made for a group of people or gender. Another reason hate is counterproductive is that **you cannot be blessed by what you hate**. If you hate your job, you will rarely save a penny from it; if you hate your employer or supervisor, or employee, you will rarely receive a favor or miracle from them.

CHALLENGE #7: OLYMPIC CHAMPIONS ARE BRUISED BY TOUGH TRAINING

Unless it hurts, it will not produce the results you expect. What makes Michael Jordan an NBA legend? In the words of Tim Grover, Michael's trainer, Michael Jordan was not the most athletic basketball player but the most revered. Why? Every athlete's purpose is to win a competition, and competitions are won by those who better prepare for them. Building a champion requires unparalleled mental and physical training, and mental readiness counts for 90 percent. Athletes such as Michael Jordan knew the importance of mental strength and the power of physical fitness.

According to Grover, Michael's personal strength trainer, Michael Jordan was an incredibly competitive athlete who wanted to beat everyone on his team and be at the top of his profession. Like Sam Walton, Michael Jordan was a ruthless competitor. Michael had a daily routine to keep himself on top. He would expose his body to physical torture that started each day at 5:00 A.M. He would run, jump, lift weights, and expose himself to various physical strains to prepare his body to stay on top.

CHALLENGE # 8: SWITCH OFF "THE FOR-TIME-BEING" MODE, SELF- GRATIFICATION, DISTRACTIONS, AND TRIVIALITIES

Go the extra mile. Feeling good does not build wealth. Countless books have been written about the power of good habits. From Jack Canfield to Zig Ziglar, great writers have profusely demonstrated how success demands power habits. You cannot aim for exceptional accomplishments and stay in your comfort zone, live in the status quo, and do business as usual. Wealthy people have routines different from those of ordinary people. They work long hours, often over seventy hours a week, while most do just forty. To succeed, you must go the extra mile and do what most people refuse.

CHALLENGE # 9: MAKE PERSONAL EFFORTS TO STAY ORGANIZED.

Success demands that you stretch yourself. I once asked my students, "What holds most people back, and what is the first thing you should eliminate?" Surprisingly, they unanimously responded, "Bad company," and they were right. A lousy company creates unhealthy habits, and bad habits hold you back. Your phone is for profitable opportunities, not pointless conversations. The best way to let go of a poor habit is to replace it with a good one.

Make profitable use of your time. If you spend too much time watching soap operas, the news, sports, and talk shows, you are wasting valuable time you could be using to invest in yourself. If, as we say, "time is money," then wasting time is equal to throwing away money. You need to replace those unproductive uses of your valuable time with activities like reading self-help books or biographies, watching inspiring videos, or listening to podcasts that empower you. If you spend time with friends with whom you indulge in life's pleasures, seek now the company of people who are already where you want to be and have fun with them. If you spend long hours sleeping, you must cut down on some of that time and devote it to working on your goals.

CHALLENGE #10: BE AN ACE AT THE GAME OF WINNING AND LOSING

Wealth-building is not for the feeble mind. There is no victory without a battle, and the size of the struggle gives value to the hero.

A Wall Street Journal article on CNBC.com reported that affluent investors such as the Walton Family, US Secretary of Education Betsy DeVos and family, and many other high-profile investors lost over half a million US dollars in a misleading investment. These families invested in Theranos, a biotechnology company that allegedly announced that it had found a technology for a commercially ready portable blood analyzer. This announcement ended up being a flop. Today, the company is being sued and has laid off over 90 percent of its 800-employee workforce.

This high-profile case is not the only one. Many investors take the risk and accept that they will lose or win. In a nutshell, you cannot go to war if you are afraid to die. Wealth-building is all about taking chances and being audacious. As a wealth-builder, you are an opportunity seeker. In a sense, you are willing to try new things at your own risk. What is more, the higher chances you are ready to take, the higher rewards you demand in return.

While humans naturally abhor pain, every successful person knows that no gain comes easily. Even to heal an ailing body, some people go through homeopathy, using pain to cure the pain. Sacrificing your indulgence for the full manifestation is a necessary pathway every self-made person has traveled. You can have your way all the way. This chapter invites you to become accountable for your success and the outcome of your actions. For every harvest, you must plant a seed.

> ***LESSON LEARNED:*** *Sacrifice takes center stage in this chapter, examining the sacrifices made by audacious individuals in pursuit of their dreams. Through poignant stories of dedication and commitment, the chapter emphasizes that audacious goals often require significant sacrifices, and it encourages readers to assess their willingness to make sacrifices for their own audacious aspirations.*

YOUR TURN – DAY 6: THE AUDACITY OF SACRIFICE

Self-Reflection: **What change have you been hesitating to make in your life or career? Identify it and consider why you've been hesitant.**

- Are there goals or dreams that you have been hesitant to pursue due to the sacrifices they might require?
- What sacrifices have you made in the past to achieve significant goals, and what did you learn from those experiences?
- How do you balance personal sacrifices with the pursuit of audacious aspirations?
- Can you think of stories of individuals who made extraordinary sacrifices to achieve greatness?

Application: *List your current commitments and goals. Identify areas where you might need to make sacrifices to pursue audacious goals.*

1. **Time Audit:** Analyze how you spend your time each day. Are there non-essential activities that you can sacrifice to create more time for your audacious pursuits?
2. **Support Network:** Reach out to friends and family members to discuss the sacrifices you're considering. Seek their understanding and support.
3. **Resilience Building:** Develop strategies for coping with the sacrifices you make. How can you maintain your motivation and mental well-being?
4. **Reflection:** Regularly reflect on the sacrifices you've made and the progress you've achieved. Is the sacrifice worth the reward?

THE AUDACITY OF EXECUTION

BE THE ARCHITECT OF YOUR DESTINY

"If you are not in the process of becoming the person you want to be, you are automatically engaged in becoming the person you don't want to be."

– Dale Carnegie

> ## THE STUBBORN SELF-DISCIPLINE OF ROBERT SMITH, THE RICHEST MAN IN BLACK AMERICA

How do you become the wealthiest person in Black America? What does it take to make it to the top in the private lounge of the superrich when you still have your nappy hair, a large nose, and *colored* skin? Some would say, "He was lucky," while others would chime, "He had a lift," but when you hear what Robert says about becoming successful as a black person in America, you will have a different view.

Robert, whose success has been profusely celebrated by the mainstream media, though still unknown to many of his brethren *people of color*, once said in an interview:

> *The most important thing you can do as a young person in [the Black] community is to become an expert to become skilled in whatever it is that you are desirous of doing. And that takes countless hours and in some cases outreach for knowledge and information and in some cases it's [about] building a learned capability. To me there is no substitute for that.... There's no substitute for becoming an expert and being the best at your craft. And that's what I focused on.*
>
> **– Robert F. Smith**

Become a wizard at the art of self-management. How do you see yourself? Unless you see yourself as a system or an enterprise, you will easily be prey to your emotional and irrational cravings. However, when you shift the paradigm and see yourself as a system, you will have to accept to manage yourself as an enterprise with principles, values, operating procedures, rules, resources, responsibilities, deadlines, and accountability that do not bow to excuses. Management is the science of getting things done. Self-management is the art of getting yourself to do what must be done within planned parameters, or you become a slacker overwhelmed by self-indulgences, procrastination, excuses, and impulsiveness. Self-management is what will get you there from here. Some people call it self-discipline, self-restraint, or self-control. Those terms sound a bit repressive; I prefer self-management to them and will use them interchangeably in this section.

No one ever conquered the world without first conquering self. The exercise of self-discipline is the most painful yet rewarding road seldom taken by the citizens of Loserville. If you can become successful without self-discipline, you might as well buy the ticket for the jackpot. You are a wizard at the game of luck. Becoming successful is like picking a rose through the thorns. Something will sting you, but you do not mind because of the beauty of the rose you are focused on getting for that special person. No feeble mind or lazy soul can build wealth. It takes a Herculean mental strength and a mountain of audacity to restrain yourself and focus on achieving whatever you put your mind to.

Like Robert Smith, *superachievers are forward-charging bulls*. What do you become when two disciplinarian parents raised you? Robert J. Smith, black America's top-ranking billionaire, did not land on the Forbes List sleeping on his laurels and has an attitude you can mimic. When you learn that Robert was raised by Dr. William Robert Smith and Dr. Sylvia Myrna Smith, both teachers in Denver, Colorado, you get the idea of the home Robert grew up in. Self-discipline was not a personal choice. It was the way of life.

Self-restraint starts at home. People who make it in this life are those who resolutely know what they want and will force their way through until they get it. When Roberts wanted something, he knew how to get it. As he likes to joke about his past, Robert says he tried to earn his own money so he no longer had to wear his elder brother's clothes. Early on, Robert set his mind on building wealth. As a schoolboy and like any predestined superrich, he figured out how to make money selling baseball hats to other children. In high school, Roberts wrapped himself in sheer audacity.

The Self-made followed their own rules. Who has the guts to call the same company thirty times to apply for an internship? This is what Robert Smith did to secure an opportunity for an internship with Bell Labs. This chance exposed him to the technologies that influenced his career choice. Robert

Smith says he would not let go when he decided to intern with the company. Though he knew the requirements disqualified him, he did not believe that he should just give up.

Robert was repeatedly told that the internship was for college juniors and seniors, not high school students. He had been turned away over thirty times, but his perseverance eventually paid off. As he recalled in an interview, when an MIT student offered an internship but did not show up, Robert was called to replace him. Is this luck? If so, then I call it *provoked luck*, for opportunity must meet preparedness.

Superachievers bend human rules. A go-getter does not play by the set rules but by his own. You keep up your chin and do not buy into pessimistic predictions. Where people see the economy going down and expect their businesses to take a hit, you will say, "Not mine." You refuse to accept the roadblock. Where others say it is impossible, you will say it is possible because everything is possible if you believe it is. That is called the *power of belief or self-power*. Hence, anything you forcefully reject will find no other place but far away from you.

The self-made train themselves to become experts at their crafts. Brilliant and focused, Robert graduated with a degree in chemical engineering. He did not stop there. He pushed himself to obtain an MBA from Columbia University Business School in New York. With this background, Robert had ample negotiating room to get anything from anyone who needed his talent. He could use it to become someone else's servant to earn a paycheck or to build his fortune as most folks do. Robert landed a great career with the investment banking firm Goldman Sachs in 1994 after spending a few years with Air Products and Chemicals, Goodyear Tires, and Kraft General Foods. The salaries and perks were enticing and could have lured labor-minded pals to lie at anchor and slumber.

Fortunately, people of Robert's breed are not easily preyed on. They know how to keep their eyes on the bigger prize. Where many will rejoice at eating the crumbs that fall from the royal table, Robert knew how to sit in the king's chair at the table of abundance. Don't kick yourself out of the race. What is deplorable is the case of brilliant people who rate themselves unqualified for limitlessness. They fall for sign-on bonuses and hand in their fighting gear to go and let their genius die in the confines of corporate operating procedures. Unlike many bright minds enticed by corporate America's sumptuous offices and perks to continue laboring to build their employers' family fortune, Robert knew there were better ways to earn a living. Did it make sense to have studied hard to obtain an engineering degree and a master's degree from a prestigious university to spend your life working in someone's cubicle?

"Big hat, no cattle?" Many young, affluent people, who could be the hope to lift their communities out of the jaws of poverty, prefer to sign up for what pays them. They are content with making a six-figure income when they could make it to eight, ten, or twelve. When they look at the *Beemer* in their driveways, the six-bedroom, the annual bonus, and a pack of debt cards, they can smile and say, "Wow! Look at what I have accomplished. Me coming from the hood!" and proudly they will add, "There aren't that many people who have achieved what I have." And looking at where many came from, they can be proud of themselves. The only problem is that they could achieve more if they did not limit their view to their own selves.

Locked down by name tags, benefit packages, and the promise of promotions, many brilliant minds settle for pocket change in BIG Company. Not Robert's kind of folks. They do not look to spend their life working for Big Companies. They build their own Big Companies. For people like Robert Smith, this is ridiculous. Unfortunately, many brilliant people with prestigious parchments still sit in corporate offices, with fine suits and a matching attitude with no dough to show. As a good Texan would say, "Big hat, no cattle." If you were lucky enough to make even $200,000 a year, how much would you keep after Uncle Sam had exercised his right? If you are fortunate, you could be left with $135,000 before other withholdings. You would probably go home with a mere $120,000, no more than $10,000 monthly. That is a middle-class income, the right amount to keep you from leaving the company to strike on your own and become a fierce competitor.

Go-getters are not trapped in job security. Robert Smith knew it and got off the corporate payroll six short years after being hired by a leading investment banking firm. While Goldman Sachs went public, Robert Smith went private. In 2000, Robert Smith felt his time had come. He did not wait another day to leave Goldman Sachs to start Vista Equity Partners, a private equity firm focused on software. He was too bright to let anything wear him down, not even the loving-kindness of his grandfather. I bet many of his colleagues and relatives must have found him insane.

The self-made follow their own wisdom. As you would expect from a caring parent, Grandpa Smith thought abandoning a prestigious job was a big mistake. Other obedient grandchildren would have listened to the wise owl. After all, was this not about Robert's own welfare and job security? But Robert was too wise and savvy to let job security lock him down to keep building wealth for other people. How could he have been able to donate millions to charity? How could Robert have helped pay off $34 million of debt for the 2018 class of Morehouse College graduates and their parents had Robert continued working for others? How could he have impacted the many communities he is involved in today, supporting them with hundreds of millions of dollars, had he been an employee? "How did he do it?" you might ask.

How come so many billionaires, such as Elon Musk, Robert Smith, Dennis Richelieu, and David Stewart, who operate several companies, can accomplish so much while the cashier at the local store faces an unsurmountable challenge handling just one small task of correctly counting the cash? They live by an uncompromising power of disciplined self-manifestation.

> ### SECRET CODE #7
> ### EXERCISE THE POWER OF DISCIPLINED EXECUTION

Superachievers are laser-focused on their core expertise and remain in their lanes to the finish line. They outsource or delegate everything else. They are not generalists or Jacks-of-all-trade. They are good at one thing and experts at it. Before they diversify their holdings, these geniuses only do and excel at one talent. For Oprah Winfrey, that was the gift of speaking; Robert Smith was a financial expert; David Stewart, a computer geek; Michael Jordan, His *Airness* on the court; Annie Malone and Sarah Breedlove, the queens of hair; and Sean Combs, a.k.a Puff Daddy, the lord of the mic.

These people did what most people with talent don't do. They are visionaries who see what others do not. They knew how to leverage their natural gifts and turn them into cash machines. These Black entrepreneurs looked beyond the horizon, far beyond the barriers, discrimination, racism, bigotry, and misogyny. They did not sit to throw tantrums or find someone to blame for their suffering. They did not dwell on recounting their misery, magnifying the size of the giants in the land. They saw milk and honey and, with self-management and the power of execution, fought with their last breath to seize it.

The question is: What lesson can we all learn from these people? They do not give wings to adversity. You, too, should not give wings to the lack of education, racial discrimination, or racial profiling. Have the audacity to keep yourself mainstreamed. Do not think of yourself as a lesser human, less deserving, or an alien. These people reinvent themselves to meet their challenges and compete with anyone on a higher level. How can you explain that all white and black media celebrities put together, no one matched Oprah as the highest-paid TV anchor, racking 315 million a year as an employee? These folks, whose stories are no different from yours, see opportunities where others see challenges and roadblocks. They are African American millionaires and billionaires who rose from poverty to force themselves where they were never expected. They relentlessly pursue what they set their mind to and are testimonies that becoming a millionaire or a billionaire in black America is possible. It all starts with self-discipline from the crib, from home, for self-restraint is taught or self-taught.

FOURTEEN COUNTER-PRODUCTIVE BEHAVIORS THAT CAN UNDERMINE SELF-ACTUALIZATION.

1. *Hatred towards the rich*: you cannot become what you hate.
2. *Resentment*: holding grudges against someone can only hurt the bearer.
3. *Guilt*: dwelling on past mistakes is a counter-productive option to living.
4. *Self-pity*: the world is too busy to revolve around you.
5. *I-deserve-it mentality*: the fruit of premature self-gratification is poverty.
6. *Them-Against-Us mindset*: do not play a game you will not win.
7. *Conspiracy theories*: if the system is out against you, it won't miss you.
8. *Fear of Action*: without action, all dreams are vain fantasies.
9. *Blame mentality*: if I should hold someone else accountable for my misery, I might as well surrender.
10. *Envy*: you cannot have what you refuse to others.
11. *Impatience*: every seed must be rotten, become a tree, and yield fruit.

12. *Dishonesty*: no evil shall go unpunished under the sun.
13. *Adverse creditworthiness*: nobody builds wealth with his own money.
14. *Something-for-nothing*: for every harvest, there is a seed.
15. *Greed:*
16. *Unforgiveness:*

SELF-DISCIPLINE TRUMPS INTELLIGENCE WHEN IT COMES TO ACADEMIC AND LIFE SUCCESS

Self-discipline is the willpower to self-constraint and the predictor of success. What is the magic formula Warren Buffett used to build his massive wealth? No. There is no magic formula. There is a magical behavior, a way of life that 95 percent of people fail to live by because of a lack of direction, focus, or discipline.

What is self-discipline, and why does it matter? Self-discipline predicts academic, marital, business, and social success. Self-discipline, self-monitoring, self-control, or self-restrain is the ability to

- Self-censure and delay self-gratification.
- Plan and follow through with a set schedule.
- Find a way, not excuses, to execute a plan.
- Self-regulate and resist temptation and craving.
- Accept to pay the price for the prize even when it hurts.
- Do what must be done when it is the most inconvenient.
- Be able to control your impulses, emotions, and feelings.

Duke University psychologist Dr. Terrie Moffitt and her colleagues conducted a thirty-two-year research on 1000 respondents in New Zealand. Dr. Moffitt's findings were illuminating. The study found a strong correlation between the rate of life success, healthy lifestyle, low crime rate, low substance abuse, a higher savings rate, and a stronger financial position. How, then, do you learn self-discipline?

TEN TIPS TO TRAIN YOURSELF FOR SELF-DISCIPLINE

- Know that self-discipline is pervasive. It is a winner-take-all deal. You cannot be self-disciplined in one area of life and not in others.
- Find a compelling reason for practicing self-restraint, such as the routine of power habits. What you repeat, you become.
- Know what you want to achieve, set goals and priorities, and magnify long-term results over the pleasure of instant gratification.
- Know your weaknesses and cravings and learn to tame them.
- Know your rewards for not giving in to your cravings.
- Accept self-denial and self-censure as a way of life.
- Know your triggers and trigger-busters.
- Avoid useless exposure to temptation and negative influence.
- Repeat the positive behavior of resisting your cravings or weaknesses and reward yourself.
- Accept that change takes time and start over if you give in.

FOUR STEPS TO MANIFEST THE POWER OF EXECUTION

As Henry Ford famously stated, *"You cannot build a reputation from what you are going to do."* What makes an effective leader is not planning. It is taking bold actions and assuming their consequences. Successful people get things done. Lousy people spend time planning and never take action. Success likes actions, not just plans.

Undoubtedly, self-discipline differentiates between those who dictate what life should deliver and those who subject themselves to life's whims. Below are six steps to practice self-discipline, the inalienable ingredient of success.

STEP 1: ACTIVATE THE POWER OF FOCUS

Inspired wealth-builders pursue one goal at a time. Following too many goals at a time can only dilute your efforts and reduce your drive. Focus is the key to success. You must have the power of focus of the eagle. The eagle flies the highest in the sky, yet it feeds on the birds in the lake. When the eagle has preyed on a fish from a distance, it will no longer be distracted by anything else. It will dive into the water, catch the fish, and then fly back up and enjoy a good dinner.

You need intense and consistent actions toward your goals: your dream cannot be an off-and-on gig. Why do most people fail to enter their prophetic destiny? According to the Pareto principle (also known as the 80/20 rule), we spend 80 percent of our time doing things that bring only 20 percent of the reward we expect. Too many people waste time on trivial stuff.

Without focus, you will get nothing accomplished. Successful people have a laser focus on their goals. For Steve Jobs, focus is not about willpower *but* about being able "to say "No" even when it pisses people off." He adds that focus is "*abandoning 1000 great ideas to focus on the BIG GOAL even if that made people mad in the process.*" In his genius and corporate leadership career, Steve Jobs's attitude got him crossed with numerous collaborators. He never backed down from pursuing what he set his mind to, often through strife.

1. EXERCISE THE MAGIC POWER OF "NO"

Self-discipline is being resolutely engaged in refusing to give procrastination, self-indulgence, perfectionism, and excuses a chance.

– **Coach Greb**

You must have the courage to say "No" and resist the temptation of diving into many competing projects at a time. Here is what happens when you are not using the power of any. As soon as you start with one project, you suddenly receive so many ideas you lose track of the primary goal. Steve Jobs argued that you must have the courage to say no to brilliant ideas and focus energy and resources on accomplishing the one goal you are pursuing.

The secret of Warren Buffett's success is this: focus. Buffett believes, "You should focus on what you know best as an investor. "No concept is as powerful as the concept of focus. Focus by essence supposes that you devote yourself to one thing. Focus is vital in any industry. Can you imagine a surgeon distracted by 1,000 things while performing heart surgery? Though they may diversify their investment portfolio after making money, wealth-builders never pursue two competing goals.

Focus on the bright side of life. Look around you. A mind well cultivated is a gold mine swollen with unlimited possibilities. But the same mind can represent hell. God gave us the free will to choose. If you focus on the good things, they will produce good outcomes, but if you focus on negativity, that is what you will reap.

Anything ever built started as an idea. The plane, the boat, and the skyscrapers all started as an inspiration. The architect who builds a monument forms the concept before putting it on paper for the builders to turn it into a standing form. However, you must have a clear mind to receive inspiration because what goes into your mind is what comes out of it. If you focus on negativity, you will only see a negative result.

2. FIND AND FOCUS ON YOUR CIRCLE OF COMPETENCE

Focus on improving what you are good at. When you are bombarded with criticism and negative self-appraisal, you believe you are a good-for-nothing; you only see what is not right with you, either because someone told you or because that's all you magnify about yourself. When that happens, you focus more on your weaknesses than your strengths. No. That is a self-depleting and self-defeating approach. Instead, "dim your sunset and brighten your sunrise." Focus on maximizing your strengths. Your strength will deem your weakness away. Who ignores the excellent genius in Elon Musk? Yet the man is a terrible public speaker. He stutters every time he must explain something, but because the audience focuses less on Elon's body language than on what he says, it seems no bother. That does not seem to bother Elon, who is so busy inventing and reinventing the world.

The **circle of competence** is an investor strategy attributed to Warren Buffett, which is the key to his success. What is it? According to the website

Farnam Streets, the circle of competence helps you focus on your core expertise, avoid problems, identify opportunities for improvement, and learn from others. As notably expressed in a letter to investors, Warren Buffett stressed the importance of developing your investment strategy on not all but a few skills that you master:

> *What an investor needs is the ability to correctly evaluate selected businesses. Note that word "selected": You don't have to be an expert on every company or even many. You only have to be able to evaluate companies within your circle of competence. The size of that circle is not particularly important; knowing its boundaries, however, is vital.*

IBM founder Tom Watson, Jr. echoed this belief when he argued: "I am no genius. I'm smart in spots—but I stay around those spots." Stick to what you know. How possible is it to learn every aspect of the complex business world? It is humanly impossible to know everything, even in your area of expertise. Do you need to understand every facet of the business to become successful? There is basic knowledge we all, as common-sense users, have of the way a company should work. The sensible strategy to dominate the industry is to have an expert understanding of one specific area. If you sell rugs, you will not know every type of rug. You will probably specialize in Caspian rugs, for example, and be an expert at that. You do not need to be a jack of all trades. Expertise helps you develop excellence and depth in your core areas. Why can a medical specialist charge more than a generalist?

3. MANIFEST THE POWER OF PRECISION: FIND AND FOCUS ON ONE TARGET AT A TIME

Do something you are good at and use it to dominate. Enter a market you can monopolize. Success runs on targeting. When I studied the companies that run our economy today, I saw no one start with the desire to compete in a market that giants have already flooded. Amazon was not created to compete with the gigantic Walmart. Facebook did not begin to serve the billion people it serves today. These companies started in a small niche. Finding a niche is critical because you will be the only one or the dominant force in your field.

The wisest way an underdog can beat a giant is not to snatch the bones out of his mouth; he outwits him through innovation, inventiveness, and focused differentiation. Amazon focused its energy on being the best on the Internet, where Walmart was not even present, using its first-mover advantage. Like Xerox in the 1990s and Google, Amazon has become a verb: "*Let me xerox it,*" "*Let me google it,*" or "*Let me amazon it,*" maybe soon. Despite Walmart's gigantic investment to catch up with Amazon and ranking second right behind Amazon as of January 2024, Statista.com reported Walmart to only control 6.3 percent of the US online commerce while giant Amazon sits on a domineering 37.9 percent throne, far ahead of contenders like Home Depot, Target, eBay, Etsy, and many who are far behind with market share below three percent.

Likewise, Microsoft plunged into over-diversification and lost its focus under the leadership of Steve Ballmer. The campus trailed Apple in the iPhone market; its still-born mobile is rotting in its grave, and poor Bing was smashed by giant Google, which controls 92 percent of all online searches while Bing only controls three percent.

Inspired wealth-builders are goal-setters and go-getters. They have a clear mind about what they want. If you have no goal, you will always hit your target. If you live aimlessly, you will not get anywhere or have no way of knowing where you've gotten. The target is what determines your action plan. You cannot be faltering, changing your mind repeatedly; you must be able to decide on one course of action and pursue it.

4. PRIORITIZE WHAT MATTERS THE MOST

The ability to set out what matters most for your purpose and draw the line between what drains your energy and time and what is critical is a non-negotiable skill for everyone who wants to become self-made. It is a poor habit to consider everything important. The urgent is not always necessary, and the important is not always urgent. Warren Buffet believes you should narrow your priority list to five items; otherwise, a long list is a recipe for failure.

President Eisenhower once said, *"I have two kinds of problems: the urgent and the important."* Initially introduced as the Eisenhower (priority) matrix, Coach Stephen Covey recently introduced the priority management technique as the Time Management Matrix, often referred to as the Priority Quadrants.

THE PRIORITY MAP ADAPTED FROME INSENHOWER PRIORITY MATRIX

	URGENT	NOT URGENT
IMPORTANT	Tasks with current deadlines that have a significant impact on your core goal ***DO NOW***	Tasks with future deadlines that have a significant impact on your core goal ***SCHEDULE***
NOT IMPORTANT	Tasks with current deadlines that do not impact your core goal ***DELEGATE***	Tasks with future deadlines that do not impact your core goal ***DELETE***

Setting priorities helps you create efficiency. Successful people always start by setting goals; they establish and honor their priorities. No matter how you want to put it, you work with limited resources: time, energy, capital, skills, knowledge, and human capital. You must know how to allocate your resources; otherwise, you will be depleted of critical resources needed for your core project. As a self-made, you must be able to self-assess and correct your weaknesses. If you are under constant pressure, out of time, and seeing poor results, you probably need to reorder your priorities. Adopt a new habit of planning and executing your goal items. Success bows to your character, yet character is formed from our habits.

You can replace your poor habits with the power habits you desire. The most efficient way to change a poor habit is to replace it with a power habit, the positive habit you want to see. In this case, do not focus on the poor habit you do not wish to. Replace it with a power habit and focus your energy on nurturing the power habit.

Setting priorities helps you create balance. What is more important to you: your venture or your family? Balance is critical. As surprising as this may sound, you cannot neglect and replace your family with things, nor shower them with gifts instead of your presence and love. You must prioritize and be a great communicator. How, then, do you decide to prioritize? Learn to rate the things that vie for your time and resources by their level of importance. You must delay or eliminate things that needlessly eat up your resources. Remember, you are working at building wealth. You must avoid needless waste. You must prioritize what you devote your time and energy to.

The biggest challenges mostly come from the people closest to you. You can never separate your family from your wealth-building scheme because you risk creating a human and spiritual conflict. You need to partner with your spouse and children and make them active participants in the process. Leaving them out can only increase your challenges. Every self-made person knows how to create a balance in their family and business lives. Reasonable compromises, patience, profound love, and a good dose of firmness are the ingredients for your millionaire success cocktail. If you fail, you will be like many *busy people who have acquired riches yet* lost their families.

STEP 2: MAGNIFY THE POWER OF EXECUTION

Have you noticed how some people spend so much time talking that they have little energy to act? Billionaire Mark Cuban, Dallas Mavericks owner, serial entrepreneur, and ABC's *Shark Tank* star, believes that execution skills make a successful entrepreneur. You must be able to take your dream into an executable set of decisions. Motivational speaker and TV host Mel Robbins believes you must act on your ideas. You need to do something consistently and daily. You must be able to turn your skills and knowledge into measurable results. People who get results have long-range views, consider all aspects of a decision, and take bold steps towards accomplishing them after clearly articulating their vision to their teams. They do not overstudy a plan, risking becoming ineffective and wasteful.

1. DO NOT BE AFRAID OF MAKING MISTAKES. BE AN EXECUTOR, NOT AN ETERNAL DREAMER

What are the advantages of action? Action proves your idea and gives you the reality of the true application in the practical world. In my startup coaching business, I have come to realize that many entrepreneurs can plan more than they can execute. So, they waste precious time in planning and have minimal applications. Many people wrote several books they never published because they are too scared to launch their ideas because they are afraid of failure, suffering from an anomaly known as **atychiphobia,** an irrational fear of failing caused by the fear of inadequacy, and disappointment others, especially demanding and overbearing parents, supporters, teachers, and coaches.

Many of these people are afraid of making mistakes; others are too emotional and cannot stand criticism, so they prefer never to expose themselves. Sometimes, they give up when they launch, and things do not work out. People who make it in this world are courageous and action-driven. They "Just Do It." Jack Ma said he made 1001 mistakes, and Steve Jobs almost lost Apple because of poor decisions. Countless people who started a venture and are now prominent gurus made huge mistakes. Some turned their lemons into lemonade.

You should not just stop at one trial. What happens to the plan you worked so hard on? What happens to the grand strategies developed by the marketing department? Unless the salesperson goes into the streets to sell the product, all efforts will have been fruitless.

Christian writer Vance Havner, author of *"Don't Miss Your Miracle,"* believes, *"The venture must follow the vision. It is not enough to stare up the steps—we must step up the stairs."* Vision empowers our faith to hold on as we see things happening in the future. A grand vision boils down inside and sparks the desire to act. Motivational speaker Joel Barker puts it even better when he contends, *"Vision without action is merely a dream. Action without vision passes time. Vision with action can change the world."* As a wealth-builder, you will need a solid and detailed plan, but don't dwell on it. Planning is essential to any successful endeavor, but not enough. Planning is only the starting point. It is critical because it helps identify your goals and resources to devise a strategy to help you accomplish them effectively and efficiently. A dream without an action plan is a mere wish because wishes and fantasies do not always become a reality; what about an unexecuted plan? Self-made work around a very well-organized system of things and people facilitates the implementation of action plans because savvy entrepreneurs prioritize swift actions.

2. LIFE IS AN EXPERIMENT. IT IS LIVED THROUGH TRIALS AND ERRORS. ACCEPT TO MAKE MISTAKES

Nothing happens until there is action: too much planning, little action. Some people spend too much time planning. To succeed, you must be willing to act through trial and error, correcting your actions and learning. For Pablo Picasso, *"Action is the foundational key to all success."* Benjamin Franklin believes that *words show a man's wit, but action his meaning.* Motivational speaker Simon Sinek nails it when he argues: *"What good is an idea if it remains an idea? Try. Experiment. Iterate. Fail. Try Again. Change the world."*

Perfectionists are procrastinators who are afraid to meet the challenge of putting their product in the hands of the intended audience. They delay, trying to produce an impeccable product. Many want perfection, refuse to fail, and waste excellent learning time. The determination to arrive at perfection comes with trial and error, known as the **learning curve**. *Expertise, proficiency, and experience must travel a long distance before you can sell them.* Learn to defeat fear and not let it grow wings. American psychologist Henry Link wrote, "We generate fears while we sit. We overcome them by action."

Procrastination and fear are two of the worst enemies of success. Have deadlines and meet them, no matter what. There will always be adversity or a reason something will be in your way. Do not let procrastination eat your wealth away. Why do people procrastinate? They either fear inadequacy, criticism, or inability to plan and run a project; some people like to talk more than they can perform.

Fear keeps your idea from bursting. Unless an idea turns into action, nothing will happen. The action proves an idea. I have met several people who say they have dreams and keep talking about them. Several beautiful ideas could have transformed our lives had they been tested. Idealists do not get anything accomplished. There is a time to dream and a time to be pragmatic. No. An entrepreneur is practical, realistic, and action oriented.

3. USE STRATEGY AND SPEED: FOUR EXECUTION STRATEGIES

Inspired wealth-builders have a sense of urgency, not emergency. Forceful actions test the validity of your plan and strategy. In today's economy, sluggishness is a deadly beast. You need to act forcefully and swiftly to increase your competitive edge. The time you take your idea or product to the market will determine whether you are a challenger or a market leader. Intelligent organizations and self-made know how to leverage the first-mover advantage, the power of execution, Teutonic efficiency, and balance routines.

LEVERAGE THE FIRST-MOVER ADVANTAGE

In 2007, the phone market was inundated with several phone models, but no one saw the windows of turning the cellphone into an integrated, convenient, space-saving, and highly portable mini-computer device. Coming from behind, Apple did not think that creating another cell phone brand would give it the market share it needed. The company decided to pitch into what it does best: innovate.

Apple decided to use its experiences with the iPad to enter a niche it would dominate and establish itself as the brand everyone wants to carry around. The iPhone looked gorgeous in its design and offered a versatile platform where you could listen to your old Walkman, Shop online, and video talk to your grandma while on vacation in Hawaii. Year after year, Apple used its first mover advantage to distance itself from the pack, far away from Samsun, which used the **late mover** strategy, but American consumers still preferred Apple. Likewise, Microsoft's Windows has lorded over the operating system market for decades, the same way Amazon controls the US online shopping ecosystem.

Time, indeed, is money. The time value of money concept claims that the more you wait to invest, the less opportunity you give your investment to grow. Only time will tell of the painter's craft. Unless a painter is put to the test of labor and time, telling all about his skills, there is no way of knowing how good or bad he is. Millionaires plan carefully and act forcefully with speed. Acting allows you to test the waters and sharpen your knowledge, skills, and experience. Acting fast gives you a first-mover advantage, the benefit of being the first to introduce a product, concept, or service before someone else or your competitors do.

4. HARNESS THE "RIGHT NOW" MINDSET

Practice the art of baby steps. Sometimes, the size or complexity of the task can throw you off. To tackle this, break your tasks up into small steps or pieces you can manage. Then, start with the task you fear the most. Every time you complete a task, celebrate the victory and move on to the next job until you complete the whole project. This process demands planning.

Start today with what you have. A wealth-builder does not wait for the time to be right, the resources to be perfect, or for everything to be in place. Millionaires start in a garage with what they have. As Nike puts it, they *"just do it."* Are you still sleeping on your millionaire idea and waiting for the time to be right? How many of you believe that the time is not right? Or do you think you do not have what it takes? These are great excuses, and excuses build nothing but poverty. That is the most common excuse that delays success. Never expect to have the right resources, time, or everything; you are procrastinating and will do nothing.

5. KNOW AND HEDGE AGAINST YOUR WEAKNESSES: EVERY HERO HAS A TRAGIC FLAW THAT WILL CAUSE HIS DOWNFALL

No matter how strong, every hero has a weakness. In literature, we call it the hero's tragic flaw. How was Deliliah able to cause Samsung's demise? She found his weak spot. Samson's love for Delilah made him lower his guard: unaware of the woman's duplicity and evil mission, Samson, who thought he had found the love of his life, trusted and revealed the secret of his strength to Delilah. Delilah did not hesitate to tell the Philistine army, who fought Samson until he succumbed.

Likewise, King David's kingdom was weakened by his lustful endearment of a married woman named Bathsheba, the wife of his most loyal soldier, Uriah. David's curse led his eldest son Amon to rape his half-sister before being killed by his third son Absalom. Absalom did not state there. He went into his father's concubines before being killed in an attempted coup to overthrow his father, David.

King Solomon, succeeding his father, King David, stunned the world and God. His unparalleled wisdom and wealth raised him to the pinnacle of success, fame, admiration, and wealth. Unfortunately, against God's warning, his lust for foreign women caused his disgrace and downfall, thereby breaking the covenant with God when he promised to David as long as they abide by the covenant and do not go after other God, saying:

> *"For thus says the Lord: 'David shall never lack a man to sit on the throne of the house of Israel* **(Jeremiah 33:17)**.

Every human has his summer and winter, and knowing yours will save your life. Mine was pathetic.

For many people, self-discipline, unfortunately, is learned in the school of hard knocks. When I was younger, I had a formidable challenge. There was no doubt about my intelligence, and I knew I had that unique ability to get things done to perfection when I put my mind to them. Getting things done was not the problem; getting them started was my greatest struggle. I would put them off until the last minute, but something drastic forced me to change this poor habit. In my last semester of business school, I waited too long and failed to submit my marketing project by the due date. The professor refused to grade my assignment and gave me a "0" for the project, which dropped my grade to a "C" in her subject. Despite my pleading with the professor, she would not have it. The consequences were enormous. My GPA (Grade point average) dropped from 3.7 to 3.5, which is a big deal in grad school. What if I wanted to apply for a scholarship for a Ph.D. program or any other studies? That did it.

Furious and disappointed in myself, I vowed never to let that happen again, but don't we say that a habit is second nature? I struggled throughout the year to deal with this thief called procrastination until it started stealing opportunities, progress, and wealth from me. I decided to be radical and thought of der Fuhrer's method: Blitzkrieg.

Having lived in Germany, I've had a chance to observe the manifestation of something called ***Teutonic Efficiency***. The Germanic power of execution. What is Teutonic efficiency, and how does it impact the self-made?

6. THE SELF-MADE ARE GOVERNED BY "TEUTONIC EFFICIENCY"

Studying entrepreneurs and wealth-builders worldwide led me to a striking discovery: people of Germanic descent control the world economy, especially in the Western Hemisphere. The question is, what do we call Germanic descent? As you may have noted, the Germanics, not Germans, conquered and controlled most European territories from Central through Northern Europe, including countries like Germany, the United Kingdom, the Kingdoms of Lichtenstein, Luxembourg, Switzerland, Northern Belgium, the Netherlands, and most of Scandinavia including Sweden, Denmark, Norway, and Finland. These people are known for their efficiency, hard work, chivalric code of honor, and respect for the rule of law. They thrive on meritocracy rather than relationships.

Likewise, countries or territories they politically or economically influenced and controlled exhibit the same attitudes and attributes. Look around Africa, for example, and you get the picture.

Economically strong countries were under British rule in one way or another: Nigeria, Kenya, South Africa, and Egypt are prime examples. In the northern hemisphere, you have the United States and Canada. In Asia, city-states like Hong Kong and Taiwan and countries such as India, Malaysia, and similar territories are prosperous oases in a desert of pauperism. Territories or countries the Germanics conquered share the same **Teutonic efficiency** and demonstrate a higher innovation, entrepreneurialism, business, and economic prowess. Conversely, to some extent, Nations of Greco-Latin culture controlled by France, Spain, Portugal, Italy, and Greece experienced *coughing* economies. These countries generally rank at the bottom of the development scale: most of Sub-Saharan Africa and Latin America are potent examples of such a reality. Haiti, Niger, Burundi, and Djibouti are examples of countries classified at the bottom of the Human Index Development. Of the thirty-two nations ranking at the bottom of the Human Development Index, fifteen are from French-speaking Africa, over half of the French colonies.

7. WORK ETHICS, ENTREPRENEURIALISM, MERITOCRACY, AND THE DESIRE TO CONQUER THE UNKNOWN

Why do people with a high level of Teutonic efficiency succeed at a higher rate? They *have an attitude of self-reliance, determinism, work ethic, hard toil, integrity, surrender to the laws of life, alignment to the code of success, intolerance for mediocrity, and the desire to conquer the next frontier.* How do you think American settlers conquered the territories of the Far West?

A 2020 survey painted a picture of English-speaking Africa versus French-speaking Africa. The report indicated that French Africans see relationships as the pathway to success, while English-speaking people believe education and hard work are the ways to rise the social ladder. No wonder English-speaking countries such as Nigeria, South Africa, Ghana, and Kenya emphasize good education and consequently dominate the African economy. In the United States, Nigerians are the leading nationality in terms of stellar education and prestigious university attendance.

On the global marketplace, aside from Chinese and, to some extent, Japanese companies, that share the Germanic spirit of business entrepreneurism control the lion's share with America, Germany, Switzerland, the United Kingdom, Saudi Arabia, Hong Kong, Singapore, Taiwan, and India, lording over other nations. Many US Fortune 500 companies were built by people of German descent: Pfizer, Merk, Tesla, Walmart, Amazon, etc…

On the global wealth ranking list, world billionaires and millionaires are generally concentrated in nations with a higher work ethic, the rule of law, relatively low corruption, and a high level of meritocracy. Countries such as Luxembourg, Liechtenstein, Switzerland, the United States, and Germany, as well as territories like Hong Kong and Tawain, have concentrations of *seven and ten-digit high earners.*

APPLY THE SCORE EFFICIENCY MODEL.

What is the SCORE Model, and how did it come about? Upon comparing the productivity of many workers in corporate and industrial settings, I posed the fundamental question: how to arrive at the best and highest use of people's effort to maximize output, satisfaction, and goal achievement with minimal waste, accident, burnout, and turnover?

Still under study, the SCORE model was developed to create the most desirable work methods, both for the worker and the organization. SCORE stands for Strategic, Compelling, Organized, Result-oriented, and Empowering. A task must be **strategic**: you must work around a system for a definite goal, not just moving the busy body; **compelling** and meaningful: you must find a good reason to engage in the task; **organized**: the work must be planned; it must be chunked up, scheduled, timed, and scaled to maximize output with minimal input. It must be **result-driven**: every activity must be a part of a chain of coordinated tasks that participate in achieving a set of measurable goals. Based on known metrics. **Empowering** and engaging: the work you do must not only benefit the shared goal; it must be rewarding in the form of personal and professional growth, recognition, pride, and or satisfactory material compensation beyond ordinary pay.

Teutonic Efficiency is only possible when we apply the power of execution: the *Blitzkrieg Execution Method*, another model I developed that helped me overcome procrastination and personal indulgences.

8. THE BLITZKRIEG EXECUTION METHOD (BEM)

How did Germany defeat its enemies to the point of conquering almost all of Europe? Hitler had one strategy of enemy force annihilation known as Blitz-Krieg (Lightning-War). The Webster's Dictionary defines Blitzkrieg as a

> *"War conducted with great speed and force, specifically: a violent surprise offensive by massed air forces and mechanized ground forces in close coordination."*

How would the same method apply, and why does it make sense? A question asked a group of corporate executives if they preferred a visionary or execution leader; over three-quarters responded that they preferred execution to vision.

Having suffered from procrastination, pathetic perfectionism, and atyphobia- the fear of failing, I looked for a way to cure myself. I looked at different methods until I felt on military strategies, one being blitzkrieg. I worked to make these my work method while writing my book. Seeing that I was taking too much time to complete my book and having decided to devote my career to writing, I realized I needed to be efficient. So here is what I did.

HOW I DEVELOPED THE BLITZKRIEG EXECUTION METHOD (BEM 7-70-1)

(Blitzkrieg Execution Method 7 days, 70 Hour – 1 Book)

Having already outlined most of my books, I needed a system to complete research, proofread, edit, and send them to my publishing team. I usually worked at least twelve hours a day, so I decided to stay more focused and efficient. My grand goal was to complete four books and nine mini-books within three months. I was not interested in publishing them. I wanted to ensure I tackled the most challenging part: writing the books. That was all I wanted to accomplish.

That meant I had to complete one book by week, working ten hours from 8 am to 9 pm, with an hour lunch break.

The beginning was painful: not the work, but turning off all forms of distraction, my son's games, dinner time, church, or any other. Any time missed had to be put back to the point where I worked till 3 AM or seven depending on how I used the rest of the day. I

I focused my energy and time on one book at a time. Initially, my most complicated challenges were handling family demands: being a father, a husband, a dad, and a provider of all sorts of needs. But when I completed, not without pain, the first book and sent it to my team, I knew it was possible. The books I spent a decade writing were on their way to being read.

My system was simple. I had streamlined every step of the work process, which included in-house writing, edition, proofreading, and editing, then meeting with the focus group on Saturday, and finally sending the work to the professional editing team – what a waste! They did not do much. My team did a better job.

I knew I had to think about design and marketing, which was not my core expertise. So, that was none of my worries. I delegated that task to a team that outsourced it to an expert. That freed me to focus my time and energy on what mattered the most at the time, and that was my formidable challenge: completing my books.

With the BEM technique, I completed three books and six minibooks within four months. I rested for a month and resumed writing. The next step was to focus on marketing and selling the books as a series.

From losing to procrastinating, I designed a system, streamlined my tasks, delegated accessory tasks, and focused all my time and energy on my core expertise. The system is still under test and will be bettered along the way. The Blitzkrieg Execution Method forced me to be efficient, focused, and organized while helping me maximize my productivity.

9. MAXIMIZE YOUR PRODUCTIVITY

Value progress over movement. Many people confuse productivity with activity. You have limited time for anything you do. Efficiently organizing your time to achieve progress is critical. The question is, is what I am doing leading toward reaching my goal and purpose? When you start or manage a company, you must always understand the concept of efficiency using the Key Performance Indicator. An example of KPI for a manager could be efficient capital (ROI) or asset utilization (ROA). If all things equal, an employee produces $ 2000,000 of output in six months and another in twelve, whom would you instead hire in terms of output? Productivity is measured in terms of output given a particular input level, including time. Start measuring your efficiency by doubling your productivity year in and year out; do not quit when things get tough.

10. "JUST DO NOT QUIT. SIR DYSON DID NOT."

You may have to go to the drawing board several times to learn a trade. You may face a lot of losses and lose hope. But bear in mind that Rome was built, destroyed, and built again; do not forget that more than one trial may be necessary to meet success. Failure is part of success if you have grit. Grit increases the positive energy that impacts your propensity and ability to work harder and fail forward.

Grit is an energizing tool for wealth-builders. Be great at failing so your story can inspire many generations. Every successful person has had to go to the drawing board several times. English inventor, Sir Dyson of Dyson Vacuum, can teach you something in this arena when he recalls:

> There are countless times an inventor can give up on an idea. By the time I made my 15th prototype, my third child was born. By 2,627, my wife and I were really counting our pennies. By 3,727, my wife was giving art lessons for some extra cash. These were tough times, but each failure brought me closer to solving the problem.
> — **Sir Dyson**

STEP 3: RESET YOUR PROSPERITY THERMOSTAT

Your mind is a factory as it can produce the instructions it receives the most. The law of attraction contends that your mind will attract the things it focuses on most. You understand that this includes negativity as well. The output of your mind is only the result of the input it receives. Millionaires focus their attention on producing more positive outcomes in a balanced way.

1. DEVELOP AND LIVE BY A SUCCESS CONSCIOUSNESS

Reset your mind to produce your desired results. Rewire the circuitry of your mind. The mind is a set of interconnected circuits, known as neurons, that transmit lights of information to and from the body. Why do you need to reprogram your mind? The secret to manifesting your reality lies in tapping into your mind's creative power. A part of the mind known as the subconscious mind is the depository of all your life experiences, learning, and emotions. It is like a mainframe computer with unlimited storage capacity.

As you grow and experience life, the subconscious mind will store your living reality. In due time on demand, like a factory, the subconscious mind will produce the condition and environment that meet the stored input. If all you expose yourself to is poverty, do not expect your mind to create the conditions that foster prosperity, for the subconscious mind is stubborn and feeds on the past, says psychologist Joe Dispenza.

You will only see what you magnify. Therefore, be disciplined enough to expose yourself to the reality you want to see, have a *prosperity mindset*, be jovial, use positive words, do recommendable deeds, and think positive thoughts. Most importantly, focus on what you desire, not what you do not want. The creative power of the mind will draw to you the circumstances that match the state of your mind, as the Holy Scriptures state, "Beloved, I pray that you may prosper in all things and be in health, just as your soul prospers." (3 John: 2.) You will be surprised how the very things you are trying to avoid are what you end up doing. Why? Irrespective of your desire, you manifest what your mind focuses its intention on. If all you have in your visor is a failure, do not expect success. You will only view what you focus your mind on. If you see the glass half-full, it will be, and the condition that meets the state of your mind will surround you.

2. DEVELOP A REPUTATION FOR EXCELLENCE

Develop a reputation for excellence. Mediocre seeds can only yield a poor harvest. If you are going to work with God, you better espouse a culture of excellence. God is a God of excellence. He harbors mediocrity or averageness. A lot of people are content with an average life, and they are satisfied with it. All that God created is perfect and excellent. It is only humans who destroy God's earth.

Solomon had known what no other man had ever known. He had the favor of God, who protected his kingdom. During his reign, the Israelites waged no wars against their neighbors. It was as if all those who attacked Israel had suddenly vanished. Instead, kings from other nations poured admiration and gold onto Solomon. They revered his wisdom, wealth, and, indeed, the divine hand of God on him. They also knew of the military power of his army in the cavalry, chariots, and ships.

His people revered Solomon. He had peace, unity, divine anointing, wealth, fame, respect, and a bright future. Yet, he committed an abomination that displeased God.

Solomon did not shy away from living his passion for excellence. King Solomon surprised God more than anyone. He knew how to touch God's heart and rendered Him the most significant praise with the temple of Jerusalem. Solomon wanted to experiment with the delicacies of life. In his songs, he encourages you to live life to the fullest.

In his quest for understanding, Solomon achieved an unparalleled level of accomplishment. Magnifying whatever he undertook, he studied various subjects, including botany, poetry, and music.

Whatever you do, be the best at it. Solomon raised a magnificent temple to God, built himself a lavish palace, wrote three thousand proverbs, married one thousand wives, and had 300 concubines. He drank some of the best wines and wore sumptuous clothes. Solomon's army had no comparison in stature and equipment. He surpassed anyone in wisdom, wealth, and achievement. Solomon consciously did all this with one purpose: the passion of discovery.

In the end, Solomon found that it was all vanity. He who had experimented with and experienced life, walking on and sleeping on gold, regretted all that boiled to nothing. Besides, without realizing it, Solomon had crossed the lines. He allowed himself to raise temples to the gods of his foreign women, an abomination in God's sight. He became the reflection of the insanities indulged in a spiritually corrupted man who lost God's grace.

3. DEVELOP AN IMPREGNABLE MENTAL FORTRESS

Your mind is your palace. You should never let access to it until you so desire. Developing a mental shield can only give you victory all the time. In other words, as Jim Rohne puts it, "Learn to handle your winters and your springs, protect your crops in the summer, and learn how to reap in the fall." You must build up a mental fortress that helps you face and overcome difficult situations, take advantage of opportunities, and prevent the intruder from taking your goods -because there is always an intruder seeking to steal from you and reap without guilt, excuses, and complaints. Accept full responsibility for your harvest without a blaming mentality.

Control what goes into your mind. The stories, advice, teachings, advertising, sermons, videos, experiences, music, readings, and interactions you expose yourself to influence your decisions positively or negatively.

The longer the exposure to these inputs, the stronger their power to change your personality. Don't be surprised you start reasoning like your pastor after you have spent twenty years ingurgitating his sermons. Purposed to change your behavior, advertising, propaganda, and sermons, for example, use the power of repetition to bend your willpower that weakens from so much resistance and gives in. If every Sunday, for twenty years, you hear, "Money is evil," why are you surprised you can barely put gas in your tank after church?

The most formidable way to shy yourself is to avoid exposure to ill teachings, evil thoughts, predatory advertising, half-truths, and untruths. If you see an ad, you know it will force you to buy, flip the channel, look away, or keep your distance. Your mind is the most attacked asset. Everybody knows that if they can control your mind, you are done. They can direct you like a puppet. They can feed your mind with evil, negativity, self-doubt, and dependency. Have self-discipline and discernment to know which ones to stay away from.

4. SURROUND YOURSELF WITH POSITIVE ENERGY

Be immersed in a positive environment. The mind surrenders to the principle of vibration. Your evil thoughts will vibrate and attract like energy. Some call it the law of attraction. Self-made individuals are successful because of the company of like-minded, positive people they interact with, who are self-confident, upbeat, optimistic, and energetic. Read positive materials, watch positive news, meditate, relax, and free your mind from all negativities. Listen to inspiring music quietly in a refreshing setting. *Think only of things that make you happy.* Block all negative thoughts of anger, guilt, fear, worry, and pity from entering your mind. When negative thinking comes to you, cut your breath, change the activity, and shift focus and position. You will see how you can block negative thoughts from taking control of you.

5. DISCIPLINE YOUR THOUGHTS

As aforementioned, your thoughts create our reality. You are what your mind says you are. There is power in positive thinking. The good thing is that you have control over your mind. The oppressor may beat you physically and destroy your body, but your mind will stay intact unless you let the physical bruises affect it. So, you have total governance over your mind.

As Wayne Dyer puts it in *The Power of Intention, "If you change the way you look at things, the things you look at change."* It is also about perception.

Perception is the result of your personal choice. You decide to view things one way or another. Your perception builds your emotions, which condition your actions or reactions. If you elect to see the glass as half full or half empty, it is your choice. That explains why two people exposed to the same reality can react differently. All this takes hold of our beliefs, values, and personalities.

Your life will manifest what you feed your mind. What you put into your mind is what comes out. Positive thinking is the most significant difference between failure and success. That is the fundamental difference between the poor and the rich. The poor person's mind focuses on his poor condition, while the wealth builder's mind focuses on wealth building. Positive thinking attracts positive energy and pulls you toward the positive forces that favor your success. If you are acerbic and negative, the energy around you will be forces of evil and destruction. All the wickedness you wish on others will come back to you.

6. MONITOR YOUR SELF-TALK

You are your declarations. **"What you say will be retained against you."** Our vocabulary has 50 percent more negative words. In an article entitled *"Negative Words Dominate our Language,"* Penn State University associate professor of applied linguistics and anthropology, Prof Robert Schrauf, focused on how people process words that express emotion.

Dr. Schrauf conducted his study on two groups of people of two nationalities, Mexico and the United States K, and two age groups, people in their 20s and another in their 60s. In two minutes, the participants received a group of words. Then, he asked them to classify them as positive, negative, and neutral emotions. The findings were jaw-dropping. Regardless of age and country of origin, people express 50 percent more words that denote negative feelings, 30 percent positive emotions, and 20 percent neutral emotions. As he pushed the study further, Dr. Schrauf was again surprised by another discovery. According to a survey conducted in 37 countries, only one of the seven most common emotions was positive. Can you guess which of these constantly expressed emotions is positive: fear, anger, joy, guilt, disgust, sadness, and shame?

Exercise the power of positive self-talk. Words have energy. Refrain from cursing or wishing evil on someone. Whatever comes from your mouth will vibrate in the universe and be returned to you. Resist being called or calling yourself (or anyone) pejorative slurs such as *poor, bad, evil,* etc. Steer clear of blaming words that demean you. Never tell yourself, *"I am a loser," "I am so stupid," "" I know I am going to fail,"* or *"I am poor."* Those declarations will take physical form and manifest in your life.

Conversely, make positive declarations of the results you are expecting. *"I am wealthy." "I am a millionaire." "I am a success." "I am a winner."* Those positive declarations put the universe in motion for you and cause the universal forces to work in unison to honor those words. If you declare yourself a success, you believe it and prepare your mind to see only success.

Beware what you say. Speaking is a privilege but also a power. Look around and see that all creation was designed through the power of words. Nelson Mandela once said that one significant fact he remembered about his favor is that the latter was stingy in words. He was always the last one to speak. Many think that the more they talk, the more they make sense.

Change your vocabulary. The universe has ears. If you have a chance to approach millionaires, they use a different jargon to name the same things mainstream uses.

For example, a financial coach once told his audience

> *Watch what you say. Let your words draw onto you millions. Someone who desired to be a millionaire would rather say "A quarter of a million' instead of $ 250,000.*

7. CONTROL YOUR EMOTIONS AND FEELINGS

Emotions are the external expression of your state of mind. How do you discover someone's mental state? Just look at his actions and listen to his words. The shopping mall is an ideal place to experiment with the human behavior of impulsiveness. You will see some shoppers jump on sales items, digging in their purses, wallets, or maxed-out cards to buy the items on sale. Many people will squander their meager resources simply because, as they will justify, they cannot miss a "lifetime" deal, something they never planned.

Uncontrolled emotions and poor consumer habits can lead to self-destruction and financial self-sabotage. Learn to control your impulsiveness. One outburst of anger can make you lose a great client and opportunity in the business world. We are human, and we must be ourselves, but if being yourself kills your ability to stay alive as a businessperson, the choice is clear.

Soberness and self-control are key characteristics of super-achievers. Wealth-busting habits can be altered or replaced. People adopt poor money habits because of the environment or personal indulgences. But the good news is that every habit is dynamic. It can change. If you have willpower, as we said in another part of this book, you can break a poor habit by replacing it with a new one through decision, practice, and repetition. Practice self-restraint and learn to control your temper; for example, think several times before reacting when you are under attack. If you feel irritated, never respond. If you receive an irritating message, take a day or two before responding. Never react when under emotion, be it positive or negative. Acting on impulse is a sure way to mess up. Train yourself in this area; it will make a significant difference and cause people to respect your authority.

8. LEARN TO LOSE LIKE A WINNER. YOU WILL NOT WIN ALL THE TIME

You cannot live without adversity. Adversity is a part of life. You meet it regularly in whatever you engage in. As long as you live, you will face a problem-solving need. Life's challenges are like a conveyor belt. If you stand in line, life will continuously spew challenges on you. The question, therefore, is not whether you will face adversity. The question is how you will face it and what you become of it.

Learn to accept and live with things you cannot change, learn to lose like a winner. Most people are unhappy because they believe they can control every situation and must always be in control. Many people believe that the sky will fall if they cannot win. An attitude of entitlement makes them think they must win at all costs and all the time. You must realize that winning is part of a game with three possible outcomes: you win sometimes, you lose sometimes, and sometimes you break even with zero gain and zero loss.

The advantage of this frame of mind is that you maximize the chances of winning and magnify the results because you may not always win. Sometimes, you may lose to opponents you perceive to be the weakest of all; sometimes, you win over your most dreaded adversary. Life is unpredictable. The most important thing is that after you battle with all your possible weapons, you still lose and lose with dignity. Learn to lose like a winner.

STEP 4: NURTURE YOUR EXPONENTIAL POTENTIAL

Focus your time, energy, and resources on nurturing everything that participates in your growth: People with cocky, can-do-it-alone attitudes get linear growth. Those with a leverage mindset get *exponential growth*. A leader is not a producer but an influencer. Management is the art of getting things done. The greatest gift a leader needs is the **power of nurturing.**

1. MAXIMIZE YOUR SELF-LOVE: PAMPER YOURSELF FIRST. SERVE OTHERS SECOND

An African adage says a beautiful woman can only give what she has. You cannot fulfill unless you are filled or love others if love is not in you. True altruism starts with the self. Before serving others efficiently, you must fill yourself with something valuable you can offer. We are all called on a mission to serve God by our sacrifice to others, but you will only dry out yourself if you are running on empty. Love yourself first. Pamper yourself before you can serve others.

What gives your life if not the interaction with people, not things? Unfortunately, uninspired entrepreneurs mistake bruising themselves and their relationships with the divine, family, employees, and peers. No. You should reverse course. Machines, things, and systems do not have feelings, emotions, and memories. People do. Most successful people like Elon Musk know how to make relationships a priority. Elon Musk, who works almost ninety hours a week, prioritizes spending time with his children and wife, staying in or going places together.

Your million-dollar project is not worth bruising your relationships with people you care about. You will be surprised how everything crumbles around you. To be exponentially productive, do the following:

- *Spend time with yourself.* Find a quiet place, meditate, and do something pleasing—nurturing yourself and your relationship with your inner ecosystem.

- *Frequently spend time in nature,* around water, or any place you can explore nature's beauty and refreshing cent. Walk alone with Mother Nature; she has an inspiration, healing, or a message for you.
- *As stated in the sections above, have daily encounters with the divine in prayer and meditation.*
- *Enjoy a quality, nourishing moment with your spouse* in a quiet, relaxing atmosphere away from children's distractions. Go out and enjoy your togetherness.
- *Empower your staff* daily for maximum productivity without pressuring them with quotas and deadlines.
- *Spend time visiting, entertaining,* and exchanging with your clients, suppliers, and circle of support.
- Above all, *surprise someone with a gift,* a phone call, a visit, or even something creatively and exceptionally magical.

2. INVEST IN YOUR WELLNESS: EAT WELL. THINK WELL. SLEEP WELL

The lack of self-discipline is a great challenge for many people, even for savvy wealth builders. Never beat yourself up about this. You need to create a system to make sure you cut down on waste and loss.

Focus on building yourself up: invest in your growth. You should continually seek to build the most critical asset of your wealth-building system: YOU. Invest in self-improvement. Build up good habits, learn empowering habits, and let go of self-defeating ones. Remember, a habit is a perception that becomes an emotion that then translates into an attitude that becomes a behavior. A prolonged habit that becomes a behavior will become your second nature. You have control over the center of perception and habit forming: your willpower.

The self-made's secrets of success, prosperity, good health, and longevity are hidden in the line above. No one who wants to live an amazingly fulfilling life can afford to ignore the three rules of daily living. More than anything else, three things come on top: eat well, sleep well, and think well. If you want to eliminate stress and anxiety, those three items are paramount. Feed your body with good nutrients.

Nourish your body with healthy food; that includes providing it with the appropriate dose of vitamins and minerals that keep it immune. Watch the food and fluid you take in. Spend money on healthy food if you do not want to borrow money to spend on medicine. When I turned 50, my nutritionist advised me to refrain from dairy, fat, sugar, salt, red meat, and unhealthy beverages, including soda; instead, he encouraged me to drink more water and eat greener grains, fish, and fiber. Honor your body through proper nutrition and exercise; keep away any form of toxic food and beverages.

Sleep to stay healthy. The US Center for Disease Control recommends proper sleep for everyone: nine twelve hours for school-age children, eight to ten for teenagers, seven for adults aged 18 to 60, and seven to nine for people over 61. Why so much sleep, you might wonder? Sleep is the way through which the physical and mental systems recharge. It boosts your immune system and heightens your brainpower for maximum productivity. According to the CDC, proper sleep is good medicine against several diseases, such as obesity, cardiovascular disease, depression, and diabetes. Adequate sleep can also fight anxiety, stress, mood swings, and inflammation.

Think good thoughts, and you will live longer. Our personal and lifestyle choices are six of the most devastating killer diseases of our modern time. You can prevent them by feeding your mind good brain food that includes positive thoughts, daily meditation, inspirational words, music, and prayer. Additionally, learn to forgive, stay positive, and seek every chance to laugh and stay young. Keep away all the negative feelings of guilt, anger, greed, regret, revenge, envy, and unhealthy ambition that keep you awake at night. They are your worst enemies that will precipitate you into your grave. Manifest the art of goodness, faithfulness, contentment, and fulfillment.

3. APPLY THE 100-HOUR RULE TO BUILD A WINNER'S RITUAL

Success is built on automation, a system. What would it take me to become a world-class keyboard player? You might ask how I can stop being goofy on the golf course. How long will it take me to be the best financial coach or orator? Some say it takes you years of practice to become an expert at your art; Michael Gladwell thinks 10,000 hours. Uhmm! That's some time. But there is a better way.

Anders Ericsson and collaborator Bill Chase, both PhD students, developed the idea that birthed writer Malcolm Gladwell's 10,000-hour theory outlined in his bestseller *Outliers*, though the idea was recanted later. Based on Anders and Bill's theory, it takes 100 hours of committed practice. So, If I practice for five hours a day playing golf, well, I could probably challenge Tiger Woods for a match. But not so fast. A hundred hours will demand my undivided attention, a sort of ritual to win. Based on this theory, it will only me four short weeks if I practice five hours a day and five days a week. That's it?

Though looking simple, the 100-hour rule is highly demanding. No matter how and how many hours you practice in a given time period, you must create a routine to stay consistent and disciplined. Successful people develop and follow a specific ritual in all aspects of their lives. At the corporate level, it is called the Standard Operating Procedures, a set of guidelines and procedures to implement specific business functions. Successful people have routines they follow daily at the individual level. Routines foster efficiency, orderliness, organization, and cost and timesaving.

American socio-economist, behavior scientist, and Landmark Research Group CEO Dr. Randal Bell has studied 5,000 people across several industries for over twenty-five years. In his book *Why Rich People Are Unhappy*, Dr. Randall discusses and suggests that what people need to stop losing and start winning is a tiny change. His team concluded that super-achievers have, develop, and follow routines that make them wealthy and happy.

4. OPERATE AS AN AUTOMATIC SYSTEM. SUPERACHIEVERS FOLLOW ROUTINES

The 5-AM Rule: According to the study, most affluent people wake up at 5:00 a.m., which *gives them the confidence that they have control over their lives*. They exercise early in the morning, invigorating their bodies and empowering their brain, conditioning them for high and positive energy, good humor, and self-confidence. The study indicates that those who regularly exercise, even for fifteen minutes daily, top the achievers' list. Dr. Bell adds that those with precise schedules for their day are 289 percent more likely to become millionaires than those without.

Automate yourself for consistency and scalability. Learn to value the small things. It is every drop that fills the river. When we hear about the heroic endeavors of successful superachievers, we have little time to understand that it was not all success. We often fantasize about their prowess, never connecting with the many disappointments and failures they went through. We know that Michael Jordan was one of the best NBA players the world has ever known. All we remember are the 32-point games he won. But do we remember, or do we even know that he did not always have success?

In his own words, Michael Jordan says, "I missed more than 9,000 shots in my career, have lost almost 300 games. On 26 occasions, I have been entrusted to take the game-winning shot, and I missed. I have failed over and repeatedly in my life. And that is why I succeed." Michael did not just meet success lying in bed and going to exercise when he felt like it. He disciplined himself to follow a regiment: a **Balanced Daily Routine**. Michael's trainer, Tim Grover, says that Michael was a very competitive athlete who wanted to always be at the top of his game. Hence, he would wake up at 5:00 AM daily to expose his body to strenuous exercise to stay fit. That heightened Michael's self-confidence to the point where the team could not recruit other stars because Michael said he did not need help to win games and championships.

5. DEVELOP AND FOLLOW A BALANCED DAILY ROUTINE

Working on your calling is a lifetime commitment. It is not something you do for a while and come back to whenever you find it convenient; neither can you put it on hold, nor must you put your entire life on hold to achieve it. If you have a family, you do not stop being a husband, wife, or parent. You must prioritize living a balanced life: do not neglect to spend time with your loved ones. You will be surprised how your children lived with you but never got to know you. The best way to become even more successful is to prioritize family togetherness, including your parents and relatives.

The self-made need efficiency to stay productive. They learn how to balance work-life and family life and make time to cater to their own emotional, spiritual, and physical well-being. One day, I prayed to seek balance in my life because I sensed my family complaining about my spending too much time working. My wife was particularly concerned. Realizing the unexpected consequence of workaholism, I arranged my schedule to only study, research, read, and write after everyone went to bed. It worked well. The only thing was that I had to forgo a few hours of sleep. I did not get much sleep. As I started meditating about balance, I discovered a secret: "You need to sleep well, eat well, think well, and exercise regularly."

Every successful person has a ritual and behaves as a system. How can Elon Musk run six distinct companies while still being efficient? How can Carlos Slim own over two hundred companies and not go insane? These people know how to plan, delegate, and follow routines that keep them on track. After analyzing the daily routine of several billionaires, here is my summary of what will help you live a balanced life as an entrepreneur with a family. Unfortunately, many who have not applied the plan either lost their families or are surrounded by people they are strangers to. Husband and wife sleep in the same bed but are disconnected; children grow up with their parents in the household without having a natural bond with them.

The Balance Daily Routine includes two key activities: (N) for Nurturing and (P) for Production. Wealth-builders do not do physical work; they organize and oversee the execution of result-producing actions. Some are managers and do the leg work of organizing the system and people to get things done; others are visionaries who delegate the execution of their vision to a manager or a team. In either case, they spend more time nurturing the growth of their venture. As such, they can work from anywhere in the world whenever necessary.

You should spend 80 percent of your time nurturing relationships and creating the conditions that facilitate your business's efficient and profitable operation. That includes qualifying, hiring, training, and empowering the right employees. That also means going out to find and meet with investors, partners, suppliers, bankers, and the media. Most importantly, an entrepreneur should spend most of her time building and entertaining client relations, bonding with them, and getting to know their needs, wants, and concerns. Spending your time in front of the computer will slow down your growth. Influential leaders are hand-shaking leaders: they are among the people. Successful business owners know to build this as a routine.

A wealth-builder is a maestro; you plan, research, connect, implement, and direct the flow of resources. You spend your time empowering intra-organizational production-maximizing activities and nurturing external relationships.

Highly successful people automate themselves and their activities for more efficiency. Some people have morning, daily, or evening routines at home, on the job, or when starting a project. Routines empower you for success. Above all, spend time nurturing the most critical asset in your enterprise: YOU.

Below, I compiled and summarized examples of daily routines of self-love many leaders, entrepreneurs, celebrities, and superachievers live by:

1. Daily prayer: spiritual connection with the divine
2. Daily meditation: connection with the inner self for personal power.
3. Daily physical exercise: emotional and physical balance
4. Daily reading/listening: food for creativity and brain energy and healing
5. Daily acts of kindness/giving/volunteering: boost a sense of self-worth.
6. Daily connection to laughter keeps you young and adds years to your life.

Several studies have been done about the mind and its impact on our lives. From The Secret, a bestseller written by Rhonda Byrne and made into an award-winning documentary, we learn that by the law of attraction, you attract what you focus your mind on into your life. According to this law, you are the product of your thoughts, as contended in the Bible, "As a man thinketh, so is he."

What could we achieve if we could tap into the power of execution and self-discipline? The most significant difference between success and failure is the ability to design and stick with a course of action as long as it helps achieve the set goal. No one can achieve outstanding results being distracted by so many things. The Jacks-of-all trade lad is less in demand than the expert-at-one-thing pal who profoundly understands a given area. Self-constraint is a must for every self-made, accepting the pain of forgoing instant gratification. Apply the power of sacrifice and see what you can achieve.

__LESSON LEARNED:__ Execution is a critical component of audacity, and this chapter highlights the importance of turning audacious ideas into tangible results. It explores strategies and approaches successful, audacious individuals use to execute their plans effectively. Readers are guided on *how to take action and bring their audacious visions to life.* Below is a model routine compiled from the habits of dozens of superachievers.

COACH GREB'S BALANCED DAILY ROUTINE – BDR

The BDR is an invitation to help you develop a routine that works for you and your specific circumstances. It is not a one-size-fits-all.

5:30 a.m. - *spiritual nurturing*: daily praise and meditation
6:00 - *body nurturing* - physical conditioning
6:30 – (*preparation*) - personal grooming/breakfast / (watch the news)
7:00 - (*travel to work*): *spiritual nurturing* - listening to powerful message
8:00 - *staff nurturing* - meetings/motivation/assignments.
11:00 - *client relation nurturing* - visit/call/lunch/act of kindness/gift
2:00 - (*production*): monitoring/walk-through
5:30 – (*closing*): evaluation/ planning
6:00 – (*travel home*): *mind nurturing*: listening to audiobooks.
7:00 - *body nurturing*: daily physical exercise
7:30 - *family nurturing*: family time/dinner/talk/ /kids' homework
9:00 - *kids relation nurturing*: reading to kids/family prayer time.
9:30- *spousal relation nurturing*: fun time together/intimate time/planning
10:00 - *mind/spiritual nurturing*: reading/planning/meditation.
10:30 p.m. – bedtime

TOTAL ALLOTTED: 24 HOURS

- **2 hours of spiritual nurturing** *(Meditation & Connecting with God)*
- **2 ½ hours with family** *(Nurturing family togetherness)*
- **2 ½ hours with self** *(Self-reflection and introspection)*
- **10 hours of work time** *(Production)*
- **7 hours of sleep** *(Holistic repair, rest, and rejuvenation)*

YOUR TURN – DAY 7: THE AUDACITY OF EXECUTION

Self-Reflection: **Are you typically good at holding yourself accountable for completing tasks and achieving goals?**

- Do you often struggle with procrastination or fear of taking action when faced with audacious goals?
- How organized and detailed are my plans for executing audacious ideas or projects?
- Have you learned from past failures or challenges related to execution, and how have these experiences shaped your approach to future endeavors?

Application: **Identify a specific goal or project you've been putting off due to fear or uncertainty. Describe it in detail.**

1. **Overcoming Procrastination:** What are the primary reasons for procrastination in your life? List them and brainstorm strategies to overcome them.
2. **Execution Plan:** Develop a step-by-step execution plan for your chosen goal. Include deadlines, milestones, and actionable steps.
3. **Accountability Partner:** Reach out to a trusted friend or mentor who can serve as your accountability partner during execution. Share your plan and commit to regular check-ins.

THE AUDACITY OF RESILIENCE

EVERY GOOD BATTLE IS FOUGHT TO THE END!

"And from the days of John the Baptist until now the kingdom of heaven suffers violence, and the violent take it by force."

– Matthew 11:12

> **JACK MA YUN, AN ENTREPRENEURIAL LEGEND, WHO GAVE REJECTION A NEW MEANING.**

You have the power to rise to greatness. Life is funny and can spit on you if you let it. I hear stories of kids who did not like school, or shall I say, whom school didn't like. Some struggled in elementary school and became great students in middle school; others rose to greatness in college after struggling in high school. Stories of people who had had hard times in college and rose to greatness are not uncommon. Conversely, some were brilliant students and obtained top grades, yet they amounted to nothing much in their lives. Therefore, while I teach my children to excel in school, I never miss the opportunity to empower them to express their natural talents. I expose them to whatever their passion is and let them blossom. I always remind them that school education is essential but not enough. Formative education must be complemented with transformative skills through practical training; otherwise, it becomes bland and worthless.

Jack Ma believes,

> *"The future is not made of competition of knowledge. It's the competition of creativity, imagination, learning, of independent thinking. The future is not knowledge-driven, it's wisdom-driven and experience-driven. If you think like a machine, you'll have a problem. For the past 20 years, we've made people look like machines. In the next 20 years, we'll make machines look like people."*

> SECRET CODE #8
> EXERCISE UNCOMMON TENACITY BEYOND THE FINISH LINE

The story you are about to hear will teach you how to rise from mediocrity to greatness. If you like shopping online and doing business with Chinese manufacturers, you've probably come across Alibaba.com, one of the world's largest shopping sites. If your curiosity took you a notch further, you would probably want to know about the force behind it, Jack Ma Yun, a man who gave rejection a new meaning. Jack Ma's experience with rejection can teach you one thing or two about persistence and resilience. In his own words, Jack got rejected in the following circumstances:

> *"I failed for funny things, like a key primary school test 2 times. I failed the middle school test 3 times [...] Then for three years I tried and failed University. After that, I applied to jobs and got rejected 30 times. I applied for KFC when it arrived in China. Twenty-four people came for the job, and 23 got it. I was the only one who didn't. I applied for Harvard; I got rejected ten times."*

Jack epitomizes the forcefulness the Bible writes about when it states, "And from the days of John the Baptist until now the kingdom of heaven suffers violence, and the violent take it by force" (Matthew 11:12). Life was funny with Jack, who eventually had the last laugh. In his life, Jack befriended rejection that wouldn't cut him some slack. When interviewed about his past, Jack jokingly remembered being the only one to be rejected for a position out of twenty-four applicants. Countless times, Jack was rejected for jobs, education, and funding but was never deterred. We have all been rejected. The difference with Jack is that he was mostly singled out:

- He applied for thirty jobs and got rejected for all of them.
- He was the only one rejected for a KFC job out of twenty-four applicants.
- Jack was the only one rejected for a cop job out of five applicants.
- He was rejected ten times when he applied to Harvard University.
- More than thirty venture capitalists rejected Jack Ma's startup idea.

Coming from a modest family, Jack Ma knew his future was not uncertain. He would end up living in poverty, like most of his schoolmates, those who repeatedly bullied him and tried to intimidate him because of his size at the time. Jack suffered painful humiliation as a schoolboy but eventually built his strength around his misfortune. Jack leveraged adversity and developed the character to accept rejection as a stepping stone to success.

Like Jack, you, too, have won many battles already. You may not remember, but if you take a little minute to reflect on your life, you will find a truckload of challenges you have defeated. Go ahead, mark a pause, and ponder for a minute.

Now tell me, can you count how many victories you have had so far? Countless. You are an overcomer, and no stronghold is formidable enough to stay in your way. Keep your eye off the size of your challenge and look ahead at the limitlessness of the possibilities in your hands to tame your challenge. Indeed, your mountain is weaker than you are.

After completing college, Jack Ma had no real prospect but to become a teacher. He took the job, not because he liked it, but because it was his only option, he thought. Jack Ma failed at things that you and I take for granted. He failed the middle school exam. He failed the college entrance exam. He ended up graduating from one of the lowest-ranked schools.

Jack was neither on the Dean's List nor a B-average student. So then, what audacity took him to apply to the world's most selective institution? Surprisingly, though he knew he did not stand a chance, Jack Ma dared to apply to the prestigious Harvard University. What do you think happened?

Yesterday is gone, and past failures do not determine future successes. "You've got to be kidding, Jack," you might sigh. That makes me wonder: "What?" With Harvard's extremely selective 5 percent admission rate, even brilliant students with top GPAs and stellar SAT scores get rejected. To this day, I have not come to an answer as to what went into Jack's mind when he dared to apply to Harvard, not once, not twice, but ten times. Did rejection amuse Jack, or was he trying to prove a point? Did he expect to be accepted after the ninth rejection letter?

Life is like a beautiful girl. Be gentle and know how to welcome her rejection with gentlemanliness. Keep being courteous. Rejection is not the last option. Remember that people who shape our world do things the average person might rate as weird. I do not think you need another picture to understand the character of uncommon people like Jack. How does one apply and get rejected to the same school ten times? Young people facing struggle and rejection can clone Jack's character of persistence.

Ambitious people do not let yesterday be in the way of tomorrow. Yesterday's failures do not determine tomorrow's successes. How can a person with failures and rejections of this magnitude expect more out of life? Many young people have been written off by their parents, teachers, society, and even themselves when they experience many struggles in school or their lives. These young people consider themselves doomed and opt for a full-fledged life of mediocrity and crime.

Jack's story is full of teaching. Though he did not like his job, he took it knowing there would come a day when he would part ways with it. Some people get stuck in a position they hate. Many people have jobs, not careers; they stick around for fear of losing a paycheck, grow old, and get angry at everyone. Others end up in a circus of job hopping, hoping to find a better job until they realize that any job situation is misery. Some stick around the job market until they grow physically and mentally obsolete. If you do not like your job, change it. If you can't find the promotion you expect, create it.

Jack, who had faced countless humiliating and disheartening rejections, did not just throw in the towel in self-pity. Instead, he decided to try something else. He did not want to continue teaching. Jack wanted to start something new. What would it be? A trip to the United States sparked Jack's imagination. At the start of the Internet era, American and Japanese companies had found another competition marketplace: the Internet. Jack did not like that his country, China, was nowhere to be found in this global marketplace. He created his own platform featuring Chinese companies to compete with the Japanese and American companies that had opened shop online.

TWENTY LESSONS EVERY SUPERACHIEVER HAS LEARNED

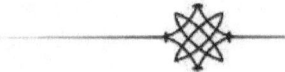

Weeping may endure for a night, but joy comes in the morning.

– Psalm 30:5

Why do most people prefer to take the easiest way out: to take a job and get paid, even if some assignments may involve rejection? Becoming an entrepreneur will cause you to experience several uncomfortable situations, many of which can be humiliating, demeaning, and hurtful.

1. LIFE WILL TEACH A LESSON BEFORE SHE LETS YOU RISE

The quality of a successful person lies not in what he has achieved but in the significance of the experience he has encountered and the power of the lesson he has learned and can teach others. Jack Ma toured the world, teaching not how to do the business of earning money but how to do the business of earning a meaningful living. You will not be successful until life has taught you a lesson you can teach others. One such lesson is: *Don't follow the money. Follow the honey, and money will follow you.*

If you want to see success in your life, pursue your passion the way a man pursues a woman he loves. He would die for her; he would give everything for her. He would give up everything just to be with her. The secret of self-made is that they do not pursue personal gain. They live and fight for a greater good, for which they accept to suffer rejection and humiliation.

Jack Ma did not have the brain of nerdy Elon Musk or Dr. Sergey Brin's parchment. So, how did he expect to make it? In our certificate-based society, we laud the geniuses and raise them above everyone else, except psychologist Angela Duckworth, author of *Grit: The Power of Passion and Perseverance.* She believes that talent and intelligence pale in front of grit. For Duckworth,

Grit is about working on something you care about so much that you're willing to stay loyal to it...it's doing what you love, but not just falling in love—staying in love."

Grit is a cocktail of perseverance, passion, resilience, determination, patience, persistence, and hard work flavored with self-belief. That's what Jack Ma demonstrated in his adventure. In 1999, Jack launched his Internet entrepreneurial career, and real challenges started. How would he raise capital? He started a capital campaign to meet with nothing but investors' vibrant rejections and ridicules, thirty of whom laughed at the idea. But Jack, who had tough skin, was not hurt to see his dream ridiculed. Determined as he promised himself to create the world's tenth-largest Internet company, Jack Ma Yun knew rejection was just part of his formatting as an entrepreneur.

The more Jack faced rejection, the more his fire to prove the naysayers wrong intensified. He knew he had the next big thing at his fingertips. How did he find out? Pure inspiration? No, Simple application of the law of life: the universe will deliver to your doors what you order through your mind, words, and actions and faithfully commit your life to. Jack Ma Yun was not a computer genius, unlike Jeff Bezos of Amazon or Sergey Bring of Google. He was an English alumnus passionate about meeting English-speaking people and serving as their guide and translator, using his only talent. He did not work in a sumptuous office but taught at a university for a meager salary. These awkward positions would serve as a point of entry into a world Jack had never expected: traveling to the United States on a Chinese government-sponsored trip and being hired to work on a government computing project.

2. DO NOT UNDERESTIMATE THE PEOPLE AROUND YOU.

In June 1999, Jack Ma started Alibaba with the people around him. Jack liked to empower the youth, so he formed a partnership of eighteen people, mainly made up of his students and friends. He selected his partners not based on their financial strengths but on their belief in the vision.

Surprisingly enough, after many unceasing courtships, life, the beautiful bride said a vribrant, "I do!" The business idea that was laughed at and rejected by more than thirty venture capitalists got a $25 million jackpot funding from American Goldman Sachs and Japanese conglomerate Softbank Group Corp in October 1999.

Jack never second-guessed himself. Despite the dizzying spiral of rejections, Jack continued to believe in his dream and could count on a team of committed people who tolerated his mistakes. Jack Ma saw his dream live on despite periods of turbulence and setbacks. Within three years, Alibaba – *along with its eighteen thieves* - brought its investors incredible dividends. The company made history when it went public in 2014. Alibaba.com broke the historical record with a $25 billion initial public offering, the highest at the time.

With a market capitalization in 2018 of $400 billion, Alibaba and its nine subsidiaries, including Alimama.com, Alipay, Taobao, and Lynx, are firmly implanted in the world's shopping culture. Today, Jack Ma is no longer a rejected man. He now has dinner with *the high class, the people who rejected him yesterday and* would never look in his direction. How funny can life be?

With a revolutionary perspective on business, Jack Ma believes that the *client is number one, followed by the employees and the stockholders*. Close to 49 percent of his company's employees are women. He believes that you should learn from your mistakes. Jack did not just land on the winning stage. He made countless mistakes and said that if he ever decided to write a book, he would title it *The 1001 Mistakes of Jack Ma*.

Jack Ma Yun's success story exemplifies every entrepreneur's challenges. Today, Jack Ma's $37 billion coffer makes him Asia's fifth-richest tycoon. This comfortable position will change soon with the growth of Alibaba Holdings. The audacity of a crazy dream from a nerd who has never coded or sold anything in his entire life, but his enthusiasm and faith to a united front of seventeen co-nerds, is now the marketplace that feeds the audacity of numerous e-commerce entrepreneurs worldwide.

3. YOU WILL BE REJECTED BEFORE YOU ARE ACCEPTED

Resilience gives you relentlessness. What about the unsung heroes whose stories of faith and self-belief make your tiny challenges pale in comparison? Do you know the man who was rejected 743 times before his first book was published? I mean *700* times, not seven times. Yes, that did happen to John Creasey, an English novelist who lived in the 1960s. He finally ended up writing over 500 books under more than twenty-eight pseudonyms.

Another remarkable story is Joanne Kathleen Rowling, known under the pen name J. K. Rowling, author of the acclaimed novel published in 1997 in the United Kingdom as *Harry Potter and the Philosopher's Stone*. Published the following year in the United States under the title *Harry Potter and the Sorcerer's Stone*, *Harry Potter* is a fantasy made into an award-winning film. After her divorce, J. K. Rowling fell to the bottom of poverty. Putting food on the table was a challenge, let alone acquiring the bare minimum, such as a computer, to type and get her story published as a book. The book was rejected over ten times but did not deter J.K. Rowling. She kept sending it to different publishers, who still would not even look at it.

Finally, a small publisher who noticed her daughter's interest in the story gave J. K. Rowling a chance, the chance that changed her life. The rest is history. J. K. Rowling became the ninth best-selling author of all time, with over 500 million copies sold worldwide. In 2011, J.K. Rowling appeared on the prestigious *Forbes* billionaire list with a net worth of $1.140 billion. In 2017, the same magazine reported her as the highest-paid writer for that year, with an income of ninety-five million US dollars. Did you say, "From rags to riches"?

4. YOU WILL FAIL MULTIPLE TIMES BEFORE YOU SUCCEED

Abraham Lincoln's name resonates when discussing the people who impacted America the most. Is this because he was the one who presided over the country during the turning point in American democracy, or is it because of the many failures he went through? President Abraham Lincoln's life evokes nothing but resilience. The man endured several business and political failures until he was finally elected to the country's highest position. That makes me give failure a new definition, a new meaning.

So, what is your definition of *failure*? Who has not failed? We start failing at the start of our lives. Do you know a baby who sat down correctly the first time and did not fall? Which one of you started walking and did not stumble? But it happened eventually. The baby turns into a toddler and becomes uncatchable. She runs down the alley and the mall alley, raising her parents' blood pressure over the danger of bumping into something. Your wealth-building scheme will fail multiple times.

After reading about the lives of superachievers, I no longer consider my shortcomings as failures. My new definition of *failure* is "not meeting the intended standards." Failing does not mean that the student does not have what it takes to pass the exam. He fell short of the standard for that specific exam on that particular day. So do not beat yourself up when failing your first twenty attempts. *Keep trying until you succeed at last, for after so many attempts, success has no choice but to give in.* How resilient are you?

HOW JAMES DYSON'S TENACITY FORCED HIS WAY THROUGH TO WEALTH

Your luck may come from adversity, don't we say? Don't hate your frustration. It might have a message or a billion-dollar envelope for you. What kind of vacuum cleaner do you have in your house today? If you have the kind that does not need a bag, you may be interested in its story. As you can probably imagine at this point in reading this book, entrepreneurs fail before they succeed. Sir James Dyson failed miserably, rejected by his fellow citizens, out of sorts, *and out of country*.

5. YOU WILL LOSE BEFORE YOU WIN

In 1978, British industrialist Sir James Dyson got frustrated with his vacuum, which would clog up and not let out the dust. Instead of magnifying the frustration, he saw a bright light run through his mind as he screamed, "Eureka!" Using his experience working with industrial cyclones, Dyson thought he had his eureka moment when he invented a bagless vacuum cleaner.

But wait! There went the second frustration. Contrary to Dyson's excitement, the European market was not impressed by what would be the next big thing. The project failed miserably in Europe, where no salespeople would sell the product. However, tenaciously, Dyson took the product to Japan and developed strategies to sell his bagless vacuum.

Dyson's tenacity paid off. After over 5000 prototypes, the project received two awards for the product in 1986. Today, Dyson vacuums are present in sixty-five countries and employ over 1000 engineers. The company is considered the Apple of the home appliance industry for its focus on innovation and creativity. According to the *New York Times*, Dyson earmarks and reinvests close to 15 percent of its revenue in research and development.

What matters is not whether you fall but what you learn from your fall and how you pick yourself up and run. You will lose all your savings in a failing business, as Soichiro Honda did when he emptied his savings and pawned his wife's jewelry for a business that kept failing.

You are undoubtedly enjoying the technological prowess of an iPhone or iPad today. If Steve Jobs had not picked himself up after being fired from his own company by the CEO he hired to run the company, we would probably still be using the old cell phone system, or maybe not. By his own account, being fired from Apple was the best thing that ever happened to him. Steve Jobs went on to create NeXT, a company that he sold to Apple, which brought him back as the CEO of the company he had created. Inspired wealth-builders are tenacious and will not let go smoothly.

6. YOUR VALUE WILL BE TESTED IN YOUR MOMENT OF TRUTH

Your moment of truth gives you a chance to uncover your identity. Honda is a company that believes in the power of shared value. **The Honda Way** is a corporate culture that, over the years, has evolved and endured. Based on absolute values and beliefs, the Honda Way provides a strong company identity and guides behavior. What are your values? What do you stand for? What is your identity? For people to follow you, they must know who you are, and you must know who you are. Your values and beliefs determine your actions, interactions, and reactions. Soichiro Honda once said,

> *Many people dream of success. I believe that success can be achieved only through repeated failure and self-analysis. Success is only one percent of your work, and the rest—bold overcoming of obstacles. If you are not afraid of them, success will come to you itself.*

7. AFTER YOU HAVE FAILED AND FAILED, SUCCESS HAS NO OTHER CHOICE BUT TO GIVE IN

"You can get it if you really want." When I was a kid, I heard a song by Jamaican reggae singer Jimmy Cliff, which shaped my view of life to this day. The song says, *"You can get it if you really want, but you must try, try, and try till you succeed at last."* The reason many people fail is that they expect to see success in the first few trials. If things do not work, they turn to something else. That's a big mistake!

All great companies have had their zones of turbulence, sometimes altering the corporate culture. An efficient leader knows how to adapt and restructure to carry out the vision. They are prepared to fail, fail, and fail some more. But in the end, people will hold them up high, hailing their prowess. Success is in the challenge. Do not quit too soon. Sales representatives know it takes at least seven calls or rejections before making a sale. An entrepreneur is a salesperson. You must accept rejection and fail many times before succeeding, and that's all that matters.

8. YOUR PLANS WILL NOT WORK AS EXPECTED

You will need to be flexible. Business is like any game. You must, tactically and strategically, adapt your strategy constantly to meet the changes based on the game and your opponent's strategy and moves. You may play defense or offense. My biggest mistake as a rookie entrepreneur was confusing dreams with reality. I learned the hard way that you must outgrow your dream, or it will drown you. *There is a time to fantasize and a time to actualize.* When my wife and I were planning our business operation, we were so much in love and so optimistic and emotional about our business that we neglected to include the worst-case scenario and prepare for it.

You must often expect things not to work out as planned. In our business, my wife and I thought hiring great employees on paper, training them, and motivating them would prepare them for great productivity. That was a mistake. As entrepreneurs, we had to swallow the bitter pill we may be tempted to refuse. We failed to realize that the employee we hired to help our business had no interest in our company. When being hired, employees have motives that have nothing to do with their own. No matter how much we stressed our policies, we still found employees who could care less.

In that case, what do you do? Identify what did not work and go back to the drawing board. Firing your people is simply the worst solution. In our industry, customers get personal with our employees. A high turnover rate is merely an excellent way to drive your customers away into the hands of your former employees, now turned next-door competitors. Savvy entrepreneurs and leaders are the ones who know how to listen to the market and the environment and adapt.

You are not the only player in your environment. Several forces with competing and mutually exclusive interests are playing for or against you. You will rarely succeed if you are not flexible enough to adapt to the changing market conditions. In the post-pandemic era, brick-and-mortar companies realized that business had moved online. Customers are now comfortable perusing through the alleys of an online shop to order their next glamorous dresses for the VIP event. Many retailers closed the mall shops to develop an outstanding presence online; others have kept both.

Fast-food restaurants fought tooth and nail to keep their employees underpaid, to a point the US Congress has tried to revisit minimum wage, not without an active lobbying from corporate Ameerica. However, following COVID-19, when everyone became suddenly rich and discovered the secret of making money, many emplooyees threw away their aprons, quit, and booed their bosses. As a result, fast-food chains, warehouses, and many other employers were, for the first time in a million years, confronted with employee shortage. In the aftermath of the pandemics, restaurant managers started doubling employee pay to entice them to sign on and stay. It was not uncommon to see street signs posting $1000-3000 hiring bonuses.

Adapt or suffer. Realizing the power shift, corporate America had to swallow the bitter pill; employees now had the upper hand. Companies originally hostile to pay raise now started posting high wages when they realized everyone understood the game of wealth: **Do Your Own**. Everybody is selling something on Amazon, eBay, Shopify, or whatnot.

You do not control the local, national, and global markets. You do not know what can come from people, the supply and demand mechanism, the political environment, or the legal system.

9. SUCCESS LOVES TO BE COURTED: YOU WILL HAVE TO FIGHT FOR YOUR DREAM

A dream that does not require challenging work is probably not a dream after all. I started feeling slightly scared when I failed my first and second ventures. I was embarrassed to even talk about any new ideas. And yet, I needed an honest critic. I knew I could find one in my wife. She is very pragmatic and will tell me what is wrong with my plan, though I have often disagreed with her.

Initially, I thought I needed to hear what other people say to validate my ideas, but then I realized something: the ideas I talked the most about never got started. What was it? Well, it is psychological. I spent too much time reassessing them in words and became weak in action. Aware of this, I decided to be quiet about my ideas. I just started them without blowing a trumpet about them.

My most successful business surprised people and taught me a life lesson. All great successes have failed several times. I understood that success is a great teacher. If you meet success easily, it is probably not your lifetime dream. You will have to fight and face hardship, frustration, discouragement, desertion, disloyalty, unfairness, and mental distress to achieve your goal. You will sometimes feel like giving up. You will feel lonely—all bright minds do. You will feel abandoned by the people you expect to have your back. You may be overwhelmed by family issues and other types of responsibilities. You will not have everything in place and may feel overwhelmed by fear, worry, anxiety, and discouragement. If all these discomforting feelings and events happen to you, remember that they are not here to break you. On the contrary, they are here to build you up and prepare you for a promotion.

Which good teacher would promote her students to the next grade without testing them? What do failing schools do? They pass failing students or make the exams so easy you can pass them without looking at the paper. Life is a set of ongoing tests. All those who do not have to take the test of life are six feet under. A good student expects to be tested proudly and impatiently waits for the day of the exam. I have throughout my never-ending student life.

Superachievers are not walking on the red carpet. Jeff Bezos was in the middle of a divorce when his poor decisions tore his family apart. Jeff's affair with Fox 11 TV anchor Laura Sanchez, then married to Patrick Whitesell, was made public by the *National Enquirer* magazine. Although Jeff wanted to fire back for extorsion, he quickly retracted, fearing the story could spill over and stain his image, consequently downgrading his company stock price and sending his and his shareholders' wealth into free fall.

10. YOU WILL STEP ON BIG TOES

"You are not welcome here!" your competitors will tell you. In the competitive business world, breaking the rules and creating a dislike towards you is not uncommon. Sometimes, looking at elected officials, I wonder how you run a country where you know half of the population hates you. I looked at poor President Obama and President Trump and concluded that not everybody would like you. If you have skin-deep feelings, you'd better find a job out of the spotlight. As a leader and business owner, you will be despised for one reason or another. Steve Jobs's staff hated him. The US Congress is not unconcerned by some of Mark Zuckerberg's business dealings. Dr. Mohammad Hunus's selfless microfinance program to help alleviate poverty in Bangladesh has been harshly criticized.

People will not always like how you do business; someone will find you unfair; others will even despise you for no reason. Competitors, employees, customers. Clients, the government, or civil society will come against you one way or another. So, be prepared to receive them. Why does Google's parent company, Alphabet, jump on every small company if not to thwart competition?

When a new gas station opens across the streets, do the existing owners go with a baked cake to welcome the newcomer into the neighborhood? Absolutely not! Remember that your presence bothers and irritates someone to whom you have done nothing. The new gas station is viewed as a threat to the one across the street. Why does Google fear Amazon so much? Amazon has beaten Google in its backyard regarding product search: 60 percent of product searches are done on Amazon.com. Google's CEO Eric Schmidt does not see this well, nor does he welcome Apple's rising competition against its Android, though Google currently leads the market by a wide margin of 67 percent.

11. YOU WILL BE BROKEN AND HUMBLED

Derision and humiliation are typical challenges superachievers face, and billionaire Michael Jordan's story is no different. When Michael Jordan went for basketball tryouts for the Emsley A. Laney High School varsity team at age fifteen, the coach told him his 5'10 height was too short. This rejection crushed Michael, but did not let it stop him. The humiliation of not seeing his name on the selected player roster became a source of motivation for him to keep exercising harder. Eventually, we all know what happened to his career.

The 32-point-a-game sky surfer Michael racked All-Star, MVP titles, six championship titles, and a hefty bank account to prove it. Billionaire Michael went from being rejected to the highest-career-earning basketball player in history. He became an NBA legend and made over a billion-dollar fortune in his career. What makes people like Michael Jordan so successful in their careers? *They are passionate about exercising their God-given talents.*

A student once said he did not understand why some of these people who had all their wealth were not enjoying it as he thought they should. Billionaire Warren Buffett is reported to still live in a house he bought for less than $32,000 in 1958, now worth $1.43 million. Zuckerberg wears the same simple hood daily.

Success must be humbling, not boastful. My reply was simple. Not all wealthy people behave like Warren Buffett. Bill Gates, Jeff Bezos, and many others have invested in properties, jets, and luxury. Still, I added that success that does not humble you is not real success. Superachievers do not blow their own trumpets. They do not take themselves as seriously as the world seems to take them.

Most successful people seem humbled by success; they will not say they met success quickly. Prosperity is not measured in what you have gotten but in what you have become. Wealth is not about material possessions but how you see and do things. That's why successful people care so much more about their public image and personas than all the jets or mansions in which they are submerged.

How much do you value yourself? You must continue being humble to serve as a desirable brand, not a nauseating, repulsive, cocky pal who gets on everybody's nerves. It is only through humility that you can brand yourself. Once you have a name, you can sell paper flowers, and a horde of fools will line up to buy them. Why does Air Jordan sell multiple the price of its competing brands? Michael skillfully branded himself; most of his wealth came from his endorsement and goodwill. You have become wealthy due to your battles on the way to success. Battles will humble you, for you will lose some and gain some. But in the end, you will have gained more.

12. ACHIEVING YOUR DREAM CANNOT BE A SECOND JOB OR A HOBBY

One thing I regret in my life is not taking the jump sooner. I spent over thirty years of my life chasing subsistence over existence. I know my passion has always been to develop and run businesses. I enjoy creating companies.

Pursuing your dream requires commitment and endurance. Wealth-building through active or passive investments requires mental stamina, a substantial amount of money, and an adequate amount of time. You may not initially have all the capital you need – rarely anyone does - but you have authority over what you do with your time. You can rent it or use it for yourself. That demands a lot of critical decision-making, the core job of any entrepreneur. When do you draw the line between being on payroll to earn the seed to cover your overheads until you can make it or taking a leap of faith and jumping into the unknown? There is no panacea. You know yourself and know how much pain you are willing to take. Either solution has merit and opportunity costs.

13. GETTING YOUR DREAM FUNDED IS NO CAKEWALK

Nobody builds wealth with his own money. Small, medium, and large entities all have the same need: external funding. Government bodies cannot function if they cannot borrow by issuing bonds on the international markets. That is how the USA got indebted to China. So, the issue of funding is not specific to startups. The only challenge is that starting a company requires you to be the guarantor. You will have to put up your own savings and credit in the early years of your venture. It usually takes five to ten years to see the fruit of your venture. Be forewarned. Any long trip starts with preparation. Why do 70 percent of businesses fail, as commonly stated? Unpreparedness.

Some people quit their jobs on a whim to start a business or, as they say, "Be my own boss." You do not start a business to pacify your grudge or to prove a point. You start a business because you want to solve a problem. That demands planning and resources. You should never start a business without assessing your chances of survival, let alone success. Do not just copy what you hear. People who decide to strike it on their own have stashed money away in retirement-like coffers before they could even think of external funding unless they chose their parents' right at birth. Jeff Bezos did not leave D.E. Shaw to struggle in the streets of Seattle, Washington. He had a solid plan and a mere $300,000 loan from Dad Miguel Bezos.

Unless you are lucky like Jeff Bezos or Donald Trump, whose father handed him, as he said, a small $1,000,000 loan, you need to clearly understand that your chance of getting funded is close to winning the jackpot. No one will fund you until you prove you produce cash flow in your dream business. I frequently hear entrepreneurs with brilliant ideas and business plans looking for bank funding and investors. Think again. Which fool would hand over the keys of his Lamborghini to a teenager? Who would invest in a business whose owners have not yet proven their abilities to produce money? A lot of dreamers abandon their ideas when they cannot find funding. Only a few startups get funded through banks, investors, or public funds. You must learn to create and prove your cash flow to potential lenders or investors. Even the public Small Business Administration loan guarantees require a verifiable stream of cash inflow.

STARTUP FUNDING STATISTICS

- Over 77 percent of ventures start with the owner's personal savings.
- Thirty-three percent of small businesses are started with $5,000 or less.
- The average small business requires about $10,000 of startup capital.
- Only 0.05 percent of startups raise venture capital.
- The median age for companies seeking a seed funding round is three years.
- Startups with two co-founders rather than one raise 30 percent more capital.

Source: Fundera: Meredith Wood, February 2020

You cannot rely on someone else to fund your dream. You must rely on yourself, as presented in the statistics above. Cash flow is critical. It is the name of the game of wealth. Learn to create a cash flow stream, no matter how small; this keeps the peace at home and within. Why did I linger on a job with which I knew I had no business meddling? It was a strategic decision. When I decided to no longer work for anyone, I drafted a five-year plan and followed it. It did not work to the dot, but it did help me through the years. My business was not generating enough cash flow to sustain itself.

Others may prefer to continue working until they are comfortable enough to transition. In either case, you need to increase your work hours. Quit any time thief and focus on anything that helps your baby grow. An entrepreneur must commit at least seventy to eighty hours weekly to achieve her dream. In the initial years of your startup, all you need is bread. Forget about butter. Accept the temporary frustration of a boss you cannot stand. Use him for your gain. Accept the pain of being on someone's payroll until you build your own.

The common mistakes that make most start-ups fail are *inexperience and lack of resources*. Inexperience is the lack of skills required to start and run a business. The crucial reason for failure is the shortage of capital and time resources. Many people think they can continue being their usual selves, treat their business part-time, and expect significant returns. This is what I thought fifteen years ago. A start-up is like a baby. You do not feed your baby when it is convenient for you. If you leave your baby in her crib to go and babysit other people's babies, by the time you return, I am not sure you will still have a baby.

No matter what choice you make, know when to call it quits. You must give time to your venture. The more you focus on growing, the faster the fruit becomes ripe. Even if you are dedicated, it is practically impossible to grow your business and build your wealth while building other people's wealth.

The conclusion I drew from my analysis of most entrepreneurial ventures is that entrepreneurs take a leap of faith. They retire from their day employment to focus on their venture and let it grow. That is what Jeff Bezos did when he left a lucrative and prosperous career as the youngest vice president at D. E. Shaw. According to the adage, you cannot pursue two rabbits simultaneously.

14. ALONE, YOU WILL GO NOWHERE; SHARE THE PIE

Two are better than one because they have a good reward for their labor. For if they fall, one will lift his companion. But woe to him who is alone when he falls, for he has no one to help him up.

— Ecclesiastes 4:9–10

Why do businesses with two or more owners get funded more than those started by solopreneurs? Two heads are better than one. Bill Gates and Paul Allen united their passion to create Traf-O-Data, only to see it die and become Microsoft, which lives today. Steve Jobs and Steve Wozniak brought their genius together to start Apple Computer. Sergey Brin and Larry Page joined their brains together to create Google. Mark Zuckerberg and four other Harvard students sweated together to birth Facebook. YouTube was founded by three young men: Chad Hurley, Steve Chen, and Jawed Karim. What pattern do we see here? Business is synergy. People with different yet complementary skills united their geniuses in most businesses created in our technology-directed society.

Though very competitive, business builders can tap into the support of venture capitalists willing to take a risk on the visionary entrepreneurs' dreams. Mike Thiel of Sequoya Capital and founders of companies like Google, Yahoo, Microsoft, and many familiar names are the major players in the arena that have permeated the establishment of great ventures. Y Combinator is a leading platform that brings together investors and dreamers. The platform has birthed such companies as Airbnb and DoorDash. Not every idea finds funding, yet if it is well crafted and presented to the right investors, it may be one of the few that get funded.

Overall, you cannot start and run a viable business by yourself. You must rely on other people's skills, funds, and talents.

15. DO NOT SABOTAGE YOUR BABY THROUGH NEGLECT AND MISMANAGEMENT

An entrepreneur is a solution seeker known for a character that is a cocktail of uncommon wisdom and talent. A true entrepreneur is focused on and lives for her venture. Most day entrepreneurs do not understand the concept of long-range thinking. They start sabotaging the venture by engaging in a lavish spending lifestyle as soon as the business starts earning some money. These entrepreneurs do not understand the difference between profit and capital. They confuse their personal finance with company finance. Ultimately, they kill their baby in the womb, and the business fails because of a lack of adequate funding.

Neglect and mismanagement will kill your venture. Some entrepreneurs, also known as **absentee owners,** are too busy with other stuff, so they neglect the business. A client of mine suffered this the hard way. He had a cigarette and spirits shop as well as a day job. He did not have the material time to control his business. Business requires planning, delegating, and controlling. If you cannot control what is happening in the business, you will lose money or the business. My client reacted too late when he learned that his former employee had siphoned the shop money to open his own competing shop a few miles away.

If you leave your business in the hands of employees and do not set up the proper control system, you will be forced to close. Many business owners fail to implement the appropriate actions, such as customer relations, employee management and empowerment, quality control, marketing, sound financial management, and proper sales and data management. Ultimately, the business does not survive the founder's folly and dies.

16. THROW YOUR BREAD AT THE FACE OF THE WATER

Every seed sown in *the gr*ound must die and rot before bringing the plant that will bear the next fruit. **Before you win, you will lose**. Risk correlates with reward. What is rewarded if not for the effort and risk you take? Is risk-taking a commendable attitude?

You have probably heard stories of millionaires who risk their life savings on ventures that have yet to be proven. Many Americans invested in dot-com startup ventures during the Internet frenzy of the early 2000s. Many of them were not lucky. They lost their savings when the investments went bust, but these investors did not run away. They were resilient and persevered. They rose from their ashes and are now investing in other thriving companies, using more wisdom and caution.

Those who invested in startups like Facebook, Google, and many other thriving ventures have seen millions pouring into their coffers. If you had invested $10,000 in Facebook in 2004, today, you would have made almost five times your investment, racking a whopping $49,000 in 2019. Not bad. What about those who took a greater risk, like serial investor Peter Thiel, who invested in many technology startups?

Peter Thiel and his investors did not complain when their $500,000 investment in Facebook, the first investment the company ever received, brought them $1 billion. I bet no bottle of Champagne was left *unpopped* on May 18, 2012, when Facebook went public and made history with an IPO (Initial Public Offering) market capitalization of $500 billion. Those who bet with Zuckerberg from the dorm to the boardroom became millionaires overnight. That is the sweetened magic of investing.

Inspired wealth-builders do lose money but don't quit. They are not rolling out the red carpet. The question is not whether you will fall - because you will. The question is, "What will you do when you fall?" The key is to pick yourself up and try again and again until you succeed.

17. YOU WILL ENDURE PAIN

When I was a kid, I did not like watching boxing. I thought it was a violent sport that was not worth showing or enjoying, but this sport taught me the most instructive lesson. When Mohamed Ali (aka Cassius Clay), the prominent multiple-time champion, set foot in the ring, he knew one thing. Despite his assurance of winning the match, he was sure he would take some heavy blows from his opponent, but he did not let this deter him.

Every boxer knows he will endure pain, but he is not thinking of the pain. What matters most is the glorious moment when the referee raises his hand to declare him a champion. I remember boxer Mike Tyson biting Holyfield's ear during a boxing match in June 1997. Despite the pain and a bruised and bloody face, Holyfield was elated when declared a champion. Every winner endures pain. David suffered, the Israelites experienced pain, and every entrepreneur goes through the painful hurdles of success.

18. LIFE WILL NOT ALWAYS BE FAIR GAME TO YOU

In the business world, you will seek hungry sharks, conniving hares, and overpowering lions. All they want is food at any cost; the end justifies the means for many. Hence, do not expect things and people to be fair, honest, and loyal. Friends will become foes, and foes will become friends. Circumstances will not always be in your favor, even when you believe they should. You will be surprised and think everything's unfair. The truth is that the rich get richer, and the poor get poorer. Why? What do the rich do that the poor do not do? Should we not exercise compassion toward people experiencing poverty? God gives everyone ideas, but few know how to hone them and use them for beneficial purposes.

19. DO NOT UNDERESTIMATE HUMBLE BEGINNINGS

"A journey of a thousand miles begins with a single step."
— Lao Tzu

Everything big starts small. Greatness follows the law of compounding. Every success starts small. A business must be scalable to reach its optimum potential. It will run along a not-so-smooth growth path. Stagnation and rollercoaster growth are undesirable as they create imbalance and chaos.

Some people expect sudden growth and undeserved achievement. Many companies you admire have had years of humble beginnings, learning, setbacks, and struggles. BackRub was started by two nerds in a garage in 1996 when Sergey Brin and Larry Page decided to create a better search engine. Renamed Google in 1997, the $1745-billion giant controls 70 percent of the world search engine market. But that is not all. The company miraculously birthed its own parent, Alphabet. Voracious parent company Alphabet buys and acquires companies like you would buy groceries. In August 2021, Alphabet controlled a portfolio of 232 companies, including Motorola Mobility.

You might be bemused by Google's size today and wonder, "How in the world is that possible?" Google is not the only company with impressive growth. Amazon, Apple, and Microsoft all started small. They were not born that way. Many self-made understand the concept of baby steps. They start in their parents' garage, then their apartment, then a shared location until they can afford the sumptuous glass-door offices. Elon Musk and his brother Kimbal made their office their dormitory. It pays little to haste. Many who wanted to be in the fast lane either left the course or had a crash. Step by step, you will build your nest if you have faith.

20. IF YOU HAVE GRIT, THE PROMISE WILL NOT GO UNACCOMPLISHED.

Actors Jim Carey, Arnold Schwarzenegger, and Sylvester Stallone did not just meet sudden success. President Abraham Lincoln did not immediately become president of the United States at the first trial. Sam Walton did not build Walmart into a world giant on a speedway. The global retail leader started as a street corner shop in Rogers, Arkansas. Biblical figure Abraham did not become the father of the multitude overnight, even though he was promised thriving descendants. Despite the time it took for the promise to manifest, Patriarch Abraham never doubted that God's promise would come to pass. He expectantly continued praising God until God gave him his son Isaac.

What would come of our world if many of us could exhibit a generous dose of grit? The Holy Book is replete with examples of steadfastness. How do you lead a people with stiff neck if you do not have the patience of Moses? How do you continue convincing a stubborn leader like Pharaoh to release God's people if you lack endurance? How did Jesus follow through with the celestial plan to redeem to the price of his life if he didn't have supernatural determination?

The examples of Jack Ma, J.K Rowlings, and many others teach us the profit of resilience: if you have grit, you can conquer the world, for as Apostle Paul put it in 1 Corinthians 15:58, *"Therefore, my beloved brethren, be steadfast, immovable, always abounding in the work of the Lord, knowing that your toil is not in vain in the Lord."*

> ***LESSON LEARNED:*** *This chapter focuses on resilience, revealing how audacious individuals overcome setbacks, failures, and adversity. It shares inspiring stories of resilience, emphasizing that audacious journeys are often filled with challenges. You need to develop resilience to persevere on your audacious path.*

YOUR TURN – DAY 8: THE AUDACITY OF RESILIENCE

Self-Reflection: How do you typically react when faced with adversity or setbacks in your life or work?

- Do you tend to view challenges as opportunities for growth and development, or do you become discouraged easily?
- Who are your life's critical sources of emotional support, and how do they help you navigate challenging times?
- What self-care practices do you currently incorporate into your routine to enhance your resilience and overall well-being?

Application: Consider the most challenging experiences in your life. What were the key factors that allowed you to bounce back and persevere?

1. **Growth Mindset:** Embrace a growth mindset by viewing setbacks and obstacles as opportunities for growth. Write down a recent challenge and explore how it can be a source of growth.
2. **Support Network:** Identify individuals in your life who provide emotional support during difficult times. Reach out to them and express your gratitude.
3. **Self-Care Commitment:** Create a self-care routine that includes activities for physical, mental, and emotional well-being. Schedule these practices into your daily or weekly routine.
4. **Resilience Journal:** Start a resilience journal to document your challenges, strategies for coping, and personal growth. Regularly reflect on your journey.

THE AUDACITY OF GIVING

RELEASE THE MAGIC OF GIVING

> *"You give but little when you give of your possessions. It is when you give of yourself that you truly give."*
>
> — Kahlil Gibran

> **BILLIONAIRE DAVID RUBENSTEIN, A VESSEL OF GIVING.**

I really hope that the philanthropy movement is seen not just as wealthy people giving money away but wealthy people giving away their time, their energy, and their ideas.
– David Rubenstein

People with a scarcity mindset see giving as losing away; those with a prosperity mindset see it as attracting abundance. It takes audacity to give, and the stories of American self-made and their adherence to the principle of giving will surprise you.

At a Q&A session at Oxford University, United Kingdom, David Rubenstein made an introductory speech that stunned the audience. Co-founder of The Carlyle Group, a world-renowned leverage buyout firm, David is used to turning dirt into gold. David's success story is no different from countless others. Could you imagine that this man did not always walk on *Happy Highway?* As he told his story, I learned that billionaires faced some of the same life realities as I did. Billionaires are people just like you and me. They face the same challenges and setbacks as you do, but what sets them apart is that they rise from the ashes and move to become success stories. On their way to the top, they fall many times, and many times, they pick themselves up. Legendary entrepreneur billionaire Sam Walton of Walmart had it even better when he remembered: *"I had to pick myself up and get on with it, do it all over again, only even better this time."*

In his own words, David Rubenstein said that he began his career as an unsuccessful lawyer. He did not like it much, or should I paraphrase him, as he jokingly put it: the clients thought he should find another job. He was then hired as an aide to President Carter, but when the latter turned in the key to the White House at the close of this short four-year term, David packed up his stuff and headed for the streets. With binoculars in one hand and a bag of hope in the other, he searched through the long, twisted avenues of bumps, humps, and opportunities.

After shuffling through many hurdles, David settled for a career as a leveraged buyout investor. He bought struggling companies with his partners, fixed them up, and sold them for a profit, the same way real estate investors would flip houses. David Rubenstein made a considerable fortune in that business. As a wealthy man, he thought, what do I do with all this money? I can pass it on to my heirs, bequeath it to my estate, or give it away during my lifetime. People with a *rich mindset* would have thought differently: I, me, myself, or my family. But no, those with a *wealth mindset* leave a family legacy but more so for the general causes.

A signer of the Bill and Melinda Gates Foundation's Giving Pledge, David is proud to say,

I give away about 50 percent of my income, so my, you know, desire to give back to the country is pretty strong and I intend to give away a lot more. I've signed the giving pledge with Warren Buffett and Bill Gates, and I intend to give away the bulk of my money.

SECRET CODE #9
BE A PASSIONATE GIVER AND A VESSEL OF POSITIVE IMPACT

"The sole meaning of life is to serve humanity."
— **Leo Tolstoy**

You may not understand why the most prominent wealthy people you know prefer to leave just a tiny portion of their wealth to their children. Wealth-builders want to teach their children to fend for themselves and not live like parasites. Self-made millionaires and billionaires toiled for their money and will frown at the beggar in the street but give lavishly to noble causes that help people help themselves. Hence, education, scientific research, and health are the primary beneficiaries of charity giving. Prominent billionaires, such as Mark Zuckerberg, Bill Gates, and many others, plan to give most of their wealth away to charity during their lifetime.

David decided to enter philanthropy to, as he said, help his country fund education and medical research, providing funds to the Bill and Melinda Gates Foundation. Can you imagine how challenging life would be when you can afford the things you want to have? Being purposelessly rich is more challenging than being poor. You must strive to maintain yourself in the rich person's position, which leads to dissatisfaction and the desire for more riches. Having too much is meaningless and worthless if you cannot find an avenue to bless others in need. No wonder most people enter philanthropy after they have built wealth. It is the human thing to do and the wisest course of action, especially when research proves that giving adds joy, happiness, and years to your life.

Rubenstein emphatically explained that 85 percent of the Forbes billionaire list came from modest backgrounds. Many of them grew up in blue-collar, low-income, and dysfunctional families. Why did these people succeed? They challenge themselves to do something with their lives to be different from their parents. They want to get out of poverty to do what their parents failed to do, as opposed to wealthy kids who do not have the same drive because they lack practically nothing.

WEALTH-BUILDING IS NOT ROCKET SCIENCE, BUT IT IS A SCIENCE.

> *"But this I say: He who sows sparingly will also reap sparingly, and he who sows bountifully will also reap bountifully. So, let each one give as he purposes in his heart, not grudgingly or of necessity, for God loves a cheerful giver. And God can make all grace abound toward you, that you, always having all sufficiency in all things, may have an abundance for every good work."*
>
> **– Corinthians 9:6-8**

Since you've read so far, let me give you the four simple secrets of American self-made:

- Find your calling and pursue it with all your mind, heart, and soul.

- Be honest in your dealings. Cheat no one, but fairly deal with anyone.
- Do not pursue money; commit your life to solving people's problems.
- Make money, share it, and send it to work to grow it more.

Mark a pause and ponder: Where does America's wealth come from? America is the wealthiest nation on earth because Americans are born-givers. *They give themselves away to resolutely plow their piece of land with hard work and share the fruit of their harvest with God—t*he principle of giving dictates that he who cheerfully gives abundantly is he who receives abundantly. More than anyone, Americans have a high work ethic but also understand the biblical principle of giving to the widow, orphan, stranger, and destitute through organized charity.

The principle of giving and receiving is as simple as that. It did not say that you must be an angel to receive. Here is the best teaching anyone must own, and I repeat: if you cannot participate in the principle of giving, no matter how many days you pray, fast, or do good deeds, you will only receive what you give. You may be blessed in many areas of your life but fail to build wealth because the principle dictates that you receive what you give.

Andrew Carnegie was a ruthless businessman, often using unethical practices to undermine the competition and stay ahead. He amassed an immense fortune and then...gave it all away by the time of his death. John Rockefeller's name awakens fear in the minds of his contemporaries. Competitive to the core, he drove his competitors out of business. He amassed an immense fortune at the head of Standard Oil and then...gave it away.

World billionaires who sacrifice their lives toiling and, while doing so, break some ethical and spiritual laws end up donating their wealth to charity. Billionaires Bill Gates, Warren Buffett, and Carlos Slim have been making massive contributions to philanthropic causes they believe in donating billions to charities.

Why break one's back, ruin others' lives, and ultimately give it all away? The essential question one should pose is, "*What is the secret behind giving?* My father always reminded me, "*Giving is the magic power of abundance.*" I never really understood what he meant, but as I grew older and witnessed the power of giving and selflessness, I realized that giving is a magic tool for living a remarkable life. It is life itself.

Famed author Maya Angelou believes that she has found that among its other benefits, giving liberates the soul. Billionaire John D. Rockefeller contends that giving should not be seen as a duty but a privilege. Have you observed the lives of those who give? They are the happiest human beings on earth. They align with the laws of life as well as those of wartime former British Prime Minister Winston Church, who once said, "We make a living by what we get. We make a life by what we give." Giving is the essence of life. God gave life to the world, mothers give life, and the universe is sustained by what we each give. Giving is a science, a principle. Legendary physicist Albert Einstein can teach you one lesson or two on the issue; he believes that we should give back more than we received when he said,

"It is every man's duty to put in the world at least the equivalent of what he takes out of it."

No matter what position you take on the topic of giving, one thing must supersede any other: acknowledge and honor God as your Source.

WHAT SECRET DO THE SUPER-RICH KNOW ABOUT GIVING?

According to BBC, between March and June 2020, world billionaires donated over $7.2 billion to Covid-19 relief efforts. That sudden act of generosity did not wait to yield its fruit. In the same period, while millions lost their jobs left and right, billionaire wealth grew by 27 percent, adding close to ten billionaires each week. Just 2153 in 2019, in 2021, the number of billionaires skyrocketed to a staggering 2755, a whopping increase of 602 new billionaires. Many nations, such as Switzerland and Luxemburg, have a high concentration of millionaires and billionaires per capita, but America stands out in the country's wealth.

According to the Forbes List and Bloomberg Index data, America tops the list with 724 billionaires and the amount of collective wealth owned by Americans superrich. That begs the following question: is there a correlation between religious beliefs and wealth creation, or does religion play a role in formatting an entrepreneurial spirit, ethics, and morals that facilitate good work habits? One can even venture to ask: did God arbitrarily bless America, a Christian nation, as did the Jewish nation and some Arab nations, such as Saudi Arabia? You can even wonder: is there an American spirit of risk-taking, giving, and honoring God that favors American self-made?

In other words, as some observers contend, is it true that many superrich founded their wealth system on their faith? A World Economic Forum study states, "Fifty-five percent of Americans say they pray daily, compared to 25 percent of Canadians, 18 percent of Australians, and 6 percent of Britons." The founding fathers built America, the wealthiest nation on earth, on religious grounds and tolerance, and in "In God, We Trust" in America, even though this orientation has been sadly criticized in recent years. Bill Gates says that he raised his children according to the Christian faith at the Catholic church he and his wife, Melinda Gates, attend regularly. His philanthropic endeavors were derived from his Christian faith. As for Sam Walton of Walmart, he mimicked Jesus Christ's sense of service. His business model was based on service leadership.

Billionaire Sam Walton dipped into his Presbyterian faith to found Walmart. The thirteenth-century Mali Empire leader, Mansa Musa, often considered the world's richest man, was a devout Muslim with an estimated net worth of $400 billion today. His help of the poor demonstrated his generosity and building mosques wherever he went. Some historical accounts even note that the emperor's generous giving of gold caused inflation in Cairo and Medina. Likewise, King Solomon, a faithful servant of the LORD, considered the wealthiest man that ever lived and worth trillions of dollars, was a generous giver to individuals and public work. He lavishly honored God with the first temple of Jerusalem, which took billions to build.

AMERICA, A BLESSED NATION OF CHEERFUL GIVERS: THE STORY OF BILLIONAIRE DAVID STEWARD

Black America's second richest man, billionaire David Stewart, is co-founder and CEO of Worldwide Technologies (WWT), a multi-billion-dollar global technology giant. Growing up in Clinton, Missouri, David never expected to be where he is today. David did not attend an Ivy League university or land a six-figure career on Wall Street. He attended and received a Bachelor of Science in Business from Central Missouri State University, a public institution.

David started his career as a regular employee in several positions in production management and sales until he got stung by the entrepreneurial virus. In 1987, he launched his first company, then WWT, in 1990 with one business philosophy: *give more than you expect to receive*. David had nothing special except this philosophy of life:" Treat people better than you would want to be treated." David was surprised by wealth as he believed, lived, and conducted business on one principle of faith: ***"Share the blessing that was bestowed upon you."*** This law of life is the foundation of his upbringing and the force behind his business success, as he summed it up below:

> My wife, Thelma, and I come from humble backgrounds, and we have been blessed with more prosperity than we could have imagined when we were young. It is a blessing for us to give to others. Consequently, we spend a significant amount of our time sharing our blessings with others. We are deeply committed to serving our community. Our people at WWT are encouraged to take active roles in the community, and we financially support their efforts. As my wife often says, 'Dave's company is his pulpit to spread the word of the LORD.'
> – David Stewart

AMERICANS' WEALTH IS GROUNDED ON SPIRITUAL PRINCIPLES

> *"And you shall remember the Lord your God, for it is He who gives you the power to get wealth, that He may establish His covenant which He swore to your fathers, as it is this day."*
> – Deuteronomy 8:18

Contrary to popular belief, many American superrich built their wealth on their religious faith. Which company founder proudly declared that his fast-food restaurant did more business in six days than any competitors did in seven?

Which kid, dad, or mom does not mind staying in a long line to grab her bag of the chicken breast sandwich, magically marinated Chick-fil-A style? Eagerly and courteously served with "My pleasure" and a smile by a well-trained staff of enthusiastic young people, the delicious meal will give you a taste of heaven. Where do those young kids proudly dressed in their clean polo and gray pants get their smiles and habits from? Have you not noticed the difference when you go to other fast-food restaurants where the staff make you feel like you are a bother to them? Chick-fil-A's corporate culture of care is the foundation and business philosophy.

Who was behind America's beloved restaurant chain? Truett Cathy founded Chick-fil-A in 1967 based on his Christian belief: devotion to serving only quality. He carries the same passion in his personal life. Kindred-hearted Cathy spent fifty years coaching young boys to espouse strong Christian leadership values in his hometown of Jonesboro, Georgia. According to the online news site Baptist News, Chick-fil-A was founded on Christian principles of stewardship with a corporate purpose that reads, *"To glorify God by being a faithful steward of all that is entrusted to us and to have a positive influence on all who come into contact with Chick-fil-A."*

THE FOUR POWER TOOLS OF GIVING

Business pioneers, such as Truett Cathy, Dave Thomas, founder of Wendy's, Sam Walton of Walmart, and many more American business magnates, are committed to their faith and act as regular members of their religious organizations. Wealth-builders from Jewish and Hindu religions ranked first and second on the list of the top superrich in America, respectively. Indeed, God never said he hates the rich. On the contrary, He summons us all to build wealth and share it, for there is unlimited power in doing so, because as Jesus himself taught us, "The more we give, the more we receive, for it is more blessed to give than to receive." (Acts 20:35)

Below are the four fundamental tools that will empower you to become a cheerful giver.

POWER TOOL # 1: BE THE GIFT

"The measure of a life, after all, is not its duration, but its donation."

— **Corrie ten Boom**

Your life is a gift of God to others. Your skills, education, money, and relations will only be fruitful if they help you achieve your calling. Otherwise, they become worthless and roadblocks that hinder your access to true wealth. King Solomon, the builder of the first temple of Jerusalem, has a clear warning for offenders when he states: *"Unless the LORD builds the house, they labor in vain who build it. Unless the LORD guards the city, the watchman stays awake in vain."* (Psalm 127:1). For years, you have labored and toiled on your own for a meager harvest. Why don't you call the master of the harvest? It only makes sense to try differently.

During world crises, such as pandemics, the American government, by principle, always tries to look out for developing nations. When the COVID-19 pandemic hit the world, and America became the epicenter with millions of people infected, the US government did not defect from its tradition of helping less fortunate countries. While each country closed itself to the world to protect its citizens, and Americans were dying like flies, the American government worried about the humanitarian needs of people in other nations. Voice of America announced that the US government had released funds to provide humanitarian relief to sixty-four countries, as illustrated in Secretary of State Mike Pompeo's statement: *"Today, I am pleased to announce that the United States has made available nearly $274 million in emergency health and humanitarian funding."*

Giving out of gratitude is an American tradition to the point it is celebrated - on Thanksgiving Day. It is not just a call of Big Brother's duty to the government but a way of life for the American people. No tragedy has left the Americans unconcerned. President John F. Kennedy spoke to this tradition when he once said,

> *"The raising of extraordinarily large sums of money, given voluntarily and freely by millions of our fellow Americans, is a unique tradition. Philanthropy, charity, giving voluntarily and freely, call it what you like, but it is truly a jewel of an American tradition."*

— John Kennedy

According to Charitychoices.com, Americans donate $1 billion to charity a day. In 2017 alone, the total giving exceeded $400 billion, representing about 2.1 percent of US GDP. The site reports that households are 70 percent of the originators of charity pledges. According to the website, over half of Americans give at least 2.5 percent of their income, which is enormous considering America's high cost of living.

Despite Americans' generosity, they are portrayed as the most individualistic folks on earth based on research conducted by Dutch economist Geert Hofstede. In his 1970 *Model of Cultural Dimension* study, Professor Geert ranked America among the most individualistic nations with a 91 percent score. However, contrary to Professor Geert's study, other data rank America as the most generous nation on earth.

A recent Gallup survey of forty industrialized nations disproves Dr. Geert's half-a-century-old study regarding generosity. Giving works and creates increased well-being for the receiver and the giving. Americans are not just giving money; they volunteer their time to help common causes. A Corporation for National and Community Service study reports that over 25 percent of America individually spent 32 hours on volunteer service, totaling eight billion hours, the equivalent of $184 billion.

How can a nation whose people are considered individualistic see its superrich even think of pledging to give away half of their wealth? Launched in 2010, the "Giving Pledge" is a charity action initiated by American billionaires Warren Buffet and Bill and Melinda Gates. As of 2022, over 70 percent of the 236 signers of the Giving Pledge are North American citizens.

As of 2019, the fund received and partly disbursed over $500 million to charity causes. No wonder America has remained prosperous. Can you imagine that close to 1,900 Americans are becoming millionaires every day? America's tradition of giving teaches us a lesson: a principle works no matter what. Americans donate money, so they are financially blessed. God is a God of principle, not religion or complacency. He is faithful to His promise.

Bill Gates's wealth was shy of $60 billion at the inception of his foundation when he was co-launching the Giving Pledge in 2010. Following that announcement, Gates's wealth skyrocketed to more than double. The wealth of Warren Buffet and Mark Zuckerberg also contributed to this. In 2010, Buffett was $ 47 billion wealthy; today, in 2020, Buffett boasts a whopping $84 billion vault. As for Mark Zuckerberg, his $4 billion piggy bank of 2010 grew twenty-two folds to thrust him among the quartet of the world's wealthiest people. Today, his $88 billion treasure chest has left many forerunners in the dust.

These people who came on record to announce that they will give away most of their wealth have seen their fortunes increase multifold beyond measure. What is the lesson here, and why am I insisting on the importance of giving? It is the secret of the newfound Eldorado. It is a principle that does not fail. The more Americans give, the more they grow their wealth. If you understand and unlock the secret code of giving, wealth will walk to your doors, and here is my life philosophy that I teach my children and live by daily: *I was born to serve God through service to others, using my God-given gift to produce joy and happiness in the heart of the many.*

GIVE TO GOD FIRST, PAY YOURSELF SECOND, THE ORIGINAL GOLDEN RULE

Sow the seed of your harvest. Mainstreet told you, "Pay yourself first." Well, you need to reorder that priority. Paying God first is the primary step in wealth-building. Many entrepreneurs may not see this as necessary, but as an inspired wealth-builder, you know your wealth comes from God. Renowned railroad tycoon Andrew Carnegie made this his number one rule. From childhood, he never missed paying his tithes. He did so into wealth. The second part of the golden rule of wealth-building is to retain your income for investment. Algamish, the richest man in Babylon, built his wealth by retaining and reinvesting a portion of any increase.

In its 2019 Giving Report, payment gateway Push Pay revealed that less than a quarter of churchgoers tithe regularly. While most people donate less than three percent to their congregation, only one percent of people making over $75000 tithe ten percent. The site further reports that eight percent of churchgoers donate to charity. Coincidentally, over 80 percent of the givers have no credit card debt. Billionaire Rockefeller once said: *"I never would have been able to tithe the first million dollars I ever made if I had not tithed my salary, which was $1.5 a week."*

What did Anthony Rossi understand about the pledge to the Lord? Impoverished Italian immigrant Anthony Rossi pledged to honor God, who gave him a business idea. If you like to drink Tropicana Orange Juice, that is a business idea that came fresh, concentrated in millions of dollars from heaven.

As you pay your ten percent to God, you have magnified the power of the remaining 90 percent. How do you feel knowing you have done your part of the promise? When you are spiritually connected and energized by a sense of entitlement, you set yourself into expectation mode. The entitled expectation releases the universal law of abundance that starts manifesting before your own eyes. *The poor have not because they give not. The richest of the poor is the one who gives.* Look at the list below, and you will validate what I am talking about.

TEN BILLIONAIRES WHO TRUSTED GOD WITH THEIR TITHES

1. John D. Rockefeller, founder of Standard Oil.
2. Andrew Carnegie, founder of US Steel.
3. Anthony Talamo Rossi, founder of Tropicana Orange Juice.
4. William Colgate, founder of Colgate Company.
5. Charles Kraft, founder of Kraft Foods.
6. David Green, founder of Hobby Lobby.
7. Sam Walton, founder of Walmart.
8. James Cash Penny, founder of JC Penny.
9. Cathy Truett, founder of Chick-Fil-A.
10. Dave Thomas, founder of Wendy's Restaurants.

Beyond the business arena, giving has become a matching field for the American superrich. Many, including Bill Gates, Warren Buffet, and Mark Zuckerberg, pledge to leave almost all their wealth to charity. According to CNBC, between 2009 and 2011, America's superrich donated over nine percent of their yearly income to charity. The site reports that almost 100 percent of all the superrich gave to charitable causes in 2009.

POWER TOOL # 2: GIVING GIVES YOU MORE LIFE

"We ourselves feel that what we are doing is just a drop in the ocean. But the ocean would be less because of that missing drop."
— **Mother Theresa**

Giving is a gift. A study by a group of scientists at the University of Buffalo, New York, reported in the *Journal of American Public Health*, found a correlation between giving and living longer. Assistant Professor of Psychology Michael J. Poulain says every act of generosity, selflessness, and kindness, such as offering a gift or service, reduces mortality risk because it reduces stress levels—a group of studies on voluntarism claim that volunteering and selflessness increase well-being and life satisfaction. The research mentioned that giving one's time to others reduces mortality risk. Sixth-century Chinese philosopher and writer Lao Tzu, also known as Laozi, believes that *"The wise man does not lay up his own treasures. The more he gives to others, the more he has for his own."*

GIVING STEMS FROM A DIVINE DNA AND TOUCHES GOD'S HEART

"Blessed is he who considers the poor; The Lord will deliver him in time of trouble. The Lord will preserve him and keep him alive, and he will be blessed on the earth; You will not deliver him to the will of his enemies. The Lord will strengthen him on his bed of illness; You will sustain him on his sickbed."
— **Psalm 41:1-3**

A giving heart is the secret to true wealth. Our actions are the results of our beliefs, which originate from our faith. Yet faith derives from what we see, hear, and perceive. Humans are like chameleons who take the color of their environments. Your beliefs, attitude, and behavior are the result of your exposure. If you are exposed to goodness, you will naturally be drawn to goodness; alternatively, if you are exposed to evil, that is all you see. Wealth as a true gift from God is a fruit of the spirit and transcends human understanding. Below are truths that may enforce or contradict and change your beliefs about wealth.

1. *Wealth is attracted by positive words.*
2. *Wealth is manifested through positive thoughts.*
3. *Wealth is actualized as the result of positive deeds.*
4. *Wealth, fulfilment, is the most joyful and happiest state of your soul, mind, and spirit.*
5. *Wealth is not measured in terms of receiving but in the value of giving.*
6. *Wealth is far more than success. Success only begets happiness, not fulfillment.*
7. *The lack of money is the source of all misery. Build wealth instead.*
8. *Alignment with Divine Purpose is what creates fulfillment, the state of true wealth.*
9. *Gratefulness is the state of complete satisfaction that waters your garden. of wealth.*
10. *Poverty is not a pathway to the Heavens.*

PURPOSEFUL GIVING IS POWER

What is the purpose of giving? Steel tycoon Andrew Carnegie, an impoverished Scottish immigrant, made a fortune in America and became a renowned philanthropist. By the end of his life, he gave away all of his wealth, estimated at $309 billion, to support universities, libraries, general education, and charities. Yet his idea of philanthropy is quite unusual when he once argued:

> "In bestowing charity, the main consideration should be to help those who will help themselves; to provide part of the means by which those who desire to improve may do so; to give those who desire to use the aids by which they may rise; to assist, but rarely or never to do all. Neither the individual nor the race is improved by almsgiving."
>
> **– Andrew Carnegie**

Give to empower, not to demean. You now understand why the rich do not throw money at the panhandler. Giving must be purposed to change and better the lives of those who receive, not to make bottomless holes out of them. Giving the right way is a moral obligation for those blessed with wealth. Many people do not see that wealth as an altruist endowment. They do not see themselves as stewards, so they look down on those who depend on them.

HOW TO GIVE: GIVE WITHOUT EXPECTATION TO RECEIVE BACK

"We need to give from the perspective of empowering the recipient instead of making them dependent on us."
— **Billionaire Entrepreneur Tony Elumelu**

Many non-profit or not-for-profit organizations take on the burden of causes they believe in and give their lives away to support such causes. On the other hand, you have a large number of NGOs – Non-governmental organizations - with individualistic and egotistical motives. Under the pretense of helping humanitarian causes, these organizations receive pledges that end up in their own personal coffers. How pathetic! Reportedly, many such NGOs only direct ten percent of their endowments and giving to the actual beneficiaries. They keep 90 percent for administrative expenses, including large salaries, luxurious travel, and sumptuous buildings and offices. As the holy book says, *They have already received their recompense.*

Giving is not self-directed. We need people genuinely interested in promoting others of the jaws of poverty. Tony Emuleme is such a fellow.

Nigerian economist, banker, investor, and philanthropist spearheaded a movement in Africa no one dared. After spending many years in the investment world in Nigeria, Tony realized being the only one to be blessed while people are suffering around you is nonsense. With an acute business acumen, Tony built himself a robust financial powerhouse with Heirs Holding and many other stakes in the banking industry. What is the following obvious human action to do when you have been immensely showered with abundant wealth? You must share it, not in bottomless charity, but by teaching others how you did it and holding their hands through.

Through The Tony Elumelu Foundation, the African philanthropist empowers thousands of young women and men from all over Africa, each receiving a seed capital to launch their own ventures. Since its inception in

2015, the foundation has already funded eighteen fifteen thousand entrepreneurs and created fourteen thousand jobs in fifty-four countries.

Giving must be purpose-driven to empower others to become their best versions. Madam Walker taught other women how they could be more than they were made to be. Using their employment at her company, these African American women could care for their families, including their children's education. They were far better off than their husbands working at factories. An agent of Madam C.J. Walker could easily take home $15 to $25 a week when her husband could barely bring home $11. These women could become salon owners, sales agents, or hairstylists and no longer need to be employed as maids. In their new position, they made more money, became financially independent, and felt a sense of self-worth.

Give wings to your giving. Give in a way that dignifies the receiver. Give meaning to your giving to empower the beneficiary. Give wings to your giving so it can fly up high in the heavens:

> "So, let each one give as he purposes in his heart, not grudgingly or of necessity, for God loves a cheerful giver."
> **– 2 Corinthians 9:7**

- Give to help, not for you to receive,
- Give in a way that frees the receiver from dependency.
- Give without looking for appreciation or acknowledgment.
- Give without seeking self-interest, recognition, and domination.
- Give to please and honor God, not you.
- Give for the welfare of the receiver.
- Above all, give with a cheerful heart.

GENEROSITY EMPOWERS LIFE SUCCESS AND A STRONGER MARRIAGE

Generosity trumps selfishness in the areas of success and health. Giving increases your mental health, reduces stress, improves your married life, and empowers you to succeed. A 2011 study by the Marriage Project reports that small acts of kindness among couples, such as getting coffee for your spouse, increase happiness in the marriage.

GIVING IS MANIFESTING GODLIKENESS

Activate the principle of giving. You will only receive what you give. Everything people need to know to live in paradise on earth is written in the Holy Scriptures. We either follow those principles or dismiss them. Why does the Bible insist that "it is more pleasurable to give than receive"? The book is rich in promises for those who give, as giving honors God as you heed His call to help one another. It is trusting God as the source and accepting your role as the steward, surrendering to the lordship of God, He, who owns all riches. Giving promotes God's plan for humanity. As a God of principles who always delivers on His promises - He blesses those who give, and each one will give as he has received (2 Corinthians 9:7)

Everyone can give. Start giving where you are with what you have today. Why does the 2021 Gallup Report rank Kenya and Myanmar ahead of the US in individual giving? Those countries are not as rich as Germany or Japan, but the people have learned to care for the suffering of others. While we quote prominent givers, you do not need to wait to be wealthy to begin giving.

On the contrary, you should start giving while still searching your way up to wealth. Giving should feel like a sacrifice. It must hurt. From the people who give from their overflowing abundance to those who give from their scarcity pot, who do you think glorified the LORD? What matters the most is not what you give but how you give. A cheerful giver does not care how large or small the gift is. You will give from a generous heart, even if it is tiny. Your contribution is magnified by the love and selflessness you packaged it in. Jesus praised the old widow who gave for her scarcity while others gave from their overflowing abundance. (Mark 12:41-44)

POWER TOOL #3: INVEST IN NOBLE CAUSES

"Giving is not just about making a donation; it is about making a difference."

— Kathy Calvin

> *Philanthropy is not about giving money; it is about waking up people's consciousness. Charity alone is not enough. You must have a genuine interest in giving your time and heart to helping people change their lives through education, self-actualization, and self-realization.*
>
> — Jack Ma

Legendary entrepreneur Jack Ma founded billion-dollar e-commerce giant Alibaba in 1999 from a vision and two cents in the pocket. He now tours world-prominent college amphitheaters to share his success story and philosophy of giving back. When questioned about philanthropy, Jack replied that giving teaches people how to build wealth and become independent. It tools them to use their God-given talents.

One striking behavior pattern stood out in my study of the American superrich. Self-made Americans work hard to build wealth. Competitive to the core, many of these industry leaders will not hesitate to crush others in the way or disregard their employees' welfare. Walmart is known for underpaying its employees. Many Fortune 500 companies are insensitive when their shareholders' interests are at stake. They will not think twice when laying off hundreds or thousands of employees to maximize profits. Yet when they acquire wealth, American superachievers reverse course to give most of their fortune away.

These pioneers prefer leaving most of their wealth to charity rather than to their families. Mark Zuckerberg and Priscilla Chan have pledged to donate 99 percent of their stakes in Facebook to charity in their lifetime. Billionaire Warren Buffett, a renowned philanthropist, has pledged to leave most of his wealth to charity and has donated over $45 billion to the Bill and Melinda Gates Foundation. Bill and Melinda Gates contributed over $40 billion to fight diseases and fund education and other areas of interest. Billionaire philanthropists George Soros and Carlos Slim have individually given away 15 to 30 percent of their wealth.

GIVING IS THE NATURE OF HUMANKIND

One of my students questioned me when I was excitedly hammering the need to give and praising our celebrity givers. He asked, "Are these people giving from the bottom of their hearts? Are they genuine or doing so for an unrevealed motive?" You, too, might be tempted to ask the same question, but to what purpose? True, some have abused philanthropy with self-interest, which has cast a questionable look at some donors' acts of generosity, but one thing must be clear: giving has never been deprived of self-interest. I promote purposeful, uninterested giving, for God encourages humans to give to receive. He is the only God who sees our motives and will reward each of us accordingly. Historical non-violence activist Mahatma Gandhi once said:

> *"The best way to find yourself is to lose yourself in the service of others."*
> — **Mahatma Gandhi**

Today, even young generations of *technopreneurs* surprised by sudden wealth start early to create charities to give back. Why do they do it? Is it a strategic move to funnel their money into nontaxable donations so they can reduce their tax liabilities, as some might think? The simple answer is that humans are wired to care for others. You can observe this behavior in times of tragedy. The global forces will bury their hatchet and rally around a common cause in times of need. Americans are an excellent example of this behavior pattern. Despite their differences, Americans will rally as one common soul to help in times of tragedy.

POWER TOOL # 4: GIVE OUT OF GRATITUDE

For Roman philosopher and statesman Tullius Cicero, "Gratitude is not only the greatest of all virtues *but the mother of all others.*" The Holy Book declares that we should give thanks in all things (1 Thessalonians 5:18).

> *True giving starts with gratitude, for it is from a heart of gratitude that the hand gives.*
> — **Coach Greb**

Gratitude is the trigger of abundant blessing. It is the river that waters your garden of limitless abundance. The benefits of gratitude have been profusely researched and demonstrated, but the ones that caught my attention came from a study conducted by the University of California's Professor Robert A. Emmons. In an article titled *"Gratitude is Good*

Medicine," the UC Davis professor of psychology, Dr. Emmons, analyzed the power of gratitude as he stated:

"Gratitude can lower blood pressure, improve immune function, and facilitate more efficient sleep. Gratitude reduces the lifetime risk of depression, anxiety, and substance abuse disorders. It is a key resiliency factor in the prevention of suicide." Dr. Emmons added that gratitude works because,

> *"It allows individuals to celebrate the present and be active participants in their own lives. By valuing and appreciating friends, oneself, situations, and circumstances, it focuses the mind on what an individual already has, rather than something that's absent and is needed".*

Dr. Emmons's study also pointed out that gratitude helps fight toxic emotions, such as envy, resentment, regret, and depression, that can destroy happiness.

Below are some findings from Professor Emmons's research on the topic of gratitude:

- Merely keeping a gratitude diary reduces suicidal intention by 76 percent.
- Gratitude increases optimism by 94 percent in people with suicidal thoughts.
- It reduces depression by 16 percent and stress by 28 percent among healthcare professionals.
- Gratitude lowers heart blood pressure.
- It increases sleep by 10 percent in people battling insomnia.

Beside Dr. Emmons, other scholars have also researched the benefits of gratitude. In an article published in Forbes Magazine, Amy Morin, New York Times's bestseller and author of *What Mentally Strong People Don't Do*, explains that "gratitude improves self-esteem, opens more relationships, reduces aggression and enhances empathy."

GRATITUDE HELPS YOU VALUE PEOPLE AROUND YOU

The people around us, especially our children and spouses, are our most valuable sources of blessings. We must value them and treat them with respect and love. Remember, you cannot attract positive energy when emitting negative energy. Love is a positive energy that will attract abundance and wealth. Every day, find an opportunity to appreciate, pray for, and bless your family. Make every effort to surround yourself with positive energy that attracts wealth. Find a chance to brighten somebody's day with kindness and words of praise, thankfulness, and encouragement.

BE THANKFUL EVEN FOR THE INSIGNIFICANT THINGS YOU ARE BLESSED WITH

Harness the power of patience. You may not be satisfied with the job or position you are occupying now and may feel unworthy of the treatment you are experiencing. Remember that your life is not static; you will move to a better position at the right time. But while in the position, be grateful for a job. Many people would be happy to be in your place. Do not hate your source of income. Thanks to this job, you have a roof over your head and put food on the table. **What you hate cannot bless you.** If you hate your employer or supervisor, never expect anything positive from them - neither a raise nor favors. *People who hate their job have great difficulty managing the income they receive from that job. – Coach Greb*

Gratefulness makes you appreciate your service providers and pay your bills with joy. Often, we tend to have a conflicted relationship with our service providers when it's time to pay them. You must not. You must thank Mother Nature for allowing these companies to provide us with energy, water, protection, insurance, and education.

VALUE AND APPRECIATE YOURSELF AS A PERFECT GIFT TO HUMANITY

Sometimes, listening to adverse appraisals from others, you tend to discount your worth to humanity. No. Nothing is wrong with you. You are perfect as you are, and do not accommodate anyone's expectations of what you should be. You are the workmanship of God, *who created you as an instrument of wonder. Exercise the power of a positive self-image.* Many people fail to attract divine blessings because of their negative view of themselves. They do not love themselves enough to deserve God's help. You magnify your weaknesses more than the great gift God has put in you. You cannot attract abundance because of your negative language and thoughts about yourself. You feel unfit and mentally and spiritually ill-prepared to receive blessings. What is the point of taking your time and energy to buy a gift for someone you know will not appreciate it?

LOVE THE GIVER AND APPRECIATE THE GIFT

The actual value lies not in the gift itself but in the giver. The door to more blessings is to love the giver more than the gift. Sometimes, we may mistakenly value the gift more than we do the giver. God is the provider of all things that we have. You may and should thank the visible, physical helper, but you must primarily thank the spiritual giver, who appoints the apparent giver. God is the one who appoints His angels - who appear in the form of human beings - to bless His children. Therefore, when people thank me for my generosity, I always redirect them to acknowledge the actual giver who has appointed me to bless them.

Many spiritual teachers warn against the love of money because many people will be inclined to love money more than they love God. God is a jealous God and will not have you serve two masters. You must appreciate and treat the money you receive with care and consideration, but it should never replace your love for the source of providence. Gratefulness makes you think and act positively. It increases your faith in your source of abundance. I learned from my grandmother that you do not cut the tree branches after it has yielded their fruit. *Thank the tree and take care of it for the next harvest season.*

CULTIVATE A GRATITUDE MINDSET

Giving is an act of gratitude. Be the catalyst for a fruitful harvest. Money is a current that must flow. If you want to be a source, you cannot stop wealth from flowing freely from you to others and back to you. *Those who know how to give are the ones who shall receive* (Acts 20:35). Wealth is a reward for those who accept the Higher Source mission and yield to God's will. Most wealthy people have accomplished things that benefit humankind, their nation, city, or community. By accepting the duty to perform their godly assigned tasks, they have invented new ways to improve the ways others live. Indeed, God rewards those who are good soil that bears fruit.

GIVE GRATITUDE, BUT DO NOT EXPECT IT

The most meaningful way to give is giving without expecting a payback or reward. Give to those who cannot pay you back (Luke 14:4). Gratitude is a greater gift than the gift itself. Some people crave it and expect it. However, we often short-circuit our own blessing when we expect gratitude from others. When you open the door for someone, you naturally expect a "Thank you." What happens when the person does not acknowledge your act of gentlemanliness? You tell yourself, "That's it. I am never holding the door for anyone." Do not expect gratitude from those you bless. You are only a conduit. Be grateful you had a chance to be a blessing. Never expect your reward from humans. Expect it from above. The moment you get angry and feel cheated out of gratitude, you have already ruined your heavenly reward. Dale Carnegie put it well when he wrote,

> *Let's not expect gratitude. Then, if we get some occasionally, it will come as a delightful surprise. If we don't get it, we won't be disturbed. It is natural for people to forget to be grateful; so, if we go around expecting gratitude, we are headed straight for a lot of heartaches."*

You have just completed your training with this closing chapter. This chapter taught you about one of the most magical principles of life. Some call it the law of karma, others the law of sowing, and still others, the law of reward. Principles work no matter what. The power of principles is that they are incorruptible and give everyone a fair chance to apply them. Likewise, the principle of giving applies irrespective of the amount given and the history of the giver.

Many people are surprised at how those they consider treacherous get financially blessed. This is where you understand the power of principle. On the cross, the criminal who knew the power of repentance and faith in Jesus was forgiven. Likewise, if you are a criminal but obey the principle of giving, you will reap the benefit attached to it. Conversely, if you think of yourself as an angel but fail to exercise the principle of giving, do not expect to receive as those who do.

> ***LESSON LEARNED:*** *The final chapter discusses the concept of giving back and making a positive impact. It features stories of audacious individuals who have used their success to benefit others and society. The chapter underscores the idea that true audacity includes a sense of social responsibility, inspiring readers to consider how they can give back and make a difference in the lives of others.*

YOUR TURN – DAY 9: THE AUDACITY OF GIVING

Self-Reflection: *Have you considered the impact you can make through giving, whether it's through time, resources, or skills?*

- Do you have a clear understanding of the causes or organizations that align with your values and interests in giving?
- Have you set specific goals for your philanthropic efforts, including the amount of time or resources you would like to contribute?
- How do you plan to evaluate the effectiveness of your giving initiatives and ensure they make a meaningful difference?
- Who or what inspires you to give back to your community or a cause, and how can you translate that inspiration into action?

Application: Giving Plan: *Develop a giving plan that outlines how you can contribute to a cause or organization that resonates with you. Specify the type of support (time, resources, skills) you can offer.*

1. **Research Opportunities:** Explore volunteer opportunities or organizations aligned with your values and interests. Select one that you're passionate about and contact them to get involved.
2. **Philanthropic Goals:** Consider setting philanthropic goals for yourself, whether it's regular donations, sponsorships, or fundraising initiatives. Define your giving objectives and budget.
3. **Impact Evaluation:** Regularly assess the impact of your giving efforts. How has your support benefited the cause or community? Adjust your strategy to maximize your impact.

CONCLUSION

Thank you for taking the time to read this book. If you have followed the activity on each page, you are just a few steps away from achieving your life goals. The lesson this book taught you is the power of living under divine authority. Take the teachings of this book as your invitation to reflect on your relationship with yourself, God, and your neighbor. If God came to judge you today, would he find you worthy of His kingdom? Read the story, share it at home, church, class, or anywhere you feel fits.

Life is a school. We learn from living, reading, and listening to others. The beauty of learning is that it can be costly or free. Which one would you prefer? My purpose for writing will only be met if, because of this book, you become the person you were created to be, for there is no better version of you than the one originally designed by the Supreme Creator. I know that we fail to live life as intended in the pursuit of survival. The good thing is that some will someday connect to their divine selves at the end of the suffering. In contrast, others will live as strangers to themselves because they never dared to meet their true natures.

Life is a canvas. You paint your inspiration for the world to marvel at, spit on, or question. If you do not stand in the way of the interpretation, you will have done your part. If your conscience tells you that you did great, then you indeed did, and you should be grateful that you did what you were intended to do. The size of your bank account does not measure the value of your life. All that is called riches, the possession, and its likes pales in the face of wealth, the true measure of a life worth living.

At the end of the day, when the play called Life is over, and you are at the other end of the tunnel, we dare ask: how many dreams have you helped realize? How many passions have you helped turn into reality? How many lives have you helped save, and how many mouths have you fed? And, eventually, the ultimate question: How many souls have you helped save?

If you can answer those essential yet straightforward questions honestly and without remorse, then you have lived a life of purpose, the one worth living.

Thank you for reading and putting into practice the teachings of this book. I hope you will invite those around you to get a copy, or you can give them a copy - it will be one of the greatest gifts they will live to be grateful for.

ACKNOWLEDGEMENTS

From the bottom of my heart, I dedicate this book to my dream team: my sweetheart and best friend, Grace Agnes, for her humbling love, dedication, and support. I most joyfully bless my children, Faby, Claudia, Carrie, Cephora, and David, for their loving support along the arduous journey. My profound gratitude goes to Rev. Dr. Fred Hartley and Pastors Mike Mikanda, Joseph Blay, and Stephen Hartley for their support, advice, inspiration, encouragement, teaching, and visionary leadership.

My warmest thanks also go to the many mentors, teachers, proofreaders, and focus groups who made this book possible:

- The leadership at the One Mission Church;
- The teams at the ISBF Institute;
- The leadership at Nations of Love;
- The partners at the Coach Greb Financial Power Institute;
- The leadership at the New Alliance Church International;
- The team at Greb & Co Holdings;
- The faculty at Harvard University Extension;
- The faculty at UCLA Executive Education Program.

Finally, my encouragement and gratitude goes to you, my students, mentees, friends, and community, and especially my dear readers, for picking this book from among a myriad.

You all make the journey worthwhile.

ABOUT COACH GREB

Inspired to empower, Coach Greb is an author, entrepreneur, and financial coach who identifies himself as a scripture-based financial coach and writer. Digging into his Christian background, Coach Greb says his mission *is to connect people to their purpose and build wealth and share it for God's glory*.

Educated in humanities, business, economics, finance, and technology, Coach Greb blends his multicultural, multilinguistic, and interdisciplinary flavor in a delicious cocktail to teach employees, couples, managers, executives, and students the spiritual foundation of wealth to accomplish a life purpose. With extensive experience in education, Coach Greb excels in the art of storytelling. With witty, humorous tics and conversational styles, the author provokes, rebukes, inspires, and empowers you to change your life.

A student of Bob Proctors and John Maxwell, Coach Greb authored two series of books, *The Power to Triumph, featuring* six books that uncover the habits, insight, and strategies to build financial power. The second series, *Teach Me Money,* comprises fifteen *"Easy Steps To"* mini books that cover the fundamentals of financial security, entrepreneurship, business management, and wealth-building.

Coach Greb has been a student of prominent authors and coaches such as Bob Proctor, John Maxwell, Jack Canfield, Dale Carnegie, and Napoleon Hill.

Practical and result-driven Coach Greb writes in a plain yet elevated style that blends poetry, fiction, and non-fiction. As the founder of the Financial Power Institute, Coach Greb coined the word "Financial Power" as a new trend of wealth building that reached far beyond financial security, financial independence, or financial freedom.

BOOKS BY COACH GREB

Note to the Reader: Pre-order today!
The books from the Financial Power Series are available on Amazon, Ingram Spark, and major book retailers.

1. *The Power to Triumph: Spiritual DNA of Superachievers & Self-made Millionaires*
2. *Women of Wealth: What If Women Ruled the World for a Day?*
3. *First Millionaires: How to Build Your First Million from Scratch*
4. *Power Habits of Wealth: Live Rich. Be Rich.*
5. *Dream Beyond the Oceans: How Immigrant Can-do Attitude Built a Nation of Wealth*
6. *Road to Wealth: From the Mailroom to the Boardroom*
7. *The Power of Two: Rich Habits of Wealthy Couples*
8. *The Triumph of Audacit: How Ordinary People Become Highly Successful Selfmade*

Order your copy in English, French, or Spanish.
Available in print, audio, and downloadable formats.
Distributed in 35 countries.

Contact our Global Headquarters
Greb & Co. Holdings
ISBF/Financial Power Institute
2070 Sugarloaf Parkway
Lawrenceville, GA 30045
1.800.604.4040

FINANTV.COM COACHGREB.COM ISBFINSTITUTE.COM.COM

POWERFUL BOOKS THAT INSPIRED ME

Chapter 1: **The Audacity of Insanity**

1. *Brain Wash: Detox Your Mind for Clearer Thinking, Deeper Relationships, and Lasting Happiness* - David Perlmutter MD, Austin Perlmutter MD, et al. - Little, Brown Spark (2020).
2. *Frames of Mind: The Theory of Multiple Intelligences - Howard E Gardner* - Basic Books (2011).

Chapter 2: **The Audacity of Change**

1. *The Power of Habit: Why We Do What We Do in Life and Business* - Charles Duhigg. Random House (2012)
2. *That Will Never Work: The Birth of Netflix and the Amazing Life of an Idea* - Marc Randolph - Little, Brown and Company (2019).
3. *That Will Never Work: The Birth of Netflix and the Amazing Life of an Idea* - Marc Randolph - Little, Brown and Company (2019).
4. *The Science of Likability: 27 Studies to Master Charisma, Attract Friends, Captivate People, and Take Advantage of Human Psychology (2017)* - Patrick King - CreateSpace Independent Publishing Platform.

Chapter 3: **The Audacity of Purpose**

1. *Start with Why: How Great Leaders Inspire Everyone to Take Action* - Simon Sinek.
2. *The Purpose Driven Life: What on Earth Am I Here For?* - Rick Warren.

Powerful Books That Inspired Me

3. *Creating a World Without Poverty, Muhammad Yunus* – Public Affairs (2007).
4. *Business Secrets from the Bible: Spiritual Success Strategies for Financial Abundance Daniel Lapin, Stephen Bowlby, et al* – Wiley (2014).

Chapter 4: **The Audacity of Imagination**

1. *The Creative's Guide to Starting a Business: How to Turn Your Talent into a Career* - Harriet Kelsall.
2. *The Science of Likability: 27 Studies to Master Charisma, Attract Friends, Captivate People, and Take Advantage of Human Psychology* - Patrick King (2017).

Chapter 5: **The Audacity of Expectation**

1. *The Power of Positive Thinking* - Norman Vincent Peale. Sumaiyah Distributors Pvt Limited (2018)
2. *Onward: How Starbucks Fought for Its Life without Losing Its Soul - Howard Schultz* - Rodale Books (2012).
3. *Inner Engineering: A Yogi's Guide to Joy* - Sadhguru Jaggi Vasudev – Harmony (2016).

Chapter 6: **The Audacity of Sacrifice**

1. *Rich Habits: The Daily Success Habits of Wealthy Individuals* - Thomas C. Corley - Cresthaven Publishing (2010)
2. *Rich Habits Rich Life:* The Four Cornerstones of All Great Pursuits - Randall Bell PhD - Career Press (2016).

Chapter 7: **The Audacity of Execution**

1. *Execution: The Discipline of Getting Things Done* - Larry Bossidy and Ram Charan (2002).
2. *Amazon Unbound: Jeff Bezos and the Invention of a Global Empire* - Brad Stone - Simon & Schuster (2021).

Chapter 8: **The Audacity of Resilience**

1. *Grit: The Power of Passion and Perseverance* - Angela Duckworth, Peter D. Harms (2016).

2. *Change Your Thinking, Change Your Life: How to Unlock Your Full Potential for Success and Achievement* - Brian Tracy, Wiley ORM (2011).

Chapter 9: **The Audacity of Giving**

1. *Give and Take: Why Helping Others Drives Our Success* - Adam Grant Penguin Book (2013).
2. *Don't Miss Your Miracle* - Vance Havner - Harper & Row (1984).

www.ingramcontent.com/pod-product-compliance
Lightning Source LLC
Chambersburg PA
CBHW030227100526
44585CB00012BA/284